BEST RADIO
PLAYS OF 1988

BEST RADIO PLAYS OF 1988

The Giles Cooper Award Winners

Ken Blakeson: Excess Baggage
Terence Frisby: Just Remember Two Things: It's Not Fair and Don't
Be Late
Anthony Minghella: Cigarettes and Chocolate
Rona Munro: The Dirt Under the Carpet
Dave Sheasby: Apple Blossom Afternoon

METHUEN/BBC PUBLICATIONS

First published in Great Britain in 1989 by Methuen Drama,
Michelin House, 81 Fulham Road, London SW3 6RB and in the USA
by HEB Inc, 70 Court Street, Portsmouth, New Hampshire 03801,
and BBC Publications, 35 Marylebone High Street, London W1M 4AA.

Set in 9pt Garamond by
Tek Art Ltd

Printed and bound in Great Britain
by Richard Clay Ltd, Bungay, Suffolk

British Library Cataloguing in Publication Data

Best radio plays of 1988.
1. Radio plays in English, 1945 – Anthologies
822′.02′08

ISBN 0-413-61780-7

CONTENTS

THE GILES COOPER AWARDS: a note on the selection

Giles Cooper

As one of the most original and inventive radio playwrights of the post-war years, Giles Cooper was the author who came most clearly to mind when the BBC and Methuen were in search of a name when first setting up their jointly sponsored radio drama awards in 1978. Particularly so, as the aim of the awards is precisely to encourage original radio writing by both new and established authors – encouragement in the form of both public acclaim and of publication of their work in book form.

Eligibility

Eligible for the awards was every original radio play first broadcast by the BBC domestic service from December 1987 to December 1988 (almost 500 plays in total). Excluded from consideration were translations, adaptations and dramatised 'features'. In order to ensure that the broad range of radio playwriting was represented, the judges aimed to select plays which offered a variety of length, subject matter and technique by authors with differing experience of writing for radio.

Selection

The editors-in-charge and producers of the various drama 'slots' were each asked to put forward about five or six plays for the judges' consideration. This resulted in a 'short-list' of some 30 plays from which the final selection was made. The judges were entitled to nominate further plays for consideration provided they were eligible. Selection was made on the strength of the script rather than of the production, since it was felt that the awards were primarily for writing and that production could unduly enhance or detract from the merits of the original script.

Judges

The judges for the 1988 awards were:
   Pamela Edwardes, Drama Editor, Methuen Drama
   Richard Imison, Deputy Head of BBC Radio Drama
   Gillian Reynolds, broadcaster and drama critic of the *Daily Telegraph*
   B.A. Young, who was formerly the *Financial Times* drama critic, and who now writes on radio for the same paper.

PREFACE

A Matter of Choice

The long-awaited publication this year of the Government's White Paper on the future of broadcasting has let loose a debate about the nature of television and radio, and their relationship to society, which encompasses funding and technology, structure and supervision, impartiality and accountability, censorship and artistic freedom, language, sex and violence, but which – perhaps above all these things – turns upon the question of choice.

The individual's right to choose, particularly in the matter of how they spend their leisure time, has become a maxim of such widespread and uncritical support that it unites even the most unlikely philosophical bedfellows, from formerly doctrinaire Reithians to the most dedicated free marketeers. It is, after all, not only at the heart of much contemporary government policy but central to the thinking of a society which has abandoned very many of its traditional moral positions and reduced its respect for the institutions which upheld them.

Whereas once it was society's concern – and indeed often the broadcasters' also – to protect individuals from certain forms of speech and behaviour altogether on the grounds that they were indefensible in any context, it has now become much more a question of how those wishing to expose themselves to such speech or behaviour could most conveniently do so without the risk of others, less liberal in their views, being exposed also and being offended thereby. Consenting adults should, by and large, be allowed maximum freedom of choice within the law, even if that choice tends – in the matter of broadcasting – towards that which makes least demands on their attention or intellect. And why not? Giving the public what it wants is not merely a successful commercial policy in show business, it also has the merit of appearing to be an enlightened and liberal moral position for the showman to take.

Well, perhaps. But it has long been recognised that real freedom of choice has to depend on something more than simply recognising public taste and catering for it by as many means and as often as possible. I recall the agonised debates within the struggling circle of American public service radio drama producers in the 1970's, not only trying to identify their proper role in a broadcasting system almost completely dominated by free-market forces, but even more important, trying to work out how on earth it could be funded once they had done so. For them, the question of whether a multiplicity of stations would actually lead to a multiplicity of genuine choices was not academic, or even a matter for speculation. They lived, and still live, with the reality that it does not.

'Beethoven versus Ascertainment' was a popular subject for debate and the implication for all broadcasters was clear. If *enough* members of the public are asked sufficiently *often* to think of absolutely *anything* that they would like to hear *sometimes* on the radio, there is a chance that this kind of audience research could lead to something like a reasonably balanced output of public service radio. But that output would still lack the element of surprise, the oddball, unexpected, startling, moving, life-enriching programme which no-one had heard before and consequently couldn't ask to hear again.

Despite this, the discussion about choice in British broadcasting tends to centre on technology for the dissemination of programmes rather than the provision of opportunity and support for the people who make programmes possible. At worst, 20 radio stations, if unregulated, might all broadcast the same thing, supposing that thing had been shown to be likely to attract the largest audience. In practice, of course, market forces would greatly reduce the risk of such a thing happening, but like audience research of the kind described above, market forces are not very likely to sustain support for long-term development in untried areas of programming. Sadly, experience has shown that to be true of new radio plays all over the world where either the commercial principle or at least audience measurement have been the dominant factor in programme planning. Paradoxically, in an output such as that of BBC Radio, a policy of programming drama as a regular and frequent event in the schedules has shown that a very large audience for plays can be built and maintained.

Does this mean that choice for the listener can best be assured by a public service system dedicated to quality and cushioned, at least in part, from the market forces which might work against that ideal? History suggests that the answer to that question is 'yes' but it requires some important qualifications. Quality is not the sole prerogative of public service and true choice – as opposed to a multiplicity of similar programmes – must depend on a genuinely varied market in which the important effect of competition cannot be ignored. In the arts, no less than in commerce, monopoly can act against the public interest.

In some countries, the strength of a single organisation above all others has led to a reduction of choice to listeners who wish to hear radio drama. The fact that the producers responsible for the output seriously believe that their way of interpreting the nature of the radio play is the best is no consolation to someone who would like to hear something quite different. And the fact is that listening to plays on radio is a highly subjective experience anyway, so that any attempt to limit the form rather than exploring its numerous possibilities is to go against the very nature of the art.

It follows, I believe, that in an ideal broadcasting world there should be increased resources and opportunities for those primary creators – the writers, composers, performers and begetters of programme ideas whose imagination and experience alone are the true providers of choice. They should have the chance to offer their proposals to a number of potential customers, preferably including more than one in each area of operation, whether it be public service or commercial (or indeed a mixture of the two, since they are not in many areas exclusive concepts). It should be recognised that choice *must* include minority taste, just as the devotees of minority culture must recognise that what is widely popular is not necessarily reprehensible. Each requires different forms of support but should be accessible to everyone. In an ideal broadcasting world, grand opera should be as readily available as soap opera, without extra charge or inconvenience.

How well does today's broadcasting of radio drama match up to these ideals? There is certainly a lot of it, though it is a shame that it comes almost entirely from one organisation, the BBC. It is reasonably varied in style and form and content, though it is now very noticeable that some of the best talents of the theatre are denied – or deny themselves – the opportunities of radio broadcast because their themes, or the language in which their characters express them, are felt to be too strong for a medium which intrudes, at only casual bidding, into people's homes. In the new world of broadcasting, can the BBC put this well-intentioned paternalism before a commitment to broadcast the best, whatever its content? I think not – not, at least, without the greatest risk to its self-sought responsibility for real service to the public.

Perhaps that responsibility sometimes lies a little too heavily on our shoulders. Sometimes the greater restriction of choice seems to be for those who like their plays to be simply diverting. There is no harm, and very great skill, in telling stories which gently entertain, which amuse, uplift, charm, beguile, make us sadder, wiser or more sympathetic; which frighten us a little or make us laugh a lot. They are a most important part of our choice.

Last year, there was much debate about the placing of plays on radio: a serious discussion about what is acceptable to the majority in the evening or in the afternoon. But bowing to the majority – or perhaps more often to a vocal minority – can also be seen as a restriction of choice. I believe our broadcasting future lies in part in the recognition that much serious radio is now analogous to serious reading and requires no more general regulation than do books. Young children *may* be led astray by diving unsupervised into the disturbing waters of D.H. Lawrence or Tom Sharpe but it isn't honestly very likely that they will do so. The same is surely true of Radio 3 drama and of Radio 4's Monday Play, even when repeated in an afternoon.

Adults, of course, must make up their own minds.

As the Giles Cooper judges had to do, when confronted with so many eligible plays from 1988. In the end, they were of course subjective, following their own feelings of pleasure, amusement, stimulation; their recognition of craft. To make the right choice is seldom easy; to have the choice to make is a privilege to be preserved.

Richard Imison
(February 1989)

EXCESS BAGGAGE

by Ken Blakeson

For all the original Cyns

Ken Blakeson was born in Yorkshire in 1944. He has worked as a farm labourer, milkman, insurance clerk, teacher, radio presenter and producer and has been a full-time writer since 1981. He has written and contributed to many television series and 30 plays for radio including the much praised *Gospel According to Judas*. His controversial play about army wives, *Excess Baggage*, broadcast in 1988, became the focal point of much debate within the BBC and press when it was denied its customary repeat. Last year his first stage commission, *Homeland* opened at the Contact Theatre, Manchester and he is currently working on two new commissions for the stage and a new seven-part drama series for Radio 4, *September Song*. Ken is married with two children and lives in Harrogate.

Excess Baggage was first broadcast on BBC Radio 4 on 22 February 1988. The cast was as follows:

CORPORAL WHITTAKER/ ROWDY SOLDIER	Christopher Quinn
Q.M. SERGEANT/ORDERLY	Colin Meredith
DENNY DENNISON	Stephen Tomkinson
CYN WATSON	Samantha Bond
DAWN DENNISON	Sharon Muircroft
COLONEL ELLESWORTH	Michael Tudor-Barnes
BILL BURRIDGE	Christian Rodska
MYRA BURRIDGE	Barbara Marten
MARJORIE ELLESWORTH	Diana Olsen
COL WATSON/ADJUTANT/ CORPORAL (FAMILIES)	Kim Wall
JOHNSON	Paul Codman
2ND CORPORAL	Simon Morley
CPT CRANHAM	Paul Sirr
REBECCA	Victoria Carling
COLOUR SGT BROWN/DRIVER	Chris Larner
SOLDIER (EDDIE)/ANGUS/ PROVOST SGT	Richard Henders
WENDY	Rachel Griffiths

Director: Susan Hogg
Running time, as broadcast: 90 minutes

We are outside on the bayonet course.

CORPORAL (*shouts*). Squad will fix bayonets. (*Pauses.*) Fix bayonets!

> *Sound effects: ten men fix bayonets.*

> Squad . . . Squad shun!

Sound effects: Interior. The hall of the Dennisons' married quarters. Slightly hollow sound.

Q.M. SERGEANT. Private Dennison?

DENNY. Yes Sarg.

Q.M. SERGEANT. This form is the Married Quarters Occupants' Inventory of Accommodation Stores. For your convenience the accommodation stores are listed in rooms or commodity groups together with details of entitlement. This facilitates your checking of the inventory and it would be appreciated if you will lay your quarter out in a similar manner when you hand over. On handover the accommodation stores will be checked against the Inventory. This copy must NOT be altered and is to be produced at the handover. Got it?

DENNY. Yes, Sarg!

Exterior. Bayonet course.

CORPORAL (*shouts*). The face! The face is all important. Fix the face so! and scream! (*He screams wildly.*) You will now fix your faces so! Watson, you look like a tart! Contortion! Contortion! And scream . . .

> *Few screams.*

> Scream!!

Real screams.

CORPORAL (*chants*). Kill-kill-kill-kill-kill-kill-kill. (*They join in with him and chant.*)

ALL. Kill-kill-kill-kill-kill-kill-kill-kill-kill . . .

Interior quarters.

DENNY. Three bedrooms, Sarg!

Q.M. SERGEANT. Yes, three bedrooms . . .

DENNY. But I put in for two . . .

Q.M. SERGEANT. Well you got three, didn't you! Three bed, one bath, one reception, one dining, one hall and one shithouse . . . You!

Exterior. Bayonet range.

CORPORAL. A load of bloody tarts! It's not some whore you're poking it's the bloody enemy! You've got to mean it! You've got to hate! Hate! He's coming to rape your wife and kill your kids!

Cut to.

DAWN. Shh Crystal, don't cry, Daddy won't be long.

Outside the quarters. A nine-month-old child is crying and DAWN is trying to comfort her as CYN shouts from next door.

CYN. You don't have to stand out there you know love, you can wait in here if you like . . .

DAWN. What?

CYN. I've got the kettle on.

DAWN. I dunno . . . He said to stay here.

CYN. He'll be a good half hour yet . . .

DAWN. I'd better wait. Thanks anyway.

CYN. Suit yourself . . . it's warmer in here though and if we're going to be neighbours we might as well get to know each other.

DAWN (*unsure but relents*). Yeh . . . well just for a few minutes then, ta . . .

Exterior. Bayonet course.

CORPORAL. Right let's try again and this time, present! and charge!

All scream as they charge.

Interior quarters. Door opens to the bedroom.

Q.M. SERGEANT. Group 1 . . . Bedroom 1!
  1. Chair, dining, general purpose, two.
  2. Dressing table, with mirror, one.
  3. Stool, dressing, one.
  4. Table, bedside, two.
  5. Wardrobe, 3ft 6ins, one
  6. Bedstead, double, one.
  7, Mattress, double, one.
  8. Blanket, under, double, one.

Exterior door closes. Interior. CYN's quarters, next door.

CYN. Cyn Watson.

DAWN. Dawn . . . Dawn Dennison.

CYN. Yeh I know. Everybody knows everything here. Come through
  to the kitchen.

  They walk through and acoustic changes.

DAWN (*excited*). I wish I was in there. I can't wait to see it.

CYN. You'll see enough of it before you're finished, love, don't you
  worry.

DAWN. Is it like this?

CYN. They're all like this!

DAWN. Not bad then, eh?

CYN (*laughs*). You ought to have been with us in Germany. Now that
  is a posting!

DAWN (*positively*). Seems quite nice here . . . countryside and that . . .

CYN. All right if you're a cow. Mind there's plenty of them about an'
  all . . . Give me Germany any time. It might be full of Krauts but at
  least the booze is cheap.

  Back at the march in. Different acoustic.

Q.M. SERGEANT. Group 13, Children's Items.
  1. Cot, child, one.
  2. Chair, high, one.
  3. Playpen, one.
  4. Mattress, cot, one.
  5. Blanket, cot, two.
  6. Sheet, cot, two. Right?

DENNY. Right, Sarg!

Interior. Colonel's office. Knock on door.

COLONEL. Come!

Door opens.

ADJUTANT. Company Sar'nt Major Burridge to see you as requested, sir.

COLONEL. Thank you, Tony.

BILL *marches in, comes to attention and salutes.*

BILL. Sah!

COLONEL. At ease, Bill . . .

BILL. Thank you, sir.

He stands easy.

COLONEL. I assume Major Bentley's told you there's the possibility of B Company going to Northern Ireland shortly?

BILL. Yes sir. Second home sir.

COLONEL. Yes, well you won't be going with them this time Bill.

BILL (*not pleased*). Sir?

He opens his drawer and puts a sheet of paper on his desk.

COLONEL. Your commission's come through. Congratulations, Bill.

BILL *is really chuffed and a bit lost for words.*

BILL. I don't know what to say sir.

COLONEL. . . . and you stay with the regiment.

BILL*'s joy is audible.*

BILL. That's grand sir.

COLONEL. You'll attend a two-week course at Sandhurst starting four weeks on Monday. That should give you ample time to organise uniforms and quarters.

BILL. Yes sir.

COLONEL. Colour Sarn't Williams has been promoted to take over from you.

BILL. I'm really very grateful to you sir.

COLONEL. Pleasure to see a good man get on, Bill . . . You've worked hard for this regiment . . . We're all delighted.

BILL. Thank you sir.

COLONEL. I'm sure Mrs Burridge will be too.

BILL (*not so sure*). Yes sir.

Interior. Recreation centre. Bit echoing. Wives' club committee meeting. About seven women there.

MYRA. I know I've brought this up before at these meetings but I really do think there is a problem . . .

Some recognition from the assembly. MARJORIE ELLESWORTH *is sweetly dismissive.*

MARJORIE. If it's the regimental bus I'm afraid it's out of the question Mrs Burridge . . . The band must have precedence.

MYRA. If we could just have it say three times a week for shopping trips, Mrs Ellesworth. When the band's not using it.

MARJORIE. I think we've been over all this before you know . . .

MYRA. But it always seems to be standing outside the depot doing nothing . . . If it's a matter of making it pay . . .

MARJORIE. I'm sorry Mrs Burridge . . . I really do think we've discussed this item before and in detail. Now if we could get on to the next item . . .

MYRA *sighs.*

Interior. CYN's *quarters. Tea cups clink.*

CYN. You're lumbered if you've no car. Only place to buy stuff's the NAAFI and that's a real rip off. Got you by the short and curlies stuck out here I'll tell you.

She opens a packet of fags.

CYN. Wanna fag?

DAWN. Oh . . . no thanks. Denny doesn't like me smoking.

CYN. Oh!

DAWN. Bit of a fitness fanatic.

Silence as CYN *lights her fag with a match and exhales.* DAWN *is nervous.*

DAWN. Nice furniture and that in here though isn't it? I didn't expect to get anything like this.

CYN (*laughs*). Don't worry, you won't. This is our own . . . we wharfed the army stuff.

DAWN. Eh?

CYN. Put it into store.

DAWN (*suddenly concerned*). Isn't it any good then?

CYN. It's okay if you've nothing else. Best to have your own if you can afford it then you've no worries at march out. You've to pay for anything you damage or break you know.

DAWN. Fair enough, I suppose.

CYN. Unless you have bad periods or the kids pee the bed. Cost me fifty quid for a new mattress when I haemorrhaged with our Jason.

You wouldn't mind if they put a new one in once you'd gone, but some of the new mattresses I've been issued with at march in must've been paid for three or four times over.

DAWN. You mean somebody's on the fiddle?

CYN. Just the army innit? My old man burns 'em now if they charge us.

DAWN. Denny'd spot anything like that. He's fanatical about things being clean. Anyway he knows we can't afford to be paying for someone else's damage.

CYN. He knows he can't afford to be stirring it either, not if he wants to make lance jack. Doesn't want the word round the Sergeants' Mess he's making waves does he?

Silence.

If you're worried, go and check. You're allowed in, you know.

DAWN. I thought only husbands could go.

CYN. Naw! I made sure I was at mine. Col lets the army walk all over him.

DAWN. Why did he tell me to wait outside if I'm allowed to go?

CYN. That's the way the army likes it. Doesn't want us sniffing out faults. Makes their jobs harder.

DAWN. Perhaps it's best if I just leave it up to him.

CYN. You do as you like love. It's your quarter.

DAWN's *new quarters. Still march in.*

Q.M. SERGEANT. Group 6. Other furniture, part two . . .
 1. Ladder, step.
 2. Chair, easy, low back, two.
 3. Chair, dining, general purpose, six . . .

Knock on door. He suddenly stops.

(*Shouts.*) Yes!

The door opens and DAWN *enters.*

DAWN (*nervous*). I'm sorry to bother you . . .

Q.M. SERGEANT. Problem love?

DAWN. I'm Mrs Dennison. I just want to see my husband for a minute . . .

Q.M. SERGEANT. Make it quick then will you love. I've other families to march in this afternoon apart from you.

DENNY (*goes up to her alarmed*). What are you doing here?

DAWN (*close perspective*). You seemed a long time.

DENNY (*sotto voce. Angry*). I thought I told you to wait outside.

DAWN. I just wondered if everything was all right, that's all.

DENNY. Course it's all right . . .

DAWN. You've checked everything have you?

DENNY. What do you mean 'checked'! Course I've checked.

DAWN. Only they said you have to watch for stains and stuff . . .

Q.M. SERGEANT (*off mike*). Private Dennison!

DENNY. Right Sarg. (*To* DAWN.) Look, just go, okay. I'll see you
   . . . in a minute.

DAWN. You checked the mattress?

DENNY. Yes, I've checked the mattress!

Q.M. SERGEANT (*coming over*). Some sort of problem is there?

DENNY. No problem, Sarg . . .

Q.M. SERGEANT. No need to worry love. We'll see everything's all
   right for you.

DAWN. It was just the mattress . . .

Q.M. SERGEANT. Take any punishment you can give it love.
   Specially built for couples on the job army mattresses.

DENNY (*acutely embarrassed*). Dawn!

Q.M. SERGEANT. You've been listening to some of the girls haven't
   you?

DAWN (*caught*). What do you mean?

Q.M. SERGEANT (*reassuring*). I mean there's no need to worry. We'll
   see it's all in order for you . . . me and your husband . . . and if we've
   missed anything, he can pop along and see me later.

DENNY. Okay? So, just go, eh?

DAWN (*embarrassed herself now*). Yeh . . . Right. (*Leaves for door.*) See
   you in a minute.

DENNY. Yeh.

   She closes the door after her.

   Look, Sarg . . . I'm sorry about that . . . It's her first day on camp.

Q.M. SERGEANT. Is that so?

DENNY. She's been living with her mother. She doesn't understand the
   way things are yet.

Q.M. SERGEANT. Well if I were you I'd make her understand unless
   you want to stay a private forever. Last thing a soldier needs is a
   tart running his life.

DENNY (*flares*). She's not a tart Sarg . . .

Q.M. SERGEANT. They're all tarts Dennison . . . and they'll make a tart out of you if you let 'em.

Parade ground. Section lined up.

CORPORAL (*shouts*). Married men! Company Sar'nt Major Burridge has been informed by the Colonel that he would be very appreciative of new blood in the Wives' Club.

WATSON. I'll go Corporal!

Some laughter.

CORPORAL. With your record that's where you might well end up Watson.

More laughter.

So anyone whose wife fancies it . . . (*General jeers.*) . . . thank you Watson . . . they'd be made more than welcome . . . and bear in mind that Company Sergeant Major Burridge will be representing your interests at the promotions board next week!

Some murmurs.

Right then . . . Squad . . . squad shun!

They do so.

Squad . . . fall out!

They fall out.

Interior. Burridge kitchen. MYRA *is washing up. Noisily.*

MYRA. It's a waste of time being on that bloody committee. I don't know why any of us bother going. Doesn't make any difference in the end. She always does what she wants . . . treats us like half wits. I mean she asks for suggestions and when you say anything she either ignores you or says it can't be done . . . And you get no backing. She has them exactly where she wants them. 'Yes, Marjorie, no, Marjorie . . . oh absolutely Marjorie, anyone for tennis Marjorie . . .' I'll be glad when I see the bloody back of the lot of them.

BILL. Look forget about the bus . . .

MYRA (*interrupts*). Listen, that bus belongs to everyone in the regiment Bill, not just Colonel Ellesworth's crappy old band! I didn't see him or Marjorie running jumble sales or raising money to buy it. I mean how many times did he roll his sleeves up and scrape rust off the wings? It was the wives who raised that money and their husbands who did it up in their spare time.

BILL (*trying to get his news in*). Myra . . .

MYRA. Can't you do anything Bill? I mean you've got a fair bit of pull . . .

BILL. Myra . . .

MYRA. It's just so unfair . . .

BILL. For Christ's sake. We've got a car haven't we? Forget about the bloody bus . . .

Sound of her washing up.

BILL. Listen . . . my commission came through today.

Silence. She stops washing up.

BILL. Myra? (*Silence.*)

Did you hear what I said?

MYRA (*quietly*). I heard.

BILL. Well?

She walks out slamming the door.

BILL. Myra!!

DENNY's *quarters. He is shouting.* DAWN *is crying.*

DAWN. Finished?

DENNY. Yeh.

DAWN. Everything OK? Denny?

DENNY. What are you trying to do . . . finish me off before we start!

DAWN. What?

DENNY. You've only been here three hours and you've already made me look a prat! That fat bastard'll have it all round camp by tomorrow.

DAWN. I didn't know.

DENNY. I told you! But you had to go and listen to that gobby Watson cow shooting her mouth off!

DAWN. I was thinking about the money . . .

DENNY (*angrier*). I'll worry about the money! You just see to Crystal and the house!

DAWN. I'm sorry.

DENNY. Oh, come here.

DAWN. I'm sorry love.

DENNY. Look I've been in this mob three years. I know what I'm doing. You know her old man's still a squaddie! After seven years he's still a bloody squaddie and you know why? Because they don't give stripes to blokes who marry troublemakers. Right?

He is leaving.

DAWN. Where are you going?

DENNY (*opening door*). I've got people to see.

DAWN. But it's our first night Denny!

DENNY. Look, I've got people to see. Right?

He slams the door.

Interior. Burridge bedroom. MYRA *is tidying their wardrobe with wire hangers and coats. Doing something to get away. Something meaningless.* BILL *enters.*

BILL. Myra, come downstairs.

MYRA. Needs doing.

BILL. You knew it was on the cards. (*She doesn't reply.*) I'd make a lousy civilian.

MYRA (*holds dress up*). I've had some of these years. Got this in Cyprus remember?

BILL. I can't throw up twenty-two years to ride round in a tin can for Securicor! (*She doesn't answer.*) I mean can you see me stuck outside some bank showing me medals off?

MYRA. I don't know why I've kept them. They don't fit me anymore.

BILL. Will you listen to me for Christ's sake!

MYRA. Will it change your mind if I do?

BILL. I'm a soldier Myra . . . I'm a good soldier.

MYRA. And I'm tired, Bill. Tired of being stuck in dull backwaters with my children away at school. I'm tired of talking to Marjorie bloody Ellesworth about cake decorations.

BILL. We've had some good times haven't we? Cyprus. I mean we had a great time in Cyprus.

MYRA. It's over.

BILL. It'll be different. You'll be an officer's wife.

MYRA. Super. I'll buy the tennis dress and you organise the lobotomy.

BILL. I don't understand you Myra. Most men's wives'd give their right arms for a chance like this.

MYRA. Just accept the commission and get me my house Bill. That's all.

BILL. There's no need now. We'll get a new house. They'll move us onto the officer's patch.

MYRA. Not an army house. I want my own place where I can bring up my own kids in my own way . . . That was the deal Bill . . . you get the commission, I get my house. Now I want my house.

Crowded soldiers' pub. Wall of sound. Juke box. Noise, chatter. DENNY *elbows his way to the bar, with difficulty.*

DENNY. Come on, Johnson, shift!

JOHNSON. Thought you'd be on the nest.

WATSON. Wearin' the mattress out! (*Laughter.*)

DENNY. Shut it Watson!

WATSON. What's up? Stains stopped play. (*Laughter.*)

DENNY. I said shut it!

WATSON. Please sir can I check your mattress?

DENNY (*going for him*). You bastard!

Shouts of encouragement and 'Eh! eh!' . . . JOHNSON *and* JACKO *grab him.*

JOHNSON. Grab him Jacko!

There is a tussle as JOHNSON *and* JACKO, DENNY's *mates, grab him to stop him hitting* WATSON.

JOHNSON. Not in here, Denny. Christ we'll all get done!

WATSON (*taunts*). Let him go if he fancies his chances . . .

DENNY. I'll waste you Watson . . .

WATSON (*wanting him*). Anytime Dennison . . . anytime . . .

JOHNSON. Piss off Watson, before we let him.

WATSON. Sweet dreams lover boy. I'll be listening for the creaks.

DENNY. You bastard!

DENNY *struggles free and clonks* WATSON. *A fight ensues. Fade on noise.*

DAWN's *bedroom. Door opens. Something is knocked over. It is* DENNY *who is drunk.*

DENNY. Shit!

DAWN. Denny?

DENNY *stumbles over something else.*

Denny what's happened to your face?

DENNY. Nothing.

DAWN. Denny?

DENNY. Forget it.

DAWN (*trying to help*). Denny?

DENNY. Get off. Get off!

DAWN. What is it love?

He lashes out at her. She cries out. The baby starts up.

DENNY. You it's you, you bloody tart! It's all your fault!

He hits her again.

Oh God, I'm sorry, I'm sorry love, I didn't mean to do that. I'm
sorry, OK?

DAWN. Yeh – OK . . .

Next day. Interior. WATSON's *house. Several kids are making a noise.*

WATSON. Come on for Chrissake Cyn. I haven't all day.

CYN (*throws shirt at him*). Here!

WATSON. I can't wear that! You haven't ironed it!

CYN. You're lucky it's bloody mended!

WATSON. If it wasn't for your big gob it wouldn't be ripped . . .

CYN. When are you going to start growing up Col!

WATSON. When you start to do summat round this bloody dump.
That bog's filthy.

CYN. It leaks. I keep asking you to mend it.

WATSON. I've told you, report it to the families office.

CYN. I don't like going round there.

WATSON. Well I haven't time. If you want it fixing it's up to you.

CYN. It's always up to me isn't it? Up to me to bring the kids up, up
to me to report all the faults, up to me to find the meals.

WATSON. Just shut up!

CYN. Oh yeh, you're clever with words . . .

WATSON. You're really asking for it, you are.

CYN. So are the rest of the women on this camp if what I hear's true.

WATSON. What's that supposed to mean?

CYN. You know what it means. (*To* DARREN.) Darren get your
shoes on . . . and help Sarah . . . or we'll be late for playgroup . . .

WATSON. Forgotten about Germany have we?

CYN. That was a job!

WATSON. Oh aye, we know!

CYN. If you gave me enough money instead of pissing it up against a
wall with your mates it wouldn't have happened.

WATSON. Who bought the washing machine?

CYN. Who bought the video and the hi-fi?

WATSON. Oh bloody hell, I'm going.

CYN. I need money Col.

WATSON. You've had all you're getting this week.

CYN. If you want feeding, I need money.

WATSON. I'll eat in the NAAFI.

CYN. What about us?

WATSON (*leaving*). Your problem!

CYN. Col!

WATSON. I haven't time.

He leaves and slams door.

Interior. Bathroom and bog area of the barracks block next day. Hollow and echoing. Running water, sloshing mops, bogs flushed. Some men are whistling and some singing and some moaning as the single men do their morning chores.

CORPORAL. Come on Johnson get your back into it!

JOHNSON. Don't think I'd get me back in there Corporal. It's too small.

WATSON. Might get his dick in!

Laughter.

CORPORAL. All right shut it . . . and knock off that noise Jackson! Looking for a job Watson?

WATSON. Just wandered down for muster Corporal.

CORPORAL. Well just piss off to the parade ground then. No married men on the block!

WATSON (*sotto voce*). Drop off!

CORPORAL. What was that Watson?

WATSON (*innocently*). Eh?

CORPORAL. Listen you might've done your six to my three pal, but I've got the stripes and you've got sod all so just watch yourself or I'll have you on a charge . . .

WATSON (*leaving and out of* CORPORAL's *earshot*). And I'll have you round the back of the block pal . . .

JOHNSON. Oh listen to Mr Big!

WATSON. Watch it Johnson!

JOHNSON. Don't shout at me Watson or I'll kack me kecks.

Laughter.

CORPORAL. Just the polishing, Johnson. Cut the crack! Come on Watson, I said out . . . and get yourself smartened up. Sar'nt Major Burridge is inspecting us this morning.

Interior. DENNISON's *kitchen.* DENNY *is on his way out. Finishing his last piece of toast. Radio 1 on.*

DENNY. You going out this morning?

DAWN. Dunno.

DENNY. If you do go, put some make up on.

Silence.

Don't want everybody knowing our business.

Silence.

And don't look like that . . . It's over now. Just forget it.

He drinks his tea and puts cup down on saucer.

(*Leaving*). . . . And stay out of next door's way okay! Get yourself to the Wives' Club.

DAWN *doesn't respond. He takes hold of her.*

Right?

DAWN (*quietly*). Yeh.

DENNY. Look last night was last night okay? Come on, it's over now. Just remember what I tell you . . . all right?

He gives her a brief kiss on the lips.

DENNY. All right?

DAWN. Yeh . . .

He heads for the door.

DENNY. Nobody's going to notice it with make up on . . . and if they do, tell 'em you did it in the move.

DAWN. I don't know if I want to go Denny.

DENNY. You'll enjoy yourself. Make some new friends. I'll be going for me run when I get back so I'll want to eat about six . . . and get summat decent . . . steak or summat. Need to build up muscle.

He opens the door.

DENNY. See you then.

DAWN. Yeh.

Parade ground. Early morning muster. Blokes hanging about and arriving. CORPORAL *is parading.*

CORPORAL. Come on then you lot sort yourselves out! You know how to do it! Come on Dennison move it! Move it! The man's on his way . . .

Men are sorting themselves into three ranks.

Squad . . . squad shun!

They come to attention.

(*Shouts*). In open order . . . right dress!

Front rank moves forward one pace and back rank back a pace in time. It is one sound.

(*Screams*). Still!!

CORPORAL *turns round with stamps and addresses* BILL.

(*Shouts*). Section in open order for your inspection sah!

BILL. Thank you Corporal Whittaker.

BILL *starts to walk round and the* CORPORAL *falls in behind him. He stops.*

Shave Johnson! You haven't many hairs on your face but if you're going to do the job, cut 'em all off.

He walks on and stops again.

BILL (*aggressive*). You press those denims this morning Watson?

WATSON. Yessir!

BILL. Switch the bleeding iron on next time! What's this?

WATSON. Shirt sir.

BILL. That's not a shirt Watson it's gut! You look like a bag of shit!

WATSON. Yessir!

BILL. Either get this man a new belt Corporal or have him report to the gym for extra PT.

CORPORAL. Yessir.

BILL. Looks like a fifty pee whore with one up the spout!

There is a laugh. The CORPORAL *screams.*

CORPORAL. Still!!

BILL. They're a shitty lot Corporal. I want some improvement!

CORPORAL. Yessir!

BILL. If you're not capable of sorting them out then we'll find somebody who can. (*Leaving.*) All right. Fall 'em out . . .

CORPORAL. Yessir!

The CORPORAL *walks to the front of the parade.*

Right! You heard what the Sar'nt Major said you shower of shit! I want you back here after work tonight in denims. Half hour close order drill.

WATSON. Oh Christ! Give us a break!

CORPORAL. Who said that!

Silence.

Watson! Was that you?

WATSON. No Corporal!

CORPORAL (*screams*). Don't bloody lie!

Silence.

One pace forward the man who spoke!

Silence.

All right. You will assemble at muster point tonight at five o'clock in full dress uniform for one hour's close order drill.

Silence.

No comments? (*Silence.*) Right I want you all back here in five minutes with combat jackets to pick up weapons. Squad . . . squad fall out!

They turn and stamp as they fall out. Murmurs of 'Bastard Watson' 'Keep your big gob shut'

Interior. Dennisons'. DAWN *is changing* CRYSTAL. *Radio 1 is on.*

DAWN. Come on . . . soon have you dry. Here we are then. There . . . good girl . . . Now that's better isn't it?

Bell rings, she tuts. Goes to door with CRYSTAL *on her arm and opens it.* CYN *stands there.* DAWN *isn't pleased.*

DAWN. Yes?

CYN. Oh . . . er . . . just wondered how you were getting on.

DAWN. I'm a bit busy at the moment . . .

CYN. I was just popping the kids down to playgroup. Wondered if there was anything I could pick up . . .

DAWN. No.

CYN (*sighs*). Look, I'm sorry I landed you in it love. I didn't know he'd knock you about.

DAWN (*forces a laugh*). What are you talking about? Denny doesn't knock me about. I did this moving a chair.

CYN (*sighs*). Fair enough . . . I just wanted you to know I'm next door if you get fed up.

DAWN. I don't think I'll get fed up thank you. Look, I'm sorry. I've got a lot to do.

CYN. Well you know where I am if you need any help.

DAWN. I think you've done enough already.

She shuts the door.

Interior. Armscote (where all arms are kept). It's a small room with no windows and a turfed roof.

DENNY (*shouts*). Fifteen!

A self-loading rifle is slapped into his hands. He pulls back the working parts to check there is no ammo in the breech and clicks the trigger.

JACKO (*shouts*). Seven!

Procedure is repeated.

WATSON. Thirteen!

DENNY. Unlucky for some.

They walk out of the armscote into the air. The other men are standing around.

CORPORAL. Don't point that rifle Watson.

WATSON (*to* CORPORAL). Sorry Corp! (*To* DENNY.) Don't think I'm finished with you Dennison. They won't pull me off so easy a second time.

DENNY. Be my pleasure.

WATSON. Just don't poke your head above the butts when I'm on the range, son!

CORPORAL. I heard that Watson!

WATSON. Joke, Corporal.

CORPORAL. That rifle's no joke Watson.

WATSON. Don't tell me Corporal, I've carried one down the Falls Road.

JACKO *and* JOHNSON *imitate a bugle playing the last post.*

CORPORAL. That's enough! (*To* WATSON.) Well, seeing you've so much experience Watson, you can carry the ammo . . . (DENNY *laughs.*) . . . and you can help him Dennison. That is if you're not too shagged out from testing your new mattress!

Everyone laughs, the CORPORAL *lets them.*

Right Squad . . . squad shun! By the front double march!

They set off at the double.

Fade in MYRA *on the phone.*

MYRA. Yes well that sounds about right.

Door opens.

Yes, anything between forty and fifty, preferably nearer forty.

BILL (*jokes*). Looking for another bloke?

MYRA. Yes I can. No that's quite all right. Yes, thanks. 'Bye.

She replaces the handset.

You don't need the car do you?

BILL. Where are you off?

MYRA (*leaving*). Wives' Club then town!

BILL. What's happening in town?

MYRA. I'm picking up some brochures . . . from an estate agent.

BILL. What's the hurry?

She doesn't answer.

There's plenty of time to look for houses.

MYRA. No time like the present.

BILL. I don't think you should be rushing into this just to prove a point Myra.

MYRA. I meant what I said.

BILL. Sure, but why not leave it till I get back from Sandhurst . . . I'll come with you.

MYRA. It's okay. I know what I want.

She leaves and shuts the door.

BILL (*after her*). I have to live in it as well you know. (*Pause.*) Shit!

Exterior. Ranges. The section is drawn up with rifles.

CORPORAL (*shouts*). With a magazine, ten rounds load!

Magazines are loaded.

In the standing position, at a target of 200 metres in your own time, rapid fire!

Volley of shots.

Interior. Families office.

CPL (FAMILIES). Yes love?

CYN. Mrs Watson to you.

CPL (FAMILIES). Ah! Mrs Watson. Captain Cranham wants to talk to you.

CYN. It's not a social call. I've come to report a leaking toilet.

CPL (FAMILIES) (*getting up*). Just hang on there a second . . .

He walks to a door, knocks and opens it.

(*Off mike*). Sorry to bother you sir. Just thought you might like to know Mrs Watson's here . . .

CRANHAM (*off mike*). Is she now? Thank you Corporal . . .

He walks towards her.

Well now Mrs Watson, you've got a problem?

CYN. I've already told him all you need to know.

CRANHAM. I wonder if you wouldn't mind stepping into my office for a minute. There's something I'd like to talk to you about.

CYN. Yeh well I'm in a hurry. I've a lot to do.

CRANHAM. Won't take long. Corporal see if we can't fix Mrs Watson up with a cup of tea.

CYN. Don't bother thanks.

CRANHAM. No problem. Would you like to come through?

Fade in interior. Recreation centre. Perhaps 50 wives plus twice as many kids under five. A noise of wives chattering, kids playing and crying. Cups of tea clink as they queue to be served.

REBECCA (*trying to make herself heard*). Mrs who?

DAWN. Dennison . . . My husband's in B Company.

REBECCA. What rank?

DAWN. Private.

REBECCA. Welcome to the Wives' Club then Mrs Dennison. I'm Mrs Barwick. My husband's the Adjutant . . . and that lady over there is Mrs Ellesworth, Colonel Ellesworth's wife. She runs the club . . .

DAWN. Oh . . .

REBECCA. Right . . . if you'd like to pop over to the table, Sar'nt Major Burridge's wife'll give you a cup of tea. We're having a demonstration in a few minutes but there are some more ladies you might know over there in the corner.

DAWN. I don't know anybody yet. I only moved in yesterday.

REBECCA. Well I'm sure that's a state of affairs which won't last long . . .

MARJORIE SEYMOUR *claps her hands for silence.*

MARJORIE. Ladies! . . . Ladies please . . .

REBECCA. Better get your tea. It looks as though we're starting.

Shushes echo, a few kids wail on to sounds of 'Shush Vicky' etc.

MARJORIE (*at a little distance*). Thank you ladies. Could you keep the children a bit quieter please! Thank you . . . All got a drink of some sort I hope? If not perhaps you could do so quickly and then I'll introduce Colour Sgt Brown who's kindly come along this morning to demonstrate the art of cake icing and decoration.

Interior. CAPTAIN CRANHAM's *office.*

CRANHAM. I called round at your quarter two days ago but there didn't seem to be anybody in . . .

CYN. If it's about the washing machine we've started paying it off. I've got a job three nights a week . . .

CRANHAM. It was about the job not the washing machine.

CYN. Nothing in the rules about working is there?

CRANHAM (*smiles*). Not that I'm aware of . . . It wasn't exactly the job . . . it was more the consequences of the job. (*Awkward pause.*) I'll be frank Mrs Watson, we had a phone call on Friday from someone who claims you're regularly leaving your children unattended while you go to work.

CYN. The bloody liars!

CRANHAM. There's no need to swear.

CYN. Was it that bitch over the road again?

CRANHAM. I'm afraid I can't tell you. The call was in confidence . . . but I would like to point out that although it's not illegal to leave your children on their own, you can be prosecuted if anything happens to them while you're absent . . . and if the social services find out, they could take action against you for neglect . . .

CYN. My husband babysits while I'm out.

CRANHAM. Not according to my informant . . . He's been seen to leave the house after you've gone for periods of up to two hours . . . Now I don't want to say any more at this juncture Mrs Watson. I'm just reporting to you what I've heard. If there's no truth in any of it then just ignore it.

CYN. It's a pity your 'informant' hasn't anything better to do than poke her nose into other people's business.

CRANHAM. I can't ignore what people tell me.

CYN. You ignored us when we asked if the kids could have use of the camp cinema on a Saturday morning.

CRANHAM. It was explained to you that the cinema's for military use only.

CYN. What about the sergeants' stag nights and all the porny films they show. Is that classed as military use?

CRANHAM. Yes, well we're rather getting a bit off the point now aren't we?

CYN. Yeh, get onto the cinema and the bus and we're off the point!

CRANHAM. I don't think this is getting us very far is it? (*Shouts.*) Corporal!

Door opens.

CPL (FAMILIES). Sah?

CRANHAM. Show Mrs Watson out would you? (*To* CYN.) I'm glad we've had the chance for a chat . . . Naturally, I shall be talking to your husband in due course.

CYN. Just fix the toilet, all right.

On the range. The section stands with rifles in hands but no magazines in the rifles.

CORPORAL. With a magazine of ten rounds, load!

The magazines are pushed home.

In the prone position at a target of 400 metres in your own time, rapid fire!

Ten men rattle off a magazine.

Back in the recreation room the Colour Sgt is demonstrating the art of cake icing. He is doing it very officially.

COL. SGT BROWN. Quickly, carefully and evenly. They're the words ladies . . . and the most important piece of equipment in the art of cake decoration, the revolving base which allows free and easy access of application . . . Now you're going to like this but not a lot!

Someone laughs. Few children are rabbiting on and crying – being shushed.

As you now see I am applying the white icing to the almond paste and I am wetting the knife to ensure easy smooth travel around the sides of the cake. Excuse me darlin', would you like to come and give me a bit of a hand . . . Yes, that's right, the lovely lady with the white sweater . . . and what's your name love?

Woman whispers, embarrassed.

GWENDA. Mrs Frankome.

COL. SGT BROWN. Mrs Frankome . . . That's a bit formal isn't it love? What's your christian name?

Woman whispers again.

GWENDA. Gwenda.

COL. SGT BROWN. Gwenda! Now that's better . . . Well Gwenda, how am I going to do this, love? Can you remember? No? Come on ladies, remember the motto? 'Quickly, carefully, and evenly'. Now take hold of this Gwenda . . . Well you've got to do it to know how it's done as they say . . . That's right and quickly and carefully eh? (*Innuendo intended*.) Now then while I turn, slap it on as they say . . .

Interior. DENNISON's *bedroom.* DENNY *is getting ready for bed as* DAWN *enters.*

DENNY. Has she gone down then?

DAWN. Yeh. I think she still senses it's a strange place.

DENNY. Come here!

DAWN (*laughs*). What you after?

DENNY. As if you didn't know!

DAWN. I thought all that extra square bashing would've worn you out . . .

DENNY. Fit as a lop, me.

DAWN. I might be tired after a hard day's cake decoration.

DENNY. Wasn't that bad was it?

DAWN. Oh a real turn on. You know you needed a revolving base for easy application? (*Laughs*.)

DENNY (*stops nuzzling*). Eh?

DAWN. According to Colour Sergeant Brown.

DENNY. Donkey Brown! He was screwing a Captain's wife out in Germany.

DAWN (*laughs*). Not this afternoon he wasn't. He was doing his Paul Daniels impression.

DENNY. Hey, did you see Mrs Ellesworth?

DAWN. Yeh.

DENNY. You let her know who you were?

DAWN. I didn't talk to her!

DENNY. Well you gave your name I hope! There wasn't much point in going if you didn't give your name!

DAWN. Yeh I gave me name. To some adjutant's wife.

DENNY. Mrs Barwick.

DAWN. Youngish, plenty of money.

DENNY. That sounds like her.

DAWN. They weren't that friendly really. Everybody split up, sergeants' wives one corner, us in another . . .

DENNY. Don't worry. You'll soon get settled in, get some mates.

DAWN. I don't mind it if you're here.

DENNY. Yeh. Well I won't be here all the time will I?

DAWN. Somebody said there was a club for married men and their wives . . .

DENNY. Corporals' Club. Got to make lance jack before we can get into that . . .

DAWN. You will.

DENNY. I might.

DAWN. Your athletics should help.

DENNY (*as he nuzzles*). Puts me in well with the OC but there's others . . . RSM, CSM, CO . . . I'm going to have to put myself about a bit to get that stripe . . . mean having to get used to being on your own a bit. Still be time for this though . . .

He starts to get carried away when we hear through the wall.

CYN (*through wall*). You were supposed to stay in!

WATSON. It was only half an hour!

DENNY. Bloody hell.

CYN. I felt about two feet tall!

WATSON. It's your fault. If you hadn't spent the money in the first place you wouldn't have to work!

It is obvious DAWN has become reluctant.

DENNY. Come on . . . take no notice of them . . .

DAWN. I can't Denny.

DENNY. They won't hear. Not with the noise they're making.

WATSON*'s voice comes through very loudly.*

WATSON. Yes, well why don't you piss off then. That's the best thing you could do.

CRYSTAL *wakes up and starts to cry.*

DAWN. Crystal . . .

DENNY (*hanging on*). Leave her . . .

DAWN. I can't Denny . . .

She gets out of bed.

DENNY. Bloody hell!

WATSON. Just piss off!

DENNY (*bangs on wall in frustration*). Yeh why don't you then we could all get some peace!

Fade in noise of a hundred men in an echoing gymnasium. They are talking but not too noisily. Suddenly BILL gets up.

BILL. B Company.

They all rise to their feet. Immediate stillness.

COLONEL. Thank you Sar'nt Major. Sit down men.

They sit.

COLONEL. Right chaps most of you'll have seen Regimental Orders but just to make it absolutely official, you'll be leaving this camp in six weeks' time to begin a four month unaccompanied tour of Northern Ireland. You'll be replacing a company of the Staffords in Belfast.

Any married men with doubts or problems see Captain Cranham in the Families Office. Now Ireland can be tough or it can be easy. You can dismiss most of what you read in the newspapers and a great deal of what you hear from other soldiers. I'm sure you're just as aware as I am how an ordinary story can become a good story with a bit of dramatic embellishment. Listen to your commanders, listen to your NCO's. They're the men who've been before . . . they're the men who know what they're talking about. You'll be told in due course exactly what your embarkation date is but you'll all be off for training on Monday to Wales. I won't go into the details, you'll be briefed by Sar'nt Major Burridge in due course. Just one more thing, I shall be chairing the promotion board tomorrow which means some of you will be taking on extra responsibility while we're on tour. I'm sure you'll handle it very well. Thank you Sar'nt Major.

BILL. Company!

They all rise to their feet. He walks out and the door shuts and chatter breaks out.

Still!

Silence descends.

Right. Ten minutes' break and back here for briefing.

He walks out and chatter breaks out again.

Interior. NAAFI supermarket. DAWN is wheeling a trolley round.

DAWN (*to* CRYSTAL). Now what shall we get daddy for his dinner, eh?

CYN (*off mike*). Won the pools?

DAWN. What?

CYN (*off mike*). Have to be rich to shop in this place.

DAWN. I thought the NAAFI'd be cheap.

CYN. Not when it's twelve miles to its nearest rival. (*Pauses.*) Look I know I'm not exactly flavour of the month in your house at the moment but I wanted to say I'm sorry if we've disturbed you in the last few weeks . . .

DAWN. It's okay.

CYN. Bloody bedroom walls are paper thin. When they come off exercise you can hear every married couple at it within a radius of five hundred yards.

DAWN *laughs.*

I made you laugh anyway . . . Look, do you think we could start again me and you? I'm sorry about the march in . . .

DAWN. That's okay.

CYN. I've seen you with the little girl . . . Nearly plucked up courage once or twice then I thought . . . go on Cyn get stuck in, life's too short.

DAWN. Yeh . . .

CYN. Made any friends yet?

DAWN. Not really . . . I've been to Wives' Club a few times.

CYN. Blimey you must be desperate. What was it? Donkey Brown and his revolving whatnot?

DAWN (*laughs*). Yeh.

CYN. I must have seen that demonstration 50 times. Not all he demonstrates either!

DAWN. So I hear.

CYN. Hey listen, why don't you pop round my place after you've finished here. Have a cuppa?

DAWN. Oh well . . . I don't know . . .

CYN. I won't say nothin' . . . I know your old man's warned you off me.

DAWN (*protests*). No! . . . well, yeh, he's not keen.

CYN. Snap.

DAWN. They don't get on do they?

CYN. No reason why we shouldn't though . . .

DAWN. Look, I'll tell you what, you bring your two round my place. You've not seen it since we moved in.

CYN. You sure?

DAWN. Yeh . . . I'm sure. It's all right, he's not in.

Gymnasium. Men are seated listening to BILL.

BILL. 'Tin City' (*Lets it sink in.*) Now to some of you more experienced men, those words will bring back wonderful memories and to others they'll be meaningless. 'Tin City', is what it says . . . a city built of tin . . . situated in remotest Wales and a truly wonderful place it is too. You will be spending the next five weeks in Tin City. It will be your home. It will be where you learn to deal with terrorists, hooligans, and our beloved regimental band. Now what has that fine body of privileged gentlemen to do with Tin City? I'll tell you, they will be running the place. They will be playing the inhabitants of this make-believe Belfast in remotest Wales. They will be its shopkeepers, priests, hooligans and general scruffs . . . in other words they will be the opposition and they will have no hesitation in making your lives a living hell. In fact we shall be encouraging them to do just that. If you find them unbearable now and wish to do them untold harm, you will want to beat them to pulp by the end of your spell. That is what they want you to do. Your job is to carry out your duties as a soldier under extreme stress, keeping a cool head and resisting all temptations. While you are in Tin City you will be allowed no leave, no time off, no respite. It will be twenty four hours a day, seven days a week. As the Colonel said, we leave on Monday. You may tell your wives. Right, after you're dismissed you will return to normal scheduled duties for the rest of the day so report to your muster points immediately. Dismiss!

Interior. DENNISON's *house.* CYN *and* DAWN *are drinking tea. Some noises as kids play. Maybe run in and out at times.*

DAWN. They want these cups and things back in a week. I'll need some more.

CYN. Allus get some on credit.

DAWN. We won't get credit on our wage.

CYN. Listen they're falling over each other to give you credit in this town. Any squaddie's wife can get credit 'cos they know they'll get it back if you stop paying.

DAWN. Do they come and take it back?

CYN. Don't have to. They just write to the CO and he tells the Paymaster to take it off your wage every week until it's paid. Col's docked thirty quid a week before he even sees his money.

DAWN. You're joking.

CYN. Video, hi-fi and washing machine! (*Sees she's a bit shocked.*) I'm not on me own you know. I'm just the only one who's honest about it . . . There's a sergeant down Marlborough Road in for six grand. Wife bought a new car while he was out in Cyprus. (*Laughs.*) Good for her I say.

DAWN. How do you manage with four kids then?

CYN. Got a job . . . Three nights a week pulling pints in the Elephant and Castle in town.

DAWN. That's a squaddies' pub!

CYN. Yeh.

DAWN. What about the kids?

CYN. Col looks after them or I get somebody in. There's always somebody to babysit on camp.

DAWN. Doesn't he mind?

CYN. It's his debts I'm paying off!

DAWN. Denny wouldn't let me work. Specially not in a pub.

CYN. Yeh, I know what they say but at least we're keeping afloat and it's giving me a bit extra to play with. Means I don't have to rely on that mean bastard all the time.

DAWN. I thought I might start a catalogue. I mean we're so far out and there's lots of people needing things . . .

CYN. Forget it! Every second house down this street's running a catalogue. CO's put a stop to it anyway.

DAWN. What do you mean?

CYN. You have to have his permission to run a catalogue. This is the army you know! They expect you to do as you're told here.

Training field. CORPORAL *has his section lined up.*

CORPORAL. If this had been a war zone and that had been real chemical gas or fall out you'd all be dead by now!

WATSON. Be dead anyway if somebody'd lobbed a nuclear warhead on top of us!

Some laughter.

CORPORAL. You interrupt once more Watson and so help me you'll be up in front of Sar'nt Major Burridge before this day's out. Do you understand?

WATSON. Yes Corporal. Sorry Corporal. I was just trying to make a point. Corporal.

CORPORAL. The point is that you shut up and do as your told . . . and if you are told to get into your NBC's in under seven seconds that is what you'll do. You are of no use to this regiment lying face

down on some field with a lungful of fall out! Now pay attention.
CS gas! (*Pauses.*) The hut you see to your left is at this moment
filling with CS gas. You will put on your masks . . . (*Shouts.*) when I
tell you Johnson! You will put on your masks and enter the hut.
Inside each of you will approach me in turn, lift up your mask and
give name, rank and number. When I am satisfied you have done
that correctly you will be told to replace your mask and leave. Is
that clear?

ALL. Yes Corporal.

CORPORAL. On replacing the mask you will shout 'Gas! Gas! Gas!'
Say it!

ALL. Gas! Gas! Gas!

CORPORAL (*he does it*). Gas! Gas! Gas! This dispels any gas which
has entered the mask while the operation was in progress. On leaving
the shed you will turn your face into the wind, eyes and mouth open
and breath normally. On no account rub your eyes. Right, get your
masks on and line up outside that door. Move!

*Interior. Hut. Men are lining up. They all have masks on and speak
through their masks when they speak unless otherwise directed.*

WATSON. Pillocking stupid this is. It's us who's got the tear gas not
them and you're never in a bloody room anyway . . .

CORPORAL (*shouts through mask*). Right, shut it and let's start.
Dennison!

Steps over wooden boards. Shun.

CORPORAL. Mask off!

DENNY. Dennison. (*Coughs.*) Private, 24442184, Corporal.

It is very difficult.

CORPORAL. Good lad! Mask on, mask on!

DENNY (*through mask*). Gas! Gas! Gas!

CORPORAL. Go!

DENNY *lurches out coughing inside his mask.*

CORPORAL. Next!

JOHNSON (*with real difficulty*). Johnson, private, 24592284, Corporal.

CORPORAL. Mask on!

JOHNSON (*through mask*). Gas! Gas! Gas!

CORPORAL. Go!

He departs coughing and spluttering.

CORPORAL. Next!

WATSON *walks over, lifts mask.*

WATSON (*without coughing*). Watson, private, 24437881.

Blows and replaces mask.

CORPORAL. I didn't say replace your mask, soldier. Again. And louder this time.

WATSON (*coughing now*). Watson, private, 24437881.

CORPORAL. 'Corporal'.

WATSON (*can hardly say it*). 'Corporal'.

CORPORAL. The whole thing Watson.

But WATSON *is coughing his heart out.*

CORPORAL. Right. Out! Out! Out!

Exterior. Grass. WATSON *is coughing his heart out.*

JOHNSON. You all right Watson?

WATSON. The bastard! (*Coughs.*) I got it right first time . . .

CORPORAL (*approaching*). No you didn't Watson. Name, rank, number and address the corporal! You didn't address the corporal Watson, nor did you replace or clear your mask.

WATSON (*breathing badly and coughs*). I couldn't bloody see.

CORPORAL. Why do you think we have procedures, Watson? To simulate battle conditions. That's twice you've fouled up today. Now on your feet and let's see if you can't get it right this time.

WATSON (*wheezes*). I can't.

CORPORAL. Are you refusing to obey an order Watson?

JOHNSON. He's not fit, Corporal.

CORPORAL. Then you can do it with him Johnson, hold his hand. Now on your feet.

WATSON. I can't.

CORPORAL. I'll tell you just once more. Get your mask on and in that hut!

WATSON. I can't do it . . .

CORPORAL. Right Watson. That's it. You're on report. CSM's office, four o'clock!

Exterior. CSM BURRIDGE's *office.* WATSON *is outside. This next operation is done with extreme speed and aggression.*

ORDERLY. Right, next! (WATSON *approaches.*) Beret and belt! Come on, move!

WATSON *hands them over.*

ORDERLY. Shun!

Boots.

ORDERLY (*machine gun pace as* WATSON *is almost run into the office*). Quick march! Leff-right-leff-right-leff-right-leff-right-leff-right-leff-right! Mark time! Get your knees up! Leff-right-leff-right! Halt! (*Halts.*) 24437881, Private Watson, sir!

BILL (*firm but calm*). Insubordination and refusing to obey an order. Isn't the first time you've been up in front of me Watson . . . (*Leafs file.*) Drunkenness, April, Fighting, July. More serious this time . . . refusing to obey Corporal Whittaker's order . . . can't have that. What if that'd been the field of battle Watson? Could have been fatal . . . could've killed a lot of men because you wouldn't do what you were told.

WATSON. Couldn't, sir.

ORDERLY (*screams*). Silence!

BILL. You're here to listen lad, listen, not talk. That's half your trouble isn't it? Can't keep your mouth shut! Right, it's Major Barkworth for you lad and you're on a charge. No record of insubordination before . . . but this is the third time I've seen you. That'll be five days' pay!

WATSON. Rather settle it quicker sir!

BILL. Times hard Watson?

WATSON. Yessir.

BILL. Back of the guard room in an hour.

WATSON. Thank you sir.

ORDERLY. About turn. Quick march! (*Marches him out.*) Leff-right-leff-right-leff-right-leff-right . . . (*Fades.*)

Phone rings. BILL *picks it up.*

BILL (*brusque*). Yes? (*Listens.*) Yessir. Ten minutes. Yessir! Thank you sir.

Puts phone down.

BILL. Corporal. CO wants me. Tell the rest to report nine tomorrow.

CORPORAL. Sah!

Interior. COLONEL's *office.*

COLONEL. Look Bill, I'll come straight to the point. Captain Barwick's put in a request to rejoin B Company and go to Ireland and I've agreed. That leaves me short of an adjutant, so I've asked Captain Cranham to take over as from Monday . . . (*Pause.*) . . . and I'd like you to take over from Captain Cranham as Families Officer.

Bit of a stunned silence for a second.

BILL. I'm supposed to be going to Sandhurst, Monday, sir.

COLONEL. Have to wait I'm afraid.

BILL. With respect sir, nursemaiding wives and babies isn't exactly my forte.

COLONEL. Nothing goes on in this regiment without you knowing about it Bill and there's always problems when the men go away. I think you'll make an excellent Families Officer. I've every confidence. (*He pauses.*)

BILL. Yes sir.

COLONEL. Now about your duties. Captain Cranham'll brief you fully of course and you'd better see my wife. She'll put you in the picture and we'd better move you into some quarters before Monday. Can't have you starting work from the Warrant Officers' patch.

BILL. Sir.

COLONEL. Liaise with Acting RSM Williams if you want a squad to fetch and carry and don't look so worried Bill. If I didn't think you could hack it I wouldn't be giving you the job.

BILL. No sir . . .

COLONEL. Mrs Ellesworth'll be inviting you and Mrs Burridge round to the house for cocktails sometime to meet the rest of the officers and their wives officially but I think we'll wait until the dust settles. That's all Bill! Carry on.

BILL. Sir.

Thwack as a fist hits a face. WATSON's grunt of pain as he staggers back. We are behind the guard room. Sounds of some retaliation. Another thwack and WATSON cries out again.

BILL (*breathing heavily*). Right. That's enough, Watson . . . Come on.

He helps him up.

BILL. Get yourself up . . . No charges.

WATSON (*with difficulty*). Yes sir. Thank you sir.

BILL. Go on lad, get yourself home.

Interior. Soldiers' pub.

JACKO. Seen Watson?

DENNY (*nods*). On me way out.

JOHNSON. How'd he look?

DENNY. Not a mark . . .

JACKO (*admiringly*). Clever bastard that Burridge.

DENNY. Watson deserves all that's coming to him. He's a dickhead.

JOHNSON. Bit hard Denny.

DENNY. You don't have to live next door to the bastard.

JOHNSON. Not all his fault is it? I mean he married a real slag didn't he?

JACKO. Sonny Richardson reckons she was even on the game in Germany, he'd know if anybody did.

DENNY. As long as she stays clear of my place when we're away, that's all I care about.

MYRA's *quarters. The radio is on radio 4 news as* BILL *enters.*

BILL. Myra?

MYRA. I'm here. What happened to your hand?

BILL. Nothing.

MYRA. Where've you been?

BILL. Settling an argument.

MYRA. You'll get done for that one of these days Bill.

BILL. Don't know what you're talking about. My mess kit ready?

MYRA. In the bedroom.

BILL. Right . . . Don't bother with food for me . . .

MYRA. Where are you going?

BILL. Get ready . . .

MYRA. I've fixed for us to see a house at eight . . .

BILL. I can't see a house tonight. It's Harry Bradshaw's leaving party.

MYRA. It doesn't start till nine!

BILL. RSM asked me to be there early.

MYRA. Well tell him you'll be there later.

BILL. I can't Myra. RSM's President of the Mess.

MYRA. You're going to be an officer next week for Christ's sake.

BILL. Yeh, well this week I'm still a WO2 so I do as he says.

MYRA. I would've thought that where we're going to live for the next 20 years is slightly more important than some squaddies' piss up.

BILL (*angrily*). It is not a 'piss up' and he's not a 'squaddie'. It's a regimental evening given in honour of a long serving and loyal member of this regiment.

MYRA. Something's happened hasn't it?

BILL (*sighs*). Sandhurst's off.

MYRA. What?

BILL. Captain Barwick's asked to go on the tour with B Company so Harry Cranham's taking over as adjutant. As from Monday I'm the new Families Officer.

MYRA (*loud and derisory laugh*). You!

BILL. Yes, me.

MYRA (*laughing*). You won't be able to sort the wives and kids out round the back of the guard room.

BILL. More's the pity. (*Leaves.*) We're moving at the weekend.

MYRA. What!

BILL. Colonel wants us out of here and on the officers' patch by 2400 hours Sunday.

MYRA (*doesn't believe him*). You're joking.

BILL. A squad of men'll be down here Saturday morning to help us pack.

Interior. DAWN's *house – breakfast.*

DENNY (*to* CRYSTAL). Who's Daddy's little girl then eh? Come on eat your breakfast . . . Come on, open up . . . Come on . . .

DAWN. Don't force her Denny.

DENNY. She has to learn doesn't she?

DAWN. She's only a baby still.

DENNY (*coaxing* CRYSTAL). Come on Crystal . . . Open your mouth for daddy. Oh bloody hell.

DAWN *brings two plates over and puts them down.*

DAWN. Here, get your breakfast. I'll see to her.

DENNY. What's this then?

DAWN. Beans on toast.

DENNY. Where's the bacon?

DAWN. Bacon's expensive, Denny.

DENNY. I can't survive on this crap! (*Pushes plate away.*) I've a ten mile bash today!

DAWN. I'm sorry . . .

DENNY. You know what I carry on my back? Forty pounds! That's without the rifle and two mortar bombs stuck down me trousers. I give you decent money. I need decent food.

DAWN. Denny it costs me ten quid a week on disposable nappies cos you won't let me use towelling ones.

DENNY. I can't stand being surrounded by all that crap when I come in on a night.

DAWN. It's a struggle Denny. I mean you've just spent thirty quid on a pair of trainers.

BILL. So?

DAWN. So we can't spend it and have it love.

DENNY. So how am I supposed to train without trainers?

DAWN (*upset*). I don't know . . .

DENNY. I win the inter-company mile, I get a stripe. I get a stripe and we get another twenty quid a week. Right?

DAWN. Yeh . . . I suppose so.

DENNY. So I've got to eat properly.

DAWN. I just want to know what I'm supposed to do? It's going to cost us a fortune in cups and knives.

DENNY. Look don't winge, just get me some decent food, all right? You can save next week when I'm not here!

Pause. DAWN *sounds depressed.*

DAWN. I'm going into town today. I'll get you some then.

DENNY (*quick*). I thought you were going to Wives' Club today.

DAWN (*upset*). I dunno Denny. It's boring.

DENNY. You promised. You said you'd go.

DAWN. I've got to get the crockery and that. It's cheaper in town.

DENNY. So go this afternoon.

DAWN. I've all the ironing . . .

DENNY. Do the ironing before you go. Look, it's important okay? Promotions today.

DAWN (*wearily*). Okay Denny.

DENNY. Give you summat to do while I'm away.

Interior. BURRIDGE's. *Morning.*

BILL. So it was a waste of time then?

MYRA. It wasn't what I wanted.

BILL. Glad I didn't miss Harry Bradshaw's do.

MYRA. I never asked you to miss it.

BILL. Got some lads dropping off a load of tea chests about eleven.

MYRA. They can leave them outside.

BILL. Not if it rains love, they'll be ruined.

MYRA. I'm going into town again. See another house.

BILL. I promised Johnny Williams there'd be somebody in.

MYRA. You promised me lots of things as well.

BILL. Look, he's doing us a favour!

MYRA. He's doing you a favour.

BILL (*sighs*). Why can't we just concentrate on one thing at a time.
  Let's get moved in and then we can look for a house.

MYRA. You stay in.

BILL. I'm on promotions boards all day. (*Getting angry.*) Look we
  can't move without tea chests.

MYRA. I'm quite happy to stay here until we move off the camp.

BILL. We can't. They won't let us!

MYRA. Yeh, well whose fault's that!

*Interior. DAWN's quarters later. Radio 1 is playing. DAWN is ironing
as CYN knocks and enters cheerfully.*

CYN. Hiya Miserable! Can I come in?

DAWN (*bit down*). Oh hello Cyn . . .

CYN. You should be laughing. They'll be off on Monday. Think of the
  peace.

  DAWN *half laughs.*

  The three of you get through more clothes a week than me and my
  five put together.

DAWN. He goes mad if his kit's not right.

CYN. Be doing his own soon.

DAWN (*upset*). Yeh.

CYN. He'll be all right, don't worry. Hey, fancy coming out for the
  day?

DAWN. Wouldn't mind.

CYN. Do some shopping then go round the castle, take a picnic.
  Lovely down the river.

DAWN. I can't, I promised Denny I'd go to Wives' Club.

CYN. Sod that! Let's make a day of it.

DAWN. I can't, he wants me to go.

CYN. Bloody hell!

DAWN. Listen, why don't you come with me. Keep me company.

CYN (*laughs*). I'd be about as welcome as a fart in a spacesuit.

DAWN. Go on! It's dead boring on me own.

CYN. All right then, but only if you come into town with me after.

DAWN. Yeh . . . great.

CYN. But I warn you, you won't get any Brownie points for dragging me along to Wives' Club!

Interior. Conference room in camp. COLONEL, ADJUTANT, RSM, CSM's, MAJOR's *and others, probably about twenty men.*

COLONEL. Right gentlemen, you should all have a list of names in front of you which no doubt you will all fight for. (*Laughter.*) But as usual you must realise we can only promote as many men as we are allocated places. So, there'll be some disappointments as always. I think at this point it would be appropriate for me to officially congratulate Sar'nt Major Burridge on his recent commission. (*Hear, hears, and* 'Well done Bill'.) Right, we have a large list to get through and so I suggest we start at the top and work down. Now we have two colour sergeants who need replacing. So, let's look at your recommendations . . . Major Stanford?

Fade in interior. Recreation centre. Perhaps 50 wives plus twice as many kids under five. A noise of wives chattering, kids playing and crying. Cups of tea clink as they queue to be served.

REBECCA (*trying to make herself heard*). Mrs Watson! We haven't seen you for a long time.

She pours tea.

CYN. I haven't been for a long time Mrs Barwick

REBECCA. Well, glad you could make it. Nice to see you again Mrs . . . er . . .

DAWN. Dennison . . .

REBECCA. Yes of course. Well help yourself to biscuits ladies.

They move on. REBECCA *keeps pouring and chatting.*

CYN. Cow!

DAWN. Where shall we sit?

CYN. Near the door!

DAWN (*laughs*). You're terrible.

CYN (*sighs*). Look at 'em. Kids, wives and pushchairs . . . Must be bloody mugs the lot of us.

MARJORIE SEYMOUR *claps her hands for silence.*

MARJORIE. Ladies! . . . Ladies please . . . Can I have your attention please, ladies!

Shushes echo. A few kids wail on to sounds of 'Shush'.

CYN. Eh up . . . speech from the throne . . . 'Thank you ladies, all got a drink of some sort I hope . . .'

MARJORIE (*at a distance*). Thank you ladies . . . all got a drink of some sort I hope?

DAWN *laughs. Some shushes.*

CYN. Shush your bloody self!

MARJORIE. One or two very important items today. As you know B Company leaves on Monday. This is always a difficult time for wives left on their own . . .

CYN. Poor cows.

MARJORIE. . . . and I would ask you to keep your eyes and ears open for anyone having difficulties during this time and if there is anything you think I or our Families Office ought to know, then please don't hesitate to approach us.

CYN (*sotto voce*). Plenty of spies available love, don't worry.

MARJORIE. Secondly, Captain Barwick who's been our Families Officer and who's done an absolutely splendid job has sadly left us for work in HQ Company . . .

CYN. Shame.

MARJORIE. . . . but we're delighted to welcome Company Sar'nt Major Burridge into the post . . . He takes over on Monday when he will become Lieutenant Burridge, so congratulations to him and his wife . . . Where are you Mrs Burridge?

REBECCA. Not here yet Mrs Ellesworth . . .

MARJORIE. Ah . . . well I'm sure she will be . . . Now . . . the programme for the coming months, in view of the posting . . . Mrs. Barwick?

Fade in same scene later. REBECCA BARWICK *now speaking. We hear her from* CYN's *position.* CYN *keeps making comments as* REBECCA *speaks.*

REBECCA. We are privileged. It is a very beautiful part of the country but we do realise living out here as we do does have its disadvantages as well as its obvious delights . . . and so we thought it would be useful and also practical if we continued to run the classes on budgeting in the home.

CYN (*snorts*). Be more practical to run the bus.

Few shushes and a few in agreement.

REBECCA. . . . which could include talks and demonstrations from various local people involved with food or catering . . .

CYN. Couple of chunkies from the NAAFI.

DAWN *and* CYN *laugh. So do a few of the others.*

REBECCA. . . . so you could get some useful tips which might help you to get the best out of your money . . . Anyway, that's just one suggestion. I'm sure you're going to have a lot more.

MARJORIE. Thank you Mrs Barwick.

No response.

I wonder if the ladies who found so much to say while Mrs Barwick was speaking would perhaps like to share their suggestions with us, if indeed any of them were serious.

Silence.

REBECCA (*coldly*). Well Mrs Watson?

Some whispers.

CYN. What?

REBECCA. It seemed to be you who were making the suggestions . . .

CYN. I just said it would be a good idea to run the bus, that's all.

A silence then MARJORIE *steps in.*

MARJORIE. I think in view of the fact that many of the ladies have children with them, and this is after all an informal meeting, the best way to tackle this is probably to split into smaller groups. Mrs Barwick.

REBECCA. Yes . . . fine . . .

MARJORIE. Have each group to come up with say three suggestions for the programme and present those suggestions to the committee for discussion. (*Pauses.*) Would that be acceptable?

CYN. Why can't we discuss them now? I mean we're all here.

REBECCA. Because I think, Mrs Watson, we all agree with Mrs Ellesworth's suggestion, don't we ladies?

Several murmurs of approval.

MARJORIE. In that case let's get started.

General noise and movement.

CYN (*to* DAWN). Cow! Come on, let's get out of here. It's like being back in bloody school.

Fade in promotions board.

COLONEL. We have four vacancies for lance corporal and seven names here. Privates Elerick and Dunn, A Company. Johnson and

Dennison, B Company, Harris, C Company and Meyers and Hardcastle HQ Company . . . Right let's take A Company first. Major Kirby?

Fade in bus stop. Big lorry passes with a roar, close to them. One of CYN's kids is crying.

CYN. Did you check that timetable?

DAWN. It said ten.

CYN. Where the bloody hell is it then? Jason, will you shut up.

A car approaches and passes.

DAWN. What are you doing?

CYN. Hitching a lift.

DAWN. With me and three kids!

CYN. I'm an optimist.

A car passes.

DAWN. Need to be don't you.

CYN. Don't worry about Ireland. Col's done three tours and worst he got was an ingrowing toenail.

DAWN. It's not just that. I've just moved in and he's off.

CYN. Yeh well that's the army for you innit?

DAWN. Mind I never see him when he's here, he's always working or training or out with his mates . . .

CYN. Yeh, well that's soldiers for you innit!

DAWN. He doesn't even spend time with Crystal. I couldn't keep him away from her at me mam's.

CYN. You miss your mam?

DAWN. Me Gran mostly . . . I haven't really got on with me mam since I got pregnant.

CYN. Go and see her while he's away.

DAWN. Bit early to be running back in't it? Anyway I can't afford it.

CYN. Ah well, I might have the answer to that. I had a word with Jimmy down the pub the other night . . . He's looking for a new barmaid so I put your name forward.

DAWN. You're joking!

CYN. Said you could pop in today make his mind up.

DAWN. You fixed this up didn't you?

CYN. Sort of. Still have our picnic.

DAWN. I don't know what to say.

CYN. Tenner a night you know.

DAWN. Could do with the cash. What about Crystal?

CYN. Always bring her round my place and share the babysitter.

DAWN. It's just Denny that's all.

CYN. He's away on Monday. If he comes back and you've earned a
hundred or so quid he's not going to shout about it is he?

Car approaching.

Eh up, come on mate, give us a lift!

She dashes to thumb. Car slows.

(*Off mike.*) Eh up, it's stopping.

Car stops. Engine tickover. Fade out.

*Fade in interior. Car: engine at full speed. The conversation is stilted and
awkward.*

MYRA. I'm going right through town so just tell me where you want
dropping.

CYN. Clocktower's fine, ta.

MYRA. Shopping?

CYN. Just a change . . .

This is followed by a silence.

MYRA. I'm coming back at two if that's any help.

CYN (*not too keen*). Well . . . we dunno what we're doing really . . .

MYRA. Well if I see you waiting . . .

CYN. Ta.

MYRA. There's the school bus at four if you get really desperate.

Bit of a silence. Only the engine and the kids.

Not too hot on buses round here.

CYN. They're not the only ones!

MYRA. I know what you mean.

CYN. Why don't they run the regimental bus Mrs Burridge?

MYRA. Because the band takes precedence I'm afraid.

CYN. But there's loads of wives without transport and it was our
blokes fixed it up. I mean we even raised money to buy it. Wouldn't
have done if we'd known the band was having it.

MYRA. I know. I agree with you.

CYN. Can't your husband do anything now he's Families Officer?

MYRA. I can but try.

CYN. Same if you want to make a call. There's going to be a load of girls wanting to phone their husbands when they're in Ireland and what have we got? One call box outside the main gate miles from anywhere and it's always vandalised.

MYRA. I'll tell him . . . You should really come to Wives' Club and raise these things you know.

CYN. We've just been and they didn't want to know.

MYRA. You've got to keep at them.

CYN. Do no good. They don't give a toss about us Mrs Burridge. We're second class citizens as far as the Army's concerned. (*Pauses.*) You know when they flew us home from that last tour of Germany, they put everything under a heading, right? Ammunition, men, food . . . you know what we came under?

MYRA. Excess Baggage . . .

CYN. Yeh . . . my old man thought that was dead funny.

Interior. Promotions board.

COLONEL. Right, that leaves one more vacancy and I think, in view of the tour that B Company should have it. Who have we left?

ADJUTANT. Johnson and Dennison sir.

COLONEL. Right let's have a look at their records. Should be an easy enough job . . . You know them Sar'nt Major Burridge . . . what do you think?

BILL. Dennison's a good man sir. Fine athlete . . . very keen, clean record . . . got married nine months ago . . . seems to have matured him.

COLONEL. No problems with the wife?

CRANHAM. No sir, she's only been here a matter of weeks and she's already taken an active interest in various activities.

COLONEL. Sounds like our man.

BILL. Johnson's more up top though and he has served longer.

COLONEL. Well I'll take your advice gentlemen.

By the river. Kids splashing about. Maybe the sound of a weir. The two girls are paddling, having fun.

DAWN. Give over you daft devil (*Splashing.*) Cyn! Ooh you sod. I'll get you for that!

CYN *screams and laughs as she runs through the shallows and is splashed. They end up on the bank laughing and panting. Gradually it subsides.*

DAWN. Look at kids. They think we're mad.

CYN. We are mad or we wouldn't be here . . .

DAWN. You think you did right speaking out like that?

CYN. What do I care. Hey, look we'd better think about moving if you want to see Jimmy.

DAWN. No harm in seeing him I suppose.

CYN. That's my girl. Do you good to have a job.

DAWN. I mean it is all above board and that . . .

CYN. What do you mean?

DAWN. Just barmaiding like you said.

CYN. What else? (*Dawns.*) Your old man's been having words with you hasn't he?

DAWN (*tentatively*). Just said you had a job in Germany.

CYN (*putting the record straight*). I was a waitress in a drinking club, Dawn, that's all. I served drinks to soldiers and tourists. It wasn't a knocking shop and I wasn't on the game. The only parts of me that ached after a night's work were me feet from standing and me bum from being felt by every drunken squaddie who wanted to look big in front of his mates.

DAWN is silent.

Same drunken sods who spread rumours when they got back to camp.

DAWN. I'm sorry, Cyn . . .

CYN. So am I. I'm sorry I ever took it.

DAWN. Why there though?

CYN. Paid well and we needed the money! We always need money . . . (*Pause and she laughs.*) Wasn't just the money though . . . Got me out . . . got me noticed . . . had a few laughs even . . . the other girls there were great. Course all this lot think I'm a scrubber now. Big mouthed scrubber who does a bit on the side and's blown her old man's chances but I'll tell you something, Dawn. I was just like you when I joined up . . . read the posters, seen Col in his best blue, been to passing out . . . wanting him to get on. (*Pauses.*) Just didn't seem to work out though. Too many separations, too many kids, too much gob . . . I've got a big gob, I know . . . but it can't just've been me kept him a squaddie can it? I mean it must be something to do with him as well . . . (*Forces a laugh.*) Anyway, I don't care anymore . . . I mean what have I got to lose now? Four kids under seven and a husband who'd screw a brick wall if it had legs.

There's no response from DAWN. CYN laughs.

Here! Don't look so serious! I'm not often like this. I've said me piece now . . .

DAWN. I like you Cyn. I don't care what they say.

CYN. Do you?

DAWN. Yeh . . . whatever they say.

CYN (*laughs but touched*). Ta . . . eh . . . and don't worry about him going. I'll look after you. (*Silence.*) Come on. Let's get to that pub. I think you'll like Jimmy.

Interior. DENNY's. DENNY *is waiting as* DAWN *opens the door with her Yale and enters with the push chair. She is surprised to see* DENNY.

DAWN. Denny! I didn't expect you till later.

DENNY. So I see.

DAWN. I had to catch the school bus.

DENNY. Get on okay at Wives' Club?

DAWN. Yeh, fine . . .

DENNY. Do anything interesting?

DAWN. Sat round drinking coffee mostly . . .

DENNY. Oh, somebody said they saw you with Cyn Watson.

DAWN. Oh . . . yeh . . . she was there.

DENNY. I thought I told you to stay clear of that whore.

DAWN. She's not a whore!

DENNY. That's what she says is it?

DAWN. She's all right.

DENNY (*shouts*). All right! You think she's all right!

DAWN. Denny, why are you shouting at me . . .

DENNY. I'll do more than shout at you you bitch!

He slaps her face and she cries out in pain.

(*Shouts.*) When I tell you to do summat, you do it in future and don't bloody lie to me!

He hits her again. She is crying. Baby starts crying.

DAWN. We only went to town . . .

DENNY. After you stirred it with the Colonel's wife!

DAWN. I don't know what you mean . . .

DENNY. I mean standing up and opening her gob about that bus that's what I mean! I mean losing me my chance of a stripe!

He hits her again and she cries out.

That's right. It was between me and Johnson and he got it!

She just cries and sobs bitterly.

Why the hell did I marry you!

He hits her again. And again.

You won't drag me down you bitch!

DAWN (*sobs*). Oh! . . . Crystal . . .

DENNY. Crystal! What do you care about Crystal! What do you care about anybody but yourself!

He starts to leave, she shouts after him.

DAWN. Denny!

DENNY. Piss off. Piss off round to your friends. That's all you're good for anyway. I'll be glad to get to Northern Ireland and away from the bloody lot of you.

Exterior. Departure point for troops. Parade ground trucks backing up and sergeants shouting. General hustle and bustle before main body of troops arrive.

Q.M. SERGEANT. Come on, load those lorries up. We haven't all day. Johnson! Shift yourself! (*To* CRANE.) Steady with those crates. Steady . . .

DAWN's *quarters.* DENNY *is packing his travel bag. There is an air.*

DENNY. Did you find me old trainers?

DAWN. I put 'em in your kit bag. Here. You forgot your Walkman.

DENNY. Ta . . .

DAWN. That's about it then.

DENNY. Yeh.

DAWN. I thought we might walk down to the depot with you. I could do with some fresh air.

DENNY (*quickly*). No . . . I'd rather say tara here.

DAWN (*disappointed*). I could put some make up on.

DENNY. I don't want any fuss.

DAWN. Here love, Daddy's going. Give him a kiss.

He kisses her perfunctorily. Baby mewls.

Talk to her, Denny . . . say tara.

DENNY. Tara little 'un . . .

DAWN *is quiet.*

I'd better go.

DAWN (*sighs*). Okay . . .

DENNY (*kisses her briefly*). See you.

DAWN (*softly*). Yeh. Take care.

Interior. Elephant and Castle. Lots of noise and chatter. Noisy soldier's pub.

SOLDIER. Come on love. Four pints of lager!

DAWN (*pulling pints*). I'm doing me best. Just hang on.

SOLDIER. Give us summat to hang on to and I will!

   Laughter.

DAWN. Well, you'll get served last now won't you?

SOLDIER. As long as everybody's gone home and there's just you and me.

CYN (*arriving*). You've got a lot off for a little lad!

   Jeers and cheers.

SOLDIER. Have it off wi' you anytime love!

CYN. How about now then?

SOLDIER (*taken by surprise*). What?

   Jeers and cheers and 'Go on Yorky, get stuck in Yorky'.

CYN. Now. Come on! Round the back. Shouldn't take long looking at you.

SOLDIER. You couldn't handle me love.

CYN. I'd have a job finding anything to handle by look of you!

   Laughter from men.

CYN. Well are you coming or are you all mouth and trousers like rest?

SOLDIER. Joke . . . that's all . . . just a joke.

CYN. You're the joke pal. Now just drink up and piss off.

   Cheers from rest. 'Good old Cyn'.

DAWN (*admiringly*). How'd do you do it?

CYN. Plenty of practice!

Interior. Families Office. BILL *and* MARJORIE ELLESWORTH.

MARJORIE. I know you'll be getting an official invitation Bill, but I'm telling you now so that Myra has a bit of warning. You know what we women are at times like this . . . I'm sure she'd like to buy a new dress or something like that.

BILL. Very thoughtful of you Mrs Ellesworth.

MARJORIE. You really must stop calling me that you know. It's Marjorie.

BILL. Marjorie it is then . . . By the way I've drawn up a list you might be interested in . . .

He hands it to her.

BILL. All the problem families. It's B Company I'm really concerned about . . . Thought it might be an idea to split them up between yourself and the other interested officers' wives . . . just pay the odd visit, keep checking.

MARJORIE. It's a very good idea.

BILL. I always say prevention's better than cure . . . If we see somebody's getting into trouble we can do something about it.

Wives' Club committee meeting.

MARJORIE. And so Bill and I have drawn up the list which I'll give to you at the end of this meeting. If you've any questions put them to me personally and I'll do my best to answer them. Now is there any other business? (*Silence.*) Then I declare the meeting closed. Thank you for attending.

Buzz of talk from seven or eight people.

You know your husband really is coming up trumps Myra. We should have had him doing this years ago.

MYRA. Yes, he seems to be enjoying himself.

MARJORIE. You've got the invitation?

MYRA. Yes, thank you.

MARJORIE. Should be a splendid evening . . . I've never known a ranker adapt so well before. The boys say the mess hasn't been so lively in years. (*Laughs.*)

MYRA (*trying hard*). Yes . . . Look I'm sorry but I really do have to go. Would you excuse me Mrs Ellesworth?

MARJORIE. It's Marjorie and yes of course I will. You must still be busy settling in . . .

MYRA. Yes . . . yes we are . . .

MARJORIE. Everything going smoothly?

MYRA. Oh . . . yes . . . everything's fine.

Elephant and Castle bar. Closing time. Noisy.

CYN. Right that's it you lot. Come on let's have your glasses now.

Well past time! (*To* DAWN *who is stacking glasses.*) You heard from your old man yet?

DAWN. No.

CYN. Neither have I . . . still that's nothing new. At least he won't be getting his hands on some young bit of stuff . . . not where he's gone!

DAWN. I'm worried Cyn.

CYN. Everybody has rows love. Maybe it's just as well he's posted. Might appreciate you a bit more when he gets back.

Various calls of 'Good night love', 'See you Dawn . . .'

DAWN (*calls back*). Night! It's two weeks. I was wondering about going down to the Families Office. I mean something might've happened.

CYN. They'd let you know if it had. Maybe they're busy.

SOLDIER. Eh up Dawn? Okay?

DAWN. Oh yeh, thanks Eddie.

SOLDIER. Thought I'd give you a hand.

Puts glasses on bar.

DAWN. Ta . . . I'll get the rest.

SOLDIER. No trouble!

CYN (*quietly with a smile*). He fancies you, that one. Been in every night since you started!

DAWN. Give over.

CYN. Nice looking lad. Could do worse.

DAWN. I'm not interested Cyn.

SOLDIER (*returning with more glasses*). I was saying to my mate . . . If either of you're ever stuck for a lift . . .

DAWN. Thanks but Jimmy takes us home.

SOLDIER. Or if you'd like to go out somewhere . . .

DAWN. No thanks . . .

SOLDIER. Oh right . . . sorry.

CYN. Hang on kid, I might be interested . . .

DAWN. Look, thanks anyway, but we're both married okay?

SOLDIER. Yeh, well . . . I hope you didn't mind me asking . . .

DAWN (*smiles*). No, course not . . .

SOLDIER (*leaving*). Offer's always open if you change your mind.

CYN. Bless him! I bet it took him a week to pluck up courage to ask you.

DAWN. Yeh well I'm not interested Cyn. Okay?

CYN. Okay, okay . . . don't bite me head off. Kill or cure I always
say . . . (*Shouts.*) Come on then lads! Let's be having you! We've got
homes to go to even if you haven't!

Interior. Families Office a week later. Sound of a CORPORAL *on
typewriter. Not too proficient.*

CPL (FAMILIES). Big do tonight then sir?

BILL. Yeh, should be quite a splash.

CPL (FAMILIES). Saw the chunkies taking over the food this
afternoon.

BILL. If I go now can you cope, Fred?

CPL (FAMILIES). No problem sir.

BILL. Only I've my mess kit to pick up and one or two other bits and
pieces . . .

CPL (FAMILIES). You get off sir. I'll manage.

Phone rings. CORPORAL *picks it up.*

CPL (FAMILIES) (*fairly brusque*). Families Office, Corporal
Henderson. (*Listens.*) He's just about to go. (*Listens and interrupts.*)
Hold on. (*To* BILL.) Wants to talk to you sir.

BILL (*puts papers down*). Lieutenant Burridge? Yes. (*Listens.*) How
often? (*Listens.*) You're sure of this, love? Right. Can I have your
name please? No, you don't have to . . . okay look hang on, just let
me get a pen. (*Gets a pen off desk.*) Right, Clive Road you say?
(*Writes.*) Yeh, 32 got that . . . and 34. And the names of the families
involved . . . (*She rings off.*) Hello? Hello?

He puts the phone down.

CPL (FAMILIES). Rung off?

BILL. Yeh . . . look up 32 and 34 Clive Road, Fred.

CPL (FAMILIES). What's the story sir?

BILL. She says they're leaving their kids with an underage sitter . . .
young girl.

CPL (FAMILIES). Here we are . . . (*Recognition.*) Watson, B
Company . . . well, that's par for the course. We've had them for this
before.

BILL. And 34?

CPL (FAMILIES). Dennison.

BILL (*surprised*). Dennison?

CPL (FAMILIES). Yeh . . . surprised about that. Pretty good soldier.
Got some of B Company back on R & R this week sir. In fact I
think Dennison's on the list.

BILL. Log the call then Fred.

CPL (FAMILIES). Yessir.

BILL. She says they'll be out tonight.

CPL (FAMILIES). Want me to check it?

BILL. I might just come home via Clive Road after the party . . .

Interior. Officers' Mess. There is a cocktail party going on. Perhaps 50 people in a largish room all talking. Clink of glasses. HARRY CRANHAM is standing with BILL and a few other officers who don't speak but can be heard responding to the story.

CPL. Drink sir?

ANGUS. G and T for me.

CRANHAM. Usual for me Corporal. Bill?

BILL. I'm okay thanks . . .

CRANHAM. Tell Angus that story about the taxis . . . great story this, Angus. RSM wasn't it Bill?

BILL. No, Colour Sergeant . . . Used to tell his wife he was working late . . . usual story . . . midnight and all that . . . then he'd go to work, finish at five and him and some mates used to go into Nicosia for a night out. Anyway, this particular night, about ten or eleven they're all pretty plastered and he's feeling a bit frisky so he hops in a cab and asks the cabbie to take him somewhere interesting . . . nice girl . . . bit of fun . . . all that. Anyway, it's warm in the cab and he's had a fair bit to drink and he's out like a light. When he wakes up, he finds he's stopped outside his own front door. 'I thought I told you I wanted a woman' he says to the cab driver . . . 'Yes, sir. Very good woman. Best screw in town here sir.'

ANGUS. She was on the game?

CRANHAM (*laughing*). Her and thirteen other wives of assorted ranks.

BILL. All registered with the cabbie.

CRANHAM. When their old men said they were working late they just rang up the taxi driver and told him they were open for business.

ANGUS. So what happened?

BILL. They had the wives and kids back in England within twenty four hours.

MYRA (*approaching*). And what about the men?

CRANHAM. Oh, hello Mrs Burridge.

MYRA. 'Myra', you must call me Myra now I'm an officer's wife, Harry.

CRANHAM. Oh yes, quite. Do you know Angus?

MYRA. No, what I'd like to know is what happened to the husbands . . .

BILL. No doubt they were put on a warning.

MYRA. For keeping a disruptive house or whoring?

Off mike the COLONEL *taps the table and calls for quiet.*

COLONEL. Ladies and gentlemen.

Some shushes during which MYRA *addresses* BILL.

COLONEL. Ladies and gentlemen. I'm sure everyone here is already well acquainted with Lieutenant and Mrs Burridge, who we know better now as Bill and Myra. (*Response.*) Indeed some of the younger officers will no doubt still feel a certain trepidation at the mention of his name (*Laughter.*) and perhaps relief now that our Sergeant Major is now a brother officer and a very welcome addition to this mess. (*Hear, hears.*) Now I've known Bill for nearly 20 years. He was once my platoon sergeant. He's a good man and a good soldier. I've also known Myra, less well perhaps than my wife has known her, but no one could fail to be aware of her consistent work for the regimental wives over the years and more important, the rather unfashionable but continuing support of a husband in his chosen vocation. Both Bill and Myra are people of immense character and loyalty and we hope they continue to bring both those qualities to the Regiment for many years to come. (*Hear, hears.*) Ladies and gentlemen . . . brother officers. Bill and Myra Burridge!

ALL. Bill and Myra.

Interior. Elephant and Castle. Throwing out time.

DAWN. Come on then boys let's have your glasses. Time now . . . thank you!

CYN. You do the glasses and I'll do the tables.

DAWN. Right.

CYN. Look like the cat who got the cream.

DAWN. Yeh, well. He might be home tomorrow with a bit of luck. (*Shouts.*) Come on now . . . way past time now, please!

Interior. Officers' Mess. The party is breaking up.

MARJORIE. I'm so glad we did this Myra. It's been a great success and you know Bill fits into the mess like a glove. The Colonel's very pleased.

MYRA. Oh good.

MARJORIE. He really does look splendid. You know I always say Mess Kit does something to a man.

MYRA. I always think it makes him look rather silly. And the rest of them if you want my honest opinion.

MARJORIE (*doesn't really know if this is a joke or not but laughs*). Yes, well . . . We're all very glad you both decided to stay on . . . I don't know what we'd have done without you.

MYRA. You'd have got someone else to run around Mrs Ellesworth . . .

MARJORIE. Myra, have you been drinking?

MYRA. Yes and please don't call me Myra. My friends call me Myra.

MARJORIE. I'd rather hoped we could be friends . . .

MYRA. You've had twenty years to make friends with me Mrs Ellesworth but I wasn't on the right side of the line was I? Don't you find that rather ludicrous?

MARJORIE. There are certain customs . . . traditions . . .

MYRA. No, Mrs Ellesworth, just a a lot of unnecessary nonsense . . . and a lot of outdated ideas and snobbery.

MARJORIE. Look I think it may be better if you go home . . . get some sleep . . . It's obviously been too much for you.

MYRA. Oh yes. It's definitely been that.

MARJORIE. I'm sure you'll settle in time. It always takes some getting used to.

MYRA. Oh I've no intention of getting used to it Mrs Ellesworth. Hasn't Bill told you? We're buying a house off camp, in town. We hope to be in before September.

BILL (*approaching*). Wonderful party, Marjorie. Thank you very much.

MARJORIE (*bit cool*). I'm glad you enjoyed it Bill.

BILL. First class . . . Right, you ready, love?

MYRA. I've been ready for a while.

BILL. One or two calls to make before I go home. Good night then Marjorie and thanks again. Great party.

MARJORIE. I'm glad you enjoyed it.

MYRA. Yes, it was a real experience. Good night . . . Marjorie . . .

Interior. Car. Constant speed but slowish.

MYRA. Can't we just go straight home Bill?

BILL. It won't take long.

He changes down.

Almost there. (*Slows.*) Can you make out the numbers?

MYRA. I'm so tired I can hardly see the houses.

BILL. Hang on . . .

Stops car.

There's 34.

MYRA. And there's a light on so can we please go home and get to bed.

BILL. I better just go and check.

MYRA. At half eleven at night!

BILL. The curtains aren't drawn in the bedroom.

MYRA. So what! These people have rights Bill.

BILL. Myra, there's been a report. I've got to check!

He opens car door and gets out. We follow him. He knocks on the door. After a few minutes the door opens.

DENNY. Yeh?

BILL. Private Dennison?

DENNY. Yes sir. Sorry sir.

BILL. I thought you lot weren't due back till tomorrow.

DENNY. Hitched a lift, sir.

BILL. Yeh, well sorry to bother you. Everything all right is it?

DENNY. Fine, sir.

BILL. Wife and family okay . . .

DENNY. Yes sir. Must've popped home to see her mother. Can't have heard I was coming back.

BILL. Fine . . . Well, sorry to bother you.

DENNY. Problem sir?

BILL. Got the wrong house. Night Dennison.

DENNY. Night sir.

Fade in exterior. CYN's *house.* BILL *knocking on door, we hear* WENDY's *voice through the door.*

WENDY. Go away!

BILL. Lieutenant Burridge here . . . Is that Mrs Watson?

WENDY. Mrs Watson isn't in. Go away.

BILL. Who's that?

WENDY. Wendy Ransome.

BILL. Corporal Ransome's girl?

No reply.

Are you on your own, Wendy?

WENDY. Mrs Watson says I'm not to talk to anybody or let anybody in.

BILL. You know me, Wendy. It's Lt Burridge. Now. Come on, open up.

MYRA (*joins*). For God's sake, you're terrifying the poor kid . . . Wendy, it's Mrs Burridge. You know me. I've been round to your house.

Are you on your own, Wendy?

WENDY. I'm babysitting.

MYRA. Best open up love . . . Let's have a chat, eh? It's all right, you're not in any trouble. Don't worry.

Door opens.

There, remember me?

WENDY. Yeh.

MYRA. Are you on your own?

WENDY. Yeh . . .

MYRA. And you're looking after all Mrs Watson's children?

WENDY. And Mrs Dennison's.

BILL. Mrs Dennison's? (*To* MYRA.) You go in and sit with her, Myra. I'll get Dennison, see if we can't get to the bottom of this.

Interior. CYN's *quarters.*

BILL. How old are you Wendy?

WENDY. Twelve.

BILL. And how often do you do this love?

WENDY. Three times a week.

DENNY. What?

BILL. Just for Mrs Watson?

WENDY. They always go together.

DENNY. Where? Where do they go?

BILL. Just keep your voice down and leave this to me, lad. I can understand your concern but shouting won't get us anywhere.

MYRA. Why don't you take Crystal home, Mr Dennison?

DENNY (*to* BILL). I'll wait sir. If I may sir.

BILL. As long as you keep quiet.

DENNY. Yes sir.

MYRA. It's all right Wendy . . . don't worry . . . Bill we should get this child home where she belongs.

BILL. Where is your house Wendy?

WENDY. 58 Verdun Road.

BILL. And do your parents know where you are love?

WENDY. Yeh.

BILL. How do you get home?

WENDY. Well they're not usually as late as this. Jimmy brings them home and then he drops me off.

DENNY. Jimmy!

BILL. Jimmy who?

WENDY. I don't know his other name. He works at the pub.

DENNY. Which pub?

WENDY. I don't know.

MYRA. I really think it would be better if you took Crystal home and either you or I take Wendy, Bill.

DENNY. I want to be here when she gets back.

BILL. I'll send her home when she arrives, don't worry.

As he speaks we hear car doors and some giggling and laughing outside. The door opens.

CYN. Wendy . . . get your stuff together, Jimmy's waiting to take you home . . . (*Stops dead.*) What the hell's going on in here!

DAWN. Denny! What are you doing here?

DENNY. I might ask you the same thing.

CYN. I said what's going on for Christ's sake! This is my house!

BILL (*assuming command*). Now just a minute . . . Let's take things calmly and without raising our voices!

CYN. Calmly. I come home to find you've walked into my house uninvited and you tell me to take things calmly. Christ!

BILL. I'd remind you it's an offence to leave your children in the care of a minor Mrs Watson.

CYN. Only if there's been an accident Lieutenant Burridge! And as there's been no accident I'll ask you to get out of my house. Now!

BILL. I don't see any point in anyone losing their temper . . .

CYN. Oh you don't do you? Haven't you got anything better to do than sneak round people's houses at the dead of night frightening kids half to death.

MYRA. I think it's best if we took Wendy home now Bill . . .

CYN. Yeh, well I wouldn't argue with that!

BILL. Let's not be in so much of a rush. I'll decide who goes where and when . . . Now Dennison, you get your wife and child home for a start. I'll see you tomorrow.

DENNY. Yes sir. (*They start to go.*)

DAWN. I'll go and get Crystal.

BILL. I'll decide in the morning exactly what course of action to take with all of you.

CYN. What do you mean, 'what course of action'!

BILL. She's a twelve year old child Mrs Watson and you left her in complete control of five children under seven. It's quarter past one in the morning!

MYRA. Bill, come on . . . This isn't the time.

CYN. That's right. You've nothing on me.

BILL (*angry*). Haven't I? Well I'll tell you this lady. As from tomorrow morning eight hundred hours your husband's on official family warning and you so much as breathe in the wrong direction after that and we'll have you out of here in ten minutes flat!

CYN. Just get out of my house. All of you. Get out!

DAWN's *quarters.* DAWN *enters.*

DAWN. Denny, it's great to see you.

DENNY (*interrupts*). She asleep?

DAWN. Yeh, she's fine. Denny, why didn't you let me know you'd be home tonight?

DENNY. So you could've been in?

DAWN. Yeh. Oh! It's good to see you.

She holds him. He shrugs her off.

DAWN. What's wrong?

DENNY. So who's Jimmy?

DAWN. Just a bloke works down the pub with us.

DENNY. He's not bad looking is he?

DAWN. I suppose he's all right . . . I hadn't really noticed. Denny I want to show you something . . . Here, look . . . (*She goes off mike and opens a drawer and returns.*) Look . . . there's a hundred pounds here . . . that's what I saved . . . and I've got the new plates and cutlery. It's all our own now Denny . . . I knew you wouldn't like me working but it's a tenner a night . . .

DENNY. You got all that from pulling pints?

DAWN. Yeh . . .

DENNY. That all you been pulling?

DAWN. What do you mean by that?

DENNY. I said is that all you've been pulling!

DAWN. For God's sake Denny! Denny, no!

Interior. MYRA's *quarters.*

MYRA. So they left the kids. Maybe they need the money! They have a right to work Bill.

BILL. Their kids have rights as well!

MYRA. Okay, so they did the wrong thing but you could at least find out what's been going on . . . See what they had to say instead of automatically assuming that they're guilty.

BILL. Read the files, Myra.

MYRA. Who wrote the files Bill? The army! People like Harry Cranham for God's sake.

BILL. I know the Watsons. She's been trouble since the day she was marched in!

MYRA. Yes, well slapping a family warning certificate on them's not going to solve any of their problems.

BILL. No, but it's going to solve mine. That lady steps out of line now and she loses her quarter.

MYRA. It's your job to help them.

BILL. Help! Where else would you walk into a fully furnished three bedroomed house for 24 quid a week at the age of 19?

MYRA. I'm not just talking about money . . . I'm talking about loneliness, isolation . . . being left on your own with small kids when you're not much more than a kid yourself . . . I'm talking about paying bills, doing jobs you're not used to doing . . .

BILL. That's something you just have to get used to.

MYRA. You do! You do get used to it! You take over the reins, sort things out, learn to fix plugs, mend fuses, discipline the kids, then suddenly this stranger you haven't seen for months turns up and expects to take over where he left off.

BILL. Myra, that's the army. That's the way it is.

MYRA. But you should realise it's wrong, Bill. You should be trying to change it!

BILL. I'm not a social worker Myra, I'm an officer in an infantry regiment.

MYRA. So you train and fight and file and duplicate and triplicate and somewhere along the way the families get lost or forgotten.

BILL. Look they're part of the system Myra, like the men. A regiment has to have a system to survive, and I mean life and death, Myra, not day to day. We're training them to kill, right? It's easier if they're single but if they're not we provide them with quarters which we furnish and send their kids to private schools so their education isn't disrupted . . . but we don't do it for the wives, and we don't really do it for the kids, we do it for the men because it makes them feel better and fight better.

Phone rings. He picks it up.

Lt Burridge? (*Listens.*) It's half past one in the morning Sergeant . . . Oh . . . I see. Yes. Of course. No you were perfectly right to call me. Yes . . . I'll be down directly.

Puts phone down.

MYRA. The system at work?

BILL. Dennison walked into the guard room ten minutes ago and asked for an ambulance. Said his wife had some sort of accident.

MYRA. Oh God . . .

BILL. She's on her way to the hospital now . . .

Next day in COLONEL's *office.*

COLONEL. He admits beating her up you say?

BILL. Yes sir. Said she was playing around with some bloke at the pub she worked in.

COLONEL. I've had the hospital on to me this morning. They told me you went down last night.

BILL. They usually inform the police in cases of severe beatings . . .

COLONEL. Yes, I gathered you told them we'd be dealing with it, well done, Bill.

BILL. I didn't think you'd want the police brought in sir.

COLONEL. Absolutely right. If we've any dirty washing to do let's do it ourselves.

BILL. Did they say how she is now?

COLONEL. Not as bad as she looked apparently but she has been severely beaten. They're keeping her in for observation.

BILL. So what happens now then sir?

COLONEL. Well he's brought the regiment into disrepute. We can't allow him to do that.

CRANHAM. His personal file reads well sir.

COLONEL. What we've got to decide is, is it a temporary aberration?

CRANHAM. No previous black marks, his Company Commander speaks well of him and he's recommended for promotion to lance corporal.

COLONEL. Looks like he 'cherchezed' the wrong 'femme' eh?

CRANHAM. Wouldn't be the first time sir.

COLONEL. And I don't suppose it'll be the last Harry. The question still remains, what do we do?

BILL. Could defer his promotion sir, give him enough extras to remind him and place him on a formal warning. Then if it happened again we'd withdraw his licence for married quarters.

COLONEL. Yes . . . sounds sensible.

CRANHAM. He is a good soldier sir. His OC doesn't want to lose him.

COLONEL. No . . . quite. Where is he now?

BILL. Still in the guard room sir. The Provost sergeant locked him up for the night to cool off. Mrs Burridge has the baby.

COLONEL. Right, let's have him in. I'd like you to stay Bill.

BILL. Yes sir.

Fade in DENNY *being marched in by a sergeant.*

PROVOST SGT. Leff-right-leff-right-leff. Mark time. Halt. 2442184 Private Dennison sah!

COLONEL. Thank you Sergeant. Dismissed.

PROVOST SGT. Sah!

The SERGEANT *turns about and stomps off.*

COLONEL. Bad business this Dennison. You've caused severe injuries to your wife and in the process brought this regiment into disrepute. That's something I can't tolerate. Is that clearly understood?

DENNY. Yes sir.

COLONEL. For your information, your wife is described as comfortable but they're keeping her in the hospital for observation.

No response.

Now you've got a clean record. A good record even until you went and spoiled it by this stupidity. You narrowly missed recommendation for promotion to lance corporal. (*Pauses.*) I need NCOs that are level headed Dennison, not men who fly off the handle when they're under pressure. Now from what you've told Lieutenant Burridge and from what we can gather there was a certain amount of provocation in your case and so I've decided to take the matter no further. Whether your wife decides to press charges for assault is up to her of course but we shan't involve the police. You will however be placed on official family warning notice to ensure that this domestic occurrence doesn't happen again. Do you understand?

DENNY. Yes sir.

COLONEL. And there is a form you must sign in my presence . . . Captain Cranham?

CRANHAM. Yes sir. (*Hands him the form.*)

DENNY. Permission to speak sir?

COLONEL. Go ahead.

DENNY. Request to declare myself a single person sir and return to barracks, sir.

COLONEL. You're sure about this Dennison.

DENNY. Yes sir.

COLONEL. Are you saying you intend to leave your wife and child?

DENNY. Yes sir, get divorced sir.

COLONEL. You don't think perhaps you'd better wait until you see her again. Discuss the matter.

DENNY. Nothing to discuss sir. It's over as far as I'm concerned.

COLONEL. Wait outside Dennison.

DENNY. Yes sir.

He turns and marches to the door and opens it and closes it after him.

COLONEL. What do you think?

BILL. He's perfectly at liberty to do that.

COLONEL. Did you have any idea he was going to spring this?

BILL. Not a clue, sir. Could have been talking to some of the lads in the guard room.

COLONEL. Shouldn't he discuss it with her first?

BILL. Up to him. Might be past the discussion stage, sir. Could be best for both of them.

COLONEL (*sighs*). Yes I suppose so. I'll leave it in your hands, Bill. That'll be all Harry.

BILL. We can have him back in barracks tonight and make her an IRO. I'll go and see her as soon as the hospital says it's okay.

COLONEL. Right. Let's do that then. Just one other thing Bill.

Apparently Mrs Burridge wasn't her old self last night . . . bit sharp
with Mrs Ellesworth and some of the senior officers' wives. Now
we're old friends. I don't want this to come between us so I'm
trusting you to put it right as soon as you can.

BILL. Yes sir. I'd no idea sir.

COLONEL. Could just be pressure from a change of lifestyle. Quite
understandable. Just one other thing. I'd like to make this very clear
to you. I want my Families Officer living on camp.

BILL. I understand that sir.

COLONEL. Only there was some mention of moving into town.

BILL (*laughs*). No sir. Must've been the drink. She's not really used to
it.

COLONEL. Yes, well, just keep things in line that's all Bill. Carry on!

Interior. MYRA's *quarters.*

MYRA. You're pressing charges I hope.

BILL. No.

MYRA. He's an animal. He wants locking up after what he did to that
girl.

BILL. Myra, I've had enough today, okay?

MYRA. What about her? Hasn't she had enough?

BILL. I'm going to the Mess.

MYRA. To conveniently forget!

BILL. To try and forget.

MYRA. So he declares himself single, gets off scot free and she's
dumped on the social services.

BILL. She'll be given time to sort something out.

MYRA. Meanwhile she'll become an irregular occupant of an army
quarter and her rent'll go up.

BILL. I don't make the rules.

MYRA. I know, you only carry them out. But you do it with such
enthusiasm, Bill.

BILL (*angry now*). I don't condone violence!

MYRA. Oh? And what about your alternative to fines?

BILL. That's nothing to do with wives!

MYRA. It's violence isn't it?

BILL. No, it's punishment . . . and they always had the choice. It only
needed one man to put me on the floor and I was finished.

MYRA (*sarcastically*). Marquis of Queensberry rules!

BILL. They respect me Myra.

MYRA. Oh I know. I've heard 'em. 'Hard man Sar'nt Major
   Burridge . . . but fair. Always shakes hands after he's thumped the
   shit out of you.'

BILL. Yeh and that's what it's all about. They'd follow me anywhere.

MYRA. Yeh . . . and that's what's so frightening Bill. Because when
   they stagger off home all macho and matey, they do the same things
   to their wives and kids.

BILL. I'm off to the Mess. (*He goes as if to leave.*)

MYRA. I'll be gone when you get back.

BILL (BILL *stops*). What?

MYRA. I've got a flat. It's not much but it's a start.

BILL. You're bluffing . . .

MYRA. No.

BILL (*laughs, coming back*). Hey, Myra, come on . . .

MYRA. No, don't touch me. You go to the Mess. That's what you
   want. I'll go to my flat.

BILL. You're serious.

MYRA. I paid a month's rent this afternoon. I took the money from
   the Building Society Account. I haven't taken much, don't worry I
   won't fleece you. Oh and I've got some things from here . . .
   cutlery . . . plates . . . cups. I thought we could divide stuff up later,
   when we've got more time.

BILL. Myra!

MYRA. Here's my address if you want to contact me . . . I'm going to
   see the children tomorrow to tell them what's happened. They'll be
   joining me at the end of term.

BILL. You can't. You can't just go up there . . . You can't do it just like
   that . . . it's not that simple . . .

MYRA. No it's not but I'm doing it anyway. (*Leaving.*) By the way
   I'm taking the car but you can have it once I've been up there and
   finished moving stuff in.

BILL. Myra, you can't just walk out. I mean where does this leave us?
   We've got to talk about it . . .

MYRA. I'll talk about anything you like once I'm off this camp . . .

Fade in interior. Hospital ward. MYRA *is with* DAWN.

MYRA. How are you feeling Mrs Dennison?

Silence.

Sister said it'll take a while. Not only your body that's been bruised.

Silence.

Still you've no need to worry about the baby. A very nice couple's looking after her till you get on your feet again.

Silence.

I expect you'll be going back to your mothers when you get sorted out. If she can't face that the army'll get the local authority to rehouse you here. 'Course if you do stay on the patch you'll have to go through a formal handover, officially take over the quarter from your husband, but it's only a five minute thing so it shouldn't be too embarrassing. I could arrange for someone to stand in for him if you decided you didn't want him there . . .

No reply. Pause.

You may think it's for the best love. I doubt they'd let Crystal back if he was around. (*Pause.*) She's doing well you know. Needn't have any worries in that department. They've taken really good care of her. I could arrange for them to bring her in if you'd like when you're feeling up to it. What do you think?

DAWN *speaks as if she hasn't been listening, quite matter of fact. Unemotional.*

DAWN. They've taken her away.

MYRA. Only temporarily till you get better, not because of anything you've done . . .

DAWN. I'm not fit to have her. Did you know that?

MYRA. Of course you're fit to have her. It's not your fault it's ended up like this. You've done nothing to reproach yourself . . .

DAWN (*interrupts*). Do you mind if I smoke?

MYRA (*pause*). Course not.

Pause as she fumbles with a cigarette packet and lighter.

Here, let me . . .

MYRA *lights the cigarette for her.* DAWN *inhales.*

Like I say you don't have anything to reproach yourself for . . .

DAWN (*interrupts again*). You won't tell Denny will you?

MYRA. Look, it's not your fault . . .

DAWN. Please Mrs Burridge . . . please. Promise you won't tell him . . .

MYRA. Tell him what? I don't understand . . .

DAWN. That I smoke! If he knew I was smoking again he'd kill me.

Silence. Hold silence. Cut.

JUST REMEMBER TWO THINGS:
IT'S NOT FAIR AND DON'T BE LATE

by Terence Frisby

To Auntie Rose and Uncle Jack

Terence Frisby's most famous play *There's A Girl In My Soup* was London's longest running comedy and a worldwide hit, including Broadway. His script of the film, starring Peter Sellers and Goldie Hawn, won the Screenwriters' Guild Award in 1970 for the best British comedy. His other stage plays are *The Subtopians* (1962), *The Bandwagon* (1969), *It's All Right If I Do It* (1977); and two one-act plays *Seaside Postcard* (1977) and *First Night* (1987). He has also written many plays for television and two comedy series, *Lucky Fellar* (LWT 1976) and *That's Love* (TVS 1988–89). *Just Remember Two Things . . . It's Not Fair and Don't Be Late* is his first radio play. He has acted, directed and produced, playing leading parts in the West End and all over the United Kingdom and Europe in theatre and television. He is most proud of having brought the brilliant, multi-award-winning black South African play *Woza Albert* to London's West End at the Criterion Theatre for 1983–84.

Just Remember Two Things . . . It's Not Fair and Don't Be Late was first broadcast on BBC Radio 4 on 16 April 1988. The cast was as follows:

NARRATOR	Terence Frisby
TERRY, *Child*	Charles Clarke
JACK, *Child*	Boris Hunka
UNCLE JACK	Ray Smith
AUNT ROSE	Petra Davies
MUM/MISS SHEPHERD	Polly James
DAD/DRIVER/1ST MALE VOICE COMPERE/PORTER	Danny Schiller
ELSIE/ETHEL/MRS LANGDON	Caroline Gruber
MISS POLMANOR/1ST FEMALE VOICE/CHILD/JUNE	Zelah Clarke
DAVID/KEN	Richard Peace
GRANNY PETERS/2ND FEMALE VOICE	Barbara Atkinson
HEADMASTER/REV BUCKROYD/2ND MALE VOICE/SENTRY/NEWSREADER	John Baddeley

Director: Matthew Walters
Running time, as broadcast on 16 April: 87 minutes, 27 seconds

Fade in. Interior – perhaps with a slight echo to suggest a church or hall.

TERRY (*sings*). Time like an ever-rolling stream.

   He breathes.

   Bears all its sons away.

   He breathes.

   They fly forgotten as a dream.

   He breathes.

   Dies at the opening day.

   UNCLE JACK *is about 50 with a strong South-Wales-mining-village accent.*

UNCLE JACK. That's right, boy. Not bad. If we got to bother God this Sunday let's bother him with a decent bit of sense, eh? Not all that slop about living eternally in Heaven with Him, eh? There's nothing cosy about Time bearing its sons away. Pretty agnostic, really innit, for a hymn?

   TERRY *has a South London accent, though not a very strong one.*

TERRY. What's agnostic, Uncle Jack?

UNCLE JACK. It's halfway to good sense, boy. Atheism says, 'there's no God'; agnostic says, 'I'm not sure.' I don't suppose the chap 'at wrote any hymn's a real atheist so we'll have to do with halfway house. Now, let's have it again but we'll hit 'em with a bit o'clever phrasing this time, so they listen. Look yere, take your breaths where I marked the page, see? Then they'll have to think a minute. Not that any of 'em do in church, but you never know.

TERRY. There's only one God, isn't there, Uncle Jack?

UNCLE JACK. At most.

TERRY. Then why is church and chapel different?

UNCLE JACK (*confidentially*). Well, you see, boy, church is a lot of lying, hypocritical, God-bothering, sinful Tories.

TERRY. And what's chapel?

UNCLE JACK. Chapel is church without the poetry. Come on, now, with sense this time. Breathe where I marked it and start off with a big 'un.

TERRY (*sings in one breath*). Time, like an ever-rolling stream, bears all its sons away. (*He breathes.*)

UNCLE JACK (*whispered*). Good, good.

TERRY. They fly forgotten. (*He breathes.*)

UNCLE JACK (*whispered*). Yes.

TERRY. As a dream dies at the opening day.

UNCLE JACK (*softly*). There is lovely, my Terry. There is a beautiful voice you do 'ave there. Makes me cry to yere you.

TERRY. Can I go out to play now, the soldiers are coming back from manoeuvres.

UNCLE JACK. Go on, then.

Running feet. A door opening.

Keep out of their way and breathe deeply, bach. Take good big breaths.

Door slam. It echoes as though in time rather than space. Opening credits.

NARRATOR. I was the luckiest of children: I had two childhoods. My earliest memories are of pre-war, antiseptic Welling, just in Kent but really suburban London. This brave new world of one-class, pebble-dashed estates housed young couples who had managed to raise the £25 deposit and, with their small children, escape from the grime of New Cross, Greenwich and Woolwich docks, through the newly legislated Green Belt, to fresh air and gardens. In spite of the gardens, we kids lived in the street; gangs of us on every second corner; a ball and a bike were essentials from the age of five. Then came the war and my other childhood. A few days after the last – British soldiers left Dunkirk, when my brother, Jack was seven, we became evacuees – vaccies – and were carried off to another world.

Fade in bedroom. Packing. The boys are excited. Mum is nearly cracking.

TERRY. Are you gonna stay here and fight the Germans, Mum?

MUM. Come here, Terry, while I tie this label on you.

TERRY. Aaagh, it's got my name and address on it.

MUM. That's right.

TERRY. I know who I am.

MUM. Of course you do. That's there in case – (*She stops and the bright exterior nearly cracks.*) – in case you get lost.

TERRY. I can *tell* 'em who I am.

JACK (*taunting*). 's in case the Germans gag you and you can't speak.

TERRY (*intrigued*). Honest?

MUM. Be quiet, Jack. Come here.

JACK. Ah, no. I'm not having one, too, am I?

MUM. Yes.

JACK. I'm four years older'n him.

MUM. Stand still.

TERRY. Westmoreland Secondary school. Form Two C. Huh-hah. You're a C. Rotten C's. I'm an A.

JACK. Big head.

MUM (*sharply*). Stop that. (*The boys are silent, surprised.*) Listen, you two. C's and A's don't matter. He's your brother, Terry. You do as he says. He's older than you.

TERRY (*sulkily*). I'm cleverest.

MUM. I'm clever*er*, smart Alec, and you're not. Now you do as Jack says and you stay with him. No rows. Got it?

TERRY. All right.

MUM (*mum is fighting the tears of anxiety*). And you look after him, Jack. D'you hear me?

JACK. 'Kay, Mum.

MUM. You're his big brother. Don't you stand any nonsense from him and don't you *dare* leave him. You stay together, d'you hear?

JACK. Can I bash him?

TERRY (*starts to protest*). No, I'm not going to let him –

MUM. *No.* (*She pauses.*) Well – if he's naughty – I – no. Oh, come on, you two, help me.

TERRY. I can look after myself, Mum.

MUM. All right, all right. You look after each other. How's that? D'you hear? You both look after each other.

JACK. I'm 11. I don't need him –

MUM. *D'YOU HEAR?*

Pause. Then mumbles of agreement.

That's right. That's good boys.

TERRY. You're the big head.

JACK. You wait till we get on that train.

MUM. Now, listen, both of you. Look here. See this? It's a postcard. It's a secret code. Read it, Jack.

JACK (*haltingly*). Dear Mum and Dad, arrived safe and well. Ever-y-thing fine. Love, Jack and Terry.

MUM. When you get there –

TERRY. Where?

MUM. Where you're going.

JACK (*whispers*). She doesn't know where.

MUM (*overlapping*). Find out the address. You can do that, Jack, can't you? (*Pause.*) Well, can you?

JACK. Well . . .

MUM. Just ask someone.

JACK. Oh, yeah.

MUM. That's right. Both of you. Ask. Stay together and put the address where they send you in that space there. Have you got that?

JACK. Is that all? Is that the code?

MUM. No. Now this is it. Our secret. You know how to write kisses?

TERRY. Ergh.

JACK. With a cross.

MUM. That's right. You put one kiss if it's nasty and I'll come straight there and bring you back. At once. D'you see? You put two kisses if it's all right and three kisses if it's nice. (*Her voice cracks.*) Then I'll know.

NARRATOR. Mum walked us under a canopy of barrage balloons to the 89 bus-stop by the We Anchor In Hope. They were digging up the golf course on Shooters Hill to put anti-aircraft guns there and in Oxleas Wood opposite. At Welling station several hundred yelling, rampant children were puffed away to adventure.

Fade in. Background. Many children yelling and cheering exuberantly. Steam engine starting up and drawing away.

NARRATOR. while Mum stood smiling and waving in a crowd of smiling waving mums. She told us later she went home and sobbed. Our train rumbled over the arched workshops and railway offices of South London, crossing from the Eastern Section to the Central via Nunhead, Peckham, Denmark Hill. We knew all the sections, stations and depots by heart because Dad, railway-employee Dad, had taken us over them frequently. He worked under that spider's web of lines at an office at Battersea, Stewart's Lane Carriage and Wagon Repair Depot. Essential war work.

DAD (*south London accent*). Lean out on the left side at Wandsworth Road, then when you go over my office I'll be outside there and I'll see you and wave.

NARRATOR. Ha. It seemed all South London was out there waving. Jack said he saw Dad in one place, I in another. Dad said he saw both of us but all any bystander could see

Faint children yelling and cheering from excitement.

of that train was that it sprouted yelling juvenile heads and waving arms from every aperture as we by-passed Nine Elms engine sheds, crossed onto the Western Section at Clapham Junction, gathered pace and flew westwards through Surbiton to open fields. We eventually pulled up at a station in a cutting.

Locomotive stationary, releasing steam.

Liskeard, said the boards. We couldn't even pronounce it. Cornwall, we were told. A wall of corn. It sounded all right. The evening sun shone down the length of the cutting making bars of gold through the smoke and steam of the engine as we were

Fade in: old bus.

packed into buses that fanned out of Liskeard in all directions breaking up Westmoreland Secondary School for good. Our bus followed another down a long, steep hill past a huge viaduct with another mysterious, derelict one beside it, through strange

Bus changing gears, labouring up a hill.

folded countryside with a line of moors in the distance,

Fade out bus.

to a school – small and bleak and Victorian – Dobwalls village school, just outside the village, squat and lonely. All the buildings we had seen looked so *old* after the new-minted semis of Welling. Even the people seemed older than at home.

Fade in: murmur of Cornish voices. Interior school room.

NARRATOR. A crowd was waiting for us and, as we were taken into the main classroom, these people, strange in voice and manner, pushed in after us curiously, while we stared at them.

Crowd and children moving.

VOICES (*soft, very Cornish*). Hallo, my lover.
Here, come on, move on, next.
There y'are my 'andsome.
Over there, you go.
Outside, the toilet.

HEADMASTER (*Cornish accent*). All right, children. Into the middle of the room all of you. That's right. Now come on, everybody. Find the ones you're going to take. Then tell their names to Mrs Ede or Mrs Beswetherick at the desk there so they can account for everyone with the evacuees' teachers. Miss Shepherd, their head, has their list. We don't want to lose any now, do we?

There is general background hubbub of Cornish voices and some children's voices – though not that many.

VOICES. I'll ave 'ee.
Er can come wi' I.
This one yere'll do me.
Come on, you. Want to come with me?

A child starts crying.

HEADMASTER (*calls*). Miss Shepherd, over here, could you? We seem to have had an accident.

MISS SHEPHERD (*London accent*). Yes, just a moment. Coming.

VOICES. Here y'are my handsome. Come on. What's your name, then?
Yes, I can see you're a girl.
Come on, we must get in that queue and tell 'em who you are.

FEMALE VOICE (*Cornish accent*). What about you? You coming wi' me?

TERRY. I'm with my brother.

FEMALE VOICE (*Cornish accent*). Two of you, eh?

TERRY. Yes. Him.

JACK. Yes. We're staying together.

FEMALE VOICE (*Cornish accent*). Hm. Two boys is a bit much for us. (*Moving away.*) What about you, my 'andsome. Have you got a brother or sister?

GIRL'S VOICE (*off*). No.

HEADMASTER. Now then, children, don't cluster up so tightly. Spread out a bit.

Feet. Voices.

Let's have a look at you. People have got to see you. That's it.

Auntie Rose is about 50, has a strong South-Wales accent.

AUNTIE ROSE. Yere. I'll have this one yere.

TERRY. Ow, that's my hair.

AUNTIE ROSE. Yes, I know, boy. Could do with a cut, too.

TERRY. You've got to have my brother, too.

AUNTIE ROSE. What?

TERRY. Mum said we got to stay together. She said so.

AUNTIE ROSE. Did she, now? Are you his brother?

JACK. Yes, we're staying together.

AUNTIE ROSE. Are you now?

JACK. Yes. Together.

TERRY. Both of us.

AUNTIE ROSE. That's right, then. If your Mam said. How old you boys?

JACK. Eleven.

TERRY. I'm seven.

AUNTIE ROSE. I like boys. Less trouble than girls. Girls, Oh, Dieu. (*She pronounces it dew.*) Nimby-pimby. All tears and temper. Can you top'n'tail?

JACK. What?

AUNTIE ROSE. We only got one spare bed just now. You c'n have a pillow each end. You're only little uns. You'll fit. I like little blondies. My family's dark. My son, Gwyn, is in Egypt now, fighting the Italians. Come on, both of you. You can come with me. My husband's outside. He's booked the taxi. How's that? Ever ridden in a taxi? I hadn't when I was your age. Here's my husband now. (*Calls.*) Here y'are, Jack. We got two. Brothers. They got to stay together.

UNCLE JACK. Oh, Dieu, girl. Can we fit 'em in?

AUNTIE ROSE. Easy. We'll think of something. Come on, boys, quick, before he changes his mind.

Cut to car moving. Interior.

NARRATOR. We headed through Dobwalls village out into more open country again, past a farm with a huddle of outbuildings which grimly showed their backs to the south-westerlies. Our driver broke the uncertain silence.

DRIVER (*broad east-Cornish accent*). They be everywhere, you know; they vaccies.

UNCLE JACK. Ay. All over.

DRIVER. St Neot, Menheniot; down to Duloe, up over Callington. The whole county's full of 'em. Didn't know they had so many kids in Lunnon. We got more 'n fifty to Dobwalls alone. Two down yere to Crago's farm. Three over to Polmeer's. Two boys at Miss Kitto's, the district nurse. Won't know if we'm coming 're going', will us?

UNCLE JACK. Yere that, boys? Yere what the driver says?

Silence.

Wha's up? Cat got your tongues?

TERRY. Is he talking English?

The men laugh.

DRIVER. No, tint English. Tis Cornish. Don't you fret, my handsome, we'll have you talking Cornish yet.

UNCLE JACK. I'll watch it. Not living with a Welshman they won't. I'll tan it out of 'em.

The men laugh.

NARRATOR. When we topped the brow of a hill there was a lone oak tree, not very tall but stark, with all the branches blown one way like a skinny hand.

UNCLE JACK. There we are. See? Doublebois. That's where we live. Doublebois is French – Double bois (*He tries a French pronunciation*) – means two woods. Not two boys, two woods. But we can say two boys, now, isn't it?

He laughs.

JACK. Is your name really Jack?

UNCLE JACK. 'Course it is. What d'you think? We're telling fibs?

JACK. My name's Jack, too.

UNCLE JACK. Well, there is funny.

AUNTIE ROSE. We'll have to make sure we don't muddle you up, then.

UNCLE JACK. D'you think you can manage to tell the difference?

All laugh.

What you laughing at? We look just the same, don't we?

TERRY. He's younger'n you.

UNCLE JACK. No. Not much.

JACK. I've got hair.

AUNTIE ROSE *and* DRIVER *laugh.*

DRIVER. 'A's i'. You tell 'im.

UNCLE JACK. Oh, cheeky, are we?

DRIVER. Reckon he's got your mark, Jack Phillips.

TERRY (*over-encouraged by the laughter*). And you're redder and fatter. And you talk funny.

DRIVER. Hoo-hoo. Tha's 'cos he's Welsh. They'm heathens. Can't speak English not more'n we can.

The DRIVER *and* UNCLE JACK *laugh.*

JACK. Please, I'm sorry. He didn't mean anything.

AUNTIE ROSE. 'as all right, boy. He's only saying what he sees and hears.

UNCLE JACK. There's our house, see? Last one on the end of the row there.

NARRATOR. We stared at a row of Victorian cottages in the distance; more slate and granite. They looked tiny and grim. Seven of them, as it turned out. How could seven families live in so little space? We entered and stared in wonder at a shining black range with a cat curled beside it; at a canary in a cage; at a green velvet table cloth with a little brass dustpan and crumbs brush; at a shapeless sofa; at two First-World-War shells in their cases, nearly six inches tall, standing on the mantelpiece with soldered-on army badges that had three feathers and 'Ich Dien' on a scroll; and at oil lamps – no electricity here. But the glory came last: outside, past hens in a wire-enclosed run, tucked down in a cutting right behind the wash-house and breath-takingly revealed, was the main London to Penzance railway line and Doublebois station with its goods yard and sidings. The rural silence of Doublebois was shattered at intervals as express trains roared by a few yards below us, steam and smoke belching over the cottages. Local trains chuffed, goods engines shunted and banged and clattered, shouts echoed, signals clacked and bells announced the 9.12 am up to Plymouth and the 4.20 pm down to Truro and Falmouth. Our address was 7 Railway Cottages. Our foster parents were Jack and Rose Phillips, Auntie Rose and Uncle Jack to everybody in Doublebois. He was a South Wales miner turned platelayer on the Great Western Railway. Their own son and daughter were grown up; she, married and he in uniform in the desert. That night, in the secrecy of the tiny back bedroom Jack and I stared at Mum's postcard and considered our code.

Fade in: interior boys' bedroom. They are either whispering or keeping their voices very quiet.

JACK. How many kisses shall we put?

TERRY. I vote three.

JACK. Hm. I'm not sure.

Door opening.

AUNTIE ROSE. Come on yere, you two. What's all this? Up-a-dando, into bed.

Drawer opening.

What are you hiding there?

JACK. Nothing.

Drawer close.

AUNTIE ROSE. Come on, then. Who's going at which end?

TERRY. Can I go this end, Mrs Phillips? In the corner?

AUNTIE ROSE. All right with you, young Jack?

JACK. Well.

He stops, embarrassed.

AUNTIE ROSE. Well what?

JACK. Will there be enough air for him in the corner? (*He pauses awkwardly.*) He's ever so small – smaller than he looks.

TERRY. I'm not.

AUNTIE ROSE (*most gently*). I think there will, boy. We'll open the window, is it?

JACK. Thank you, but –

TERRY. Oh, no.

JACK. I must.

AUNTIE ROSE. Must what, boy?

JACK. He gets asthma.

TERRY. I don't. Not much.

AUNTIE ROSE. All right, all right, I won't tell anyone. Now listen. Now listen, you – Jack. We'll open the window, there'll be lots of air and he'll be able to breathe there in the corner, you take my word. I know 'bout asthma. Is that all right?

JACK. Yes, thank you, Mrs Phillips.

AUNTIE ROSE. Did your Mam tell you to see about the air?

JACK. No, I thought it myself.

AUNTIE ROSE. Did you now? You're a fine boy. Now into bed, go on. No. Wait a minute. Do you say your prayers at night?

Pause.

Well. do you?

JACK (*surprised*). No.

AUNTIE ROSE. All right, then. In you get. My Jack's a heathen, too, but I'll say a prayer for both of you. Look, boys, if you want to go outside during the night, you got this yere. D'you see? Under the bed.

Chamber pot being set down on lino.

JACK. Why should we go outside?

AUNTIE ROSE. Why? Well, if you want to go down the garden, of course. To the privy.

JACK. Oh, yes. Outside. Sorry, Mrs Phillips.

AUNTIE ROSE. Auntie Rose, I said you call me. Right? (*Pause.*) Well?

JACK. But you're not our Auntie. Our Auntie's in Peckham.

AUNTIE ROSE. No, no I'm not. You're right. You call me Auntie Rose when you want to, is it?

TERRY. Coh, it's ever so soft in here.

AUNTIE ROSE. There. Look at you. As snug as bugs in a rug.

Boys laugh.

TERRY. What?

AUNTIE ROSE. 'a's what we say. As-snug-as-a-bug-in-a-rug. Only there's two bugs in my rug.

JACK (*giggling*). I'm not a bug.

TERRY. He's a bugger sometimes.

The giggles taper into silence. He has gone too far.

JACK. He didn't mean to say that. He's just stupid sometimes.

TERRY. I'm not. You are.

AUNTIE ROSE. Well he's young, isn't he. When he gets to your age he'll know better. Now I'm going to put out the candle if you're ready.

JACK. Could you leave it, please?

AUNTIE ROSE. Don't you like the dark?

JACK. No, it's not that. We got to –

AUNTIE ROSE. It's bedtime now.

JACK. We got to send a card to Mum and Dad.

AUNTIE ROSE. This one?

Drawer being opened.

JACK. Yes.

Drawer being closed.

AUNTIE ROSE. Is that your writing? It's very grown-up.

JACK. No, it's Mum's.

AUNTIE ROSE (*surprised*). She's already written the card.

TERRY. We got to put your address on it.

AUNTIE ROSE. Well, you've done it, haven't you. (*Chuckles.*) Yes, that's more like your writing. That's not how you spell Liskeard. I'll do you another card in the morning. A nice new one with a picture, how's that?

JACK (*panics*). No, no. We got to put something else on.

AUNTIE ROSE. Wha's that?

Pause.

Well?

JACK. Er – kisses.

AUNTIE ROSE (*little gentle laugh*). Well, all right, then. We can do that, too, in the morning.

JACK. *We* want to do it.

TERRY. By ourselves.

AUNTIE ROSE (*surprised*). All right, then. You do it by yourselves, then. That's right. You got something to write with?

JACK (*quickly*). Yes. Here. A pencil.

AUNTIE ROSE. All right, then. I'll leave the candle a bit and then come back again, is it, and watch you put out the candle the right way. We don't want a fire, do we? Your Mam wouldn't like that.

Door closing.

JACK (*whispers*). How many kisses?

TERRY. I vote three.

JACK. Perhaps we should take one off 'cos we've only got one bed.

TERRY. It's triffic here. 'S like being on holiday only there's no sea.

JACK. What about no electricity?

TERRY. I don't care.

JACK. And no indoor lav.

TERRY. I don't care.

JACK. How many shall we put, then?

NARRATOR. We ringed the card with kisses and posted it next morning. It made no difference, Mum still turned up unannounced within the week. Just to make sure. Jack and I were ringed with love, not that we thought in such terms, the word love would have embarrassed us. But here were two strangers who took us in and in no time at all were our other-parents – just there, taken for granted. That was their achievement. And I can still see Auntie Rose's slightly enquiring smile when we had pleased her and still feel the warmth of her body when she held us; and her hands, so much rougher than my mothers, but just as gentle. She had a saying she used most afternoons. No amount of mockery from us would make her abandon it.

AUNTIE ROSE. Oo-oh, I'm done for. I'm just going upstairs to throw myself down.

NARRATOR. And there was Uncle Jack with his ferocious secret scowls and grins; and his brusque delivery.

UNCLE JACK. If I was your father, I'd –

NARRATOR. . . . was the start to many a threat that held no terrors for Jack and me.

UNCLE JACK. Bloody Cornish.

NARRATOR. Uncle Jack would say, without rancour.

NARRATOR. Bible-punching Tories. Send 'em down the pits for a bit. Then they'd know they were born.

TERRY. What are Tories?

NARRATOR. We wondered.

TERRY. Why punch bibles?

JACK. It's just an expression. They don't actually punch 'em.

TERRY. What do they do, then?

JACK. I think they just bang them down hard in church. I've seen 'em do it with hymn books.

TERRY. Oh.

JACK. I've seen it in the pictures, too. In Westerns. They talk about punching cattle but they never do. They just punch each other.

NARRATOR. I stared at a cow in a field and imagined punching its massive forehead, wringing my fist in agony at the result.

UNCLE JACK. Bloody Churchill.

NARRATOR. Was another of Uncle Jack's remarks that seized our shocked attention.

UNCLE JACK. He sent the troops in against us at Tonypandy, didn't he. Nye Bevan, there's your man. On the opposition benches all by himself. Attlee, Morrison, Cripps: they're all in the government; part of it. Sold out.

NARRATOR. But in spite of these sentiments he seemed to support the war effort and listened, rapt, to Churchill's speeches and went drinking

UNCLE JACK *singing in background* 'Land Of My Fathers' *in Welsh, erratically.*

on Saturday nights with his allegedly Tory Cornish workmates, singing his way home from a pub in Liskeard – for Dobwalls was dry, the Wesleyans had seen to that.

UNCLE JACK. Bloody chapel. Bloody hypocrites. Four miles to wet your whistle. It's bloody antediluvian.

AUNTIE ROSE. Sssh, Jack everyone'll yere. All up the Court.

UNCLE JACK. I should hope so. Half of 'em are with me.

AUNTIE ROSE. You'll wake the boys.

UNCLE JACK. Good job. Time they learned.

TERRY. Why come to Cornwall, Uncle Jack, if you don't like it?

AUNTIE ROSE. Oh, Dieu, back to bed, you.

UNCLE JACK. Work, boy, work. No work there in the valleys. Came with the Great Western, didn't I? The Company. Got the house an' all. Tied. Huh. (*Cries, in pain.*) Tied. Like our lives.

AUNTIE ROSE. Oh-ho-ho. Plenty of time for all that in the morning. Go on up to bed, all of you. Shall I wake you for morning service, is it?

UNCLE JACK. I'll bloody kill you if you do. (*He swears in Welsh.*)

AUNTIE ROSE. Oh, big man. Couldn't kill a dozy fly with a frying pan. Go on. Bed. And you boys.

UNCLE JACK. Want to splash your boots first?

BOYS. Yes. Yes, please. Yes, I'm dying to.

NARRATOR. And Jack and I, pyjama-ed and barefoot, joined the row of men at the wire fence that overlooked the railway cutting. We thought we were men indeed to stand in such a row, barefoot on summer Saturday nights, as the last train's sounds echoed over the Fowey valley in the distance and left the dozen or so houses of Doublebois to silence. But if the bites of Auntie Rose and Uncle Jack were toothless their rebukes hit their marks. For instance: nearly three years later when most of the vaccies had drifted back to London I was, at ten, the brightest pupil in the village school, coming top in every exam with monotonous regularity. I brought home my report one term and handed it to Auntie Rose who read it and looked at me with shining eyes. Learning impressed her.

AUNTIE ROSE. Wait till Jack sees this.

UNCLE JACK. What's up?

Door shutting.

AUNTIE ROSE. We got his report. Yere. D'you want to see it? It's from the school.

UNCLE JACK. From school? That's unusual. Fancy, his report comes from school.

NARRATOR. And Uncle Jack, just back from work, stripped off his jacket, his waistcoat; rolled up his sleeves and sluiced his arms, hands, face and shining bald head; dried off; removed his boots; put on his glasses and finally sat in the armchair to read the golden report.

TERRY. I got all nines and tens. (*Pause.*) I only lost five marks in the whole exam. Every subject.

UNCLE JACK. Five, eh? What d'you lose them for?

NARRATOR. I gaped at the question, breathless. My world turned upside down. It is not what you achieve, but how far you fall short that matters.

TERRY. Er-um-well-I-er-two were silly mistakes. I really knew the answers. And three were taken off for untidiness.

UNCLE JACK. Carelessness, is it? That won't do, will it, boy? You can do better than that. Let's see all tens next time.

AUNTIE ROSE. Oh, Jack, he's top of the whole school. Some of 'em are fifteen years old, he's ten. What more d'you want?

UNCLE JACK. Bloody yokels. Clods. Cornish farm labourers. What do they know? Tens, boy, next time. Tens. And less of this untidiness. Pass me the newspaper.

NARRATOR. Uncle Jack's lesson gave me something to think about, but Auntie Rose's by-passed the mind. We had been for a walk up the lanes; her married daughter Ethel, was staying. Each of us had a jam jar to search for wild strawberries. There weren't many but I persevered and after much effort had a miserable half-jarful. I poured them on my plate at tea-time and planned to save the fattest ones till last.

Tea time.

ETHEL. Oh, I'm glad to get the weight off my feet.

UNCLE JACK. An' no mistake.

AUNTIE ROSE. You got your strawberries there, then, have you, boy?

TERRY. Yes.

AUNTIE ROSE. Aren't you going to offer them round, then? We got a guest.

NARRATOR. I flushed till the hair rose on my neck, aware of my gracelessness but also of the injustice.

TERRY. But you lot didn't bother. I mean – I picked these while you were all talking.

AUNTIE ROSE. Greed I'm bringing up yere, is it? What if I only gave you the food you got yourself?

TERRY. Sorry. Would you like some, Ethel?

ETHEL. No, thank you, Terry.

TERRY. Would you, Uncle Jack?

UNCLE JACK. No, thanks, boy.

TERRY. Auntie Rose. Would you like some?

NARRATOR. She hadn't finished her lesson.

AUNTIE ROSE. No, you have 'em boy. You obviously need 'em most.

NARRATOR. No one ate the wild strawberries.

The hamlet of Doublebois had four local children; to these were added six vaccies. The day after we arrived, Jack and I joined the other vaccies; three boys and a girl called Elsie Plummer, heavy with imminent puberty. We met the four locals: Jimmy Peters and the

three Bunney children. We all hung from the branches of a large
beech tree at the crossroads by the station. This tree commanded an
astonishing view: the Fowey valley. It was almost as heart-stopping
as the first sight of the sea on summer holiday. The main road
plunged down past a quarry into woods; the railway snaked along
the valley side on a thrilling succession of bridges and viaducts; and
the tops of trees waved and swayed into the hazy distance, beckoning
magically and majestically. Jack voiced the aching corporate longings
of the vaccies.

JACK. Let's go down the woods.

NARRATOR. There was a silence while the locals stared at us. Then –

DAVID BUNNEY (*broad east Cornish*). Wha' for?

JACK (*astounded*). What for?

DAVID BUNNEY. Yeah. Wha' for?

JACK. To play.

DAVID BUNNEY. Play wha'?

JACK. Just play.

DAVID BUNNEY. Wha's wrong wi' yere?

NARRATOR. We stared at the dingy crossroads where we stood then
away out over the enchanted valley. 'Can't you see?' 'Are you
blind?' There lay adventures, endless woods, a rushing river, fish to
catch, streams to dam, paths, tracks, the quarry to climb, creatures
and things we hadn't heard of – oh, what for?

*Background: children running and yelling from excitement, getting
more distant.*

As the locals drifted away the vaccies charged down the valley
kicking the tops off thistles and on into the dappled gloom of our
vast, new, empty playground. But the vaccies and the Doublebois
children soon found enough things in common to make friends. In the
village of Dobwalls, however, where we all went to school, it was
war. I don't know how or why it started, because we were kept in
separate schools, but it was instant and total. We ten from
Doublebois would walk to school together quite happily and as we
got to the village, separated, without conscious effort, into vaccies
and village kids.

Cricket bat on ball and children's cheers, faint.

Some well-meaning person suggested a cricket match: we walloped
them.

Fade down cricket. Fade up background cheers.

A football match followed: the score was vaccies 30-odd, village kids
two.

Fade up intensity of cheers then out.

We arranged our own private group fights in the dinner break and returned to our schools, dishevelled and bloody, to get our knuckles rapped with the edge of a ruler – more painful than the fights.

Rules whacking down. 'Oos', 'Ahs', indrawn breaths, then quick blowing from boys.

And our leader, Frank Emmett, fought their leader, Sam Finch, in single combat. A few months later the furious winter of 1940-41 took hold.

Cold low wind. Distant individual shouts of children.

The village pumps were encased in ice and the wind whipped the snow down off Bodmin Moor making six-foot drifts in the middle of Dobwalls. The children arranged a mass snowball fight one dinner break: vaccies versus village kids. It included every child in the district between the ages of five and 15 and got utterly out of hand – not that it was ever in it. Waves of schoolchildren surged up and down the village street hurling things or just shouting.

Fade in. Children cheering.

When the bell sounded, while some law-abiding souls went back to school, the rest of us spilled over into fields and chased each other to Duloe Bridge. The climax was a snowball shoot-out as the wan, winter daylight faded.

Fade children cheering.

We swaggered back into class in front of the admiring looks of the more timid kids to have the smirks wiped off our faces by Miss Shepherd and Mrs Langdon who laid their rulers mercilessly across our chapped and tingling fingers.

One day, later, there was another group transgression: chanting blasphemous versions of Hymns Ancient and Modern in public.

Ragged children's voices to the tune of 'There is a Green Hill Far Away'. *Some of the boys' voices broken.* 'There is a fair maid far away, without her knickers on. And she, poor maid, was crucified, but said she felt no pain.'

Voices, coming in stronger. 'Oh, dearly dearly, did she cost, Sam Finch had to pay double. And though she tied a knot in it, he got her into trouble'.

The tiny Miss Shepherd was finally forced to bring out the school cane and wield it on several of the bigger boys – vaccies and village kids. She was halfway down the row of proffered backsides when the cane, groaning under its excessive burden, gave up the ghost and snapped in two.

Miss Shepherd burst into tears and the row of unyielding bottoms returned to their seats. The whole village divided. Those with their own children and many others regarded the vaccies as a pestilence to be endured or resisted, but there were those who suddenly found themselves with new families: energetic, bright children who won their hearts and brought a new vitality to their village, trebling the under-16 population. Prominent among the pro-vaccie faction was Buckroyd, the Wesleyan minister. Our main classroom was in his chapel, our juniors were in a tin shack optimistically called The Hall. Our playground was his consecrated churchyard. Hide and Seek between the slabs of slate.

MISS POLMANOR. 'Tis sacrilege, Mr Buckroyd, disturbin' the dead like tha'.

BUCKROYD. I don't think the dead mind too much, Miss Polmanor.

MISS POLMANOR. They make up profane words to hymn tunes. I've heard they.

BUCKROYD. So do our children, Miss Polmanor.

MISS POLMANOR. But not so profane as they.

BUCKROYD. Well, they're more – uh-huh – inventive.

MISS POLMANOR. More sinful.

BUCKROYD. There's a war on, Miss Polmanor.

NARRATOR. And, in the rumour and gossip that always rides in tandem with war – I mean our private war – stories abounded of vaccies who behaved outrageously or were treated with cruelty.

MISS POLMANOR. Have you ever heard? Over to Tremabe they chopped off all the chickens' heads. Every living one 'on 'em. Two little savages. Only seven years old.

SECOND VOICE. No, is that so, my dear?

MISS POLMANOR. And down to Warleggan they slaughtered lambs in the fields, fired a rick. 'Tis bloody mayhem, I'm telling you – oh, sorry, Mrs. I didn't mean to – but 'tis terrible.

SECOND VOICE. Tsh, tsh, tsh, tsh.

Fade in pub background.

FIRST MALE CORNISH VOICE (*hushed and fearful*). You know that farmer up the edge of the Moor, Penmalligan. He had two vaccies billeted on he.

SECOND VOICE. Ar. Boy 'n' a maid.

FIRST VOICE. Ar. Well, he locked 'em in the linney all night then took his strap to 'em after breakfast. His breakfast. They din' get none.

SECOND VOICE. Was it their fault?

FIRST VOICE. Oh, now then, now then, they was nine and ten years old. Well, their father got to yere. In the Guards, he is. Grenadiers. Back from Dunkirk.

SECOND VOICE. Yes, they was there, I read it.

FIRST VOICE. He went AWOL, went to Penmalligan's farm punched
he all round his own farmyard, then took his kids off with him back
to Lunnon. Twas a proper job.

SECOND VOICE (*impressed*). Have you heard of anyone else giving
they vaccies what for?

FIRST VOICE. No. Everyone round yere be givin' it up for Lent.
(*They chuckle.*)

NARRATOR. And though such stories always took place in the next
village but one, the mythical guardsman was a famous and
cautionary figure.

*Children's voices, unaccompanied, singing raggedly, but triumphantly,
second half of first verse of* 'British Grenadiers': 'But of all the world's
brave heroes, there's none that can compare, (*Crescendo.*) With a tow
row row row row row row to the British Grenadier.

*Sound: The Radio Doctor: Library clip of wartime broadcast.
Woodland sounds, distant river.*

TERRY. Look, Elsie. In here.

ELSIE. Is this your camp in the woods, Terry?

TERRY. And Jack's. And the others'.

ELSIE. Can I come in?

TERRY. You mustn't tell the others I let you.

ELSIE. Cross my heart and hope to die.

TERRY. O.K.

*Cut background except close sounds: clothes, shuffles, pineneedles,
breathing.*

ELSIE. Coh, s'lovely in here. Dark. Smells of resin. No one would ever
know we were here. D'you want to play doctors?

TERRY. What's that?

ELSIE. I'll show you. Are you eight yet?

TERRY. No.

ELSIE. I'm nearly 13. I'll be doctor first.

TERRY. 'f you like.

ELSIE. Lie down, then I'll examine you. Not like that, daft. You got to
take all your clothes off first. (*Pause.*) *All* of them.

TERRY. My underpants, too?

ELSIE. 'Course.

TERRY. Don't want to.

ELSIE. You shy?

TERRY. Yes.

ELSIE. So am I. Let's undress together.

TERRY. All right.

Sound of clothes being removed.

ELSIE. Did you know boys and girls are different.

TERRY. I think so.

ELSIE. D'you know why?

TERRY. No.

ELSIE. 's to make babies. You put your – that – what d'you call that?

TERRY. My widdler.

ELSIE. Well, girls don't have one. We have a crack. See? That's 'cos
when you put your widdler in my crack then I have a baby.

TERRY. Don't be daft.

ELSIE. True.

TERRY. It wouldn't go.

ELSIE. No, I thought that.

TERRY. So, there.

ELSIE. It's still true. I don't think it works till you're married, I think.
Or grown up. Anyway, little babies come out of the end of your
widdler. All swimming.

TERRY (*giggles*). Don't be daft. You're stupid.

ELSIE. The husband has to lie on top of the wife, then it works. All
husbands and wives do it. Your mum and dad do it.

TERRY (*sullenly*). Shut up.

ELSIE. Shut up, yourself.

TERRY. I don't believe you.

ELSIE. It's how all babies come. You, me. The baby grows for nine
months in here then comes out of the woman's crack.

TERRY. Babies are too big.

ELSIE. I know. I don't get it. The woman screams so it mustn't half
hurt. I don't think I want babies.

TERRY. You made it all up.

ELSIE. The animals do it, too. You watch. I have. Up to Crago's
Farm. Nobody saw me. Crago's bull. Blige me. His widdler. You
should see. They all laughed.

TERRY. We're not like animals. We've got souls.

ELSIE. You going to play doctor, then? Now, what seems to be the
trouble, Mr Smith.

TERRY. I don't like you.

ELSIE. Yes, you do.

NARRATOR. And she was right. I did. I, sort of, loved her. She spoke with a calm authority that was thrilling and disturbing. I went home and stared at Auntie Rose and Uncle Jack. I tried to imagine them doing something so rude and unlikely. No, not possible. I thought of my parents: no, the whole picture was grotesque.

TERRY. Uncle Jack, have we got souls?

UNCLE JACK. Nobody really knows boy, though they say they do.

TERRY. Nobody in the *whole world*?

UNCLE JACK. No. But if you ask me it's all tripe. All of it. All religion. Rubbish.

TERRY. So we *are* just like the animals?

UNCLE JACK (*laughs*). I wouldn't say that, boy: we got *minds*.

NARRATOR. How could Uncle Jack know that we'd just been having our first conversation about sex?

TERRY. Auntie Rose, have we got souls?

AUNTIE ROSE. 'Course we have, my love. What d'you think we are, animals?

TERRY. Uncle Jack says we haven't.

AUNTIE ROSE. What does he know?

NARRATOR. There appeared to be nothing but confusion on the subject in the adult world, so how could Elsie know? But the assurances of her still childish, but swelling body against mine – the changes in herself she pointed out so proudly – the persistent rumours of the truth that I encountered among the older children – and the overwhelming evidence in the countryside all round us gradually undermined my incredulous resistance. So, when the bigger boys were busy elsewhere, the promise of a breathless, dry session of Doctor with Elsie – full of intimacy yet reserve – created a trembling inexplicable excitement that was quite fulfilled by the cool clinical little scenes we acted out in our pinescented surgery in the woods.

One day Jack and I joined Ken and Elsie Plummer behind the row of outside privies that sat across the foot of the gardens of Railway Cottages. A raid on Granny Peters' gooseberry bushes. Granny Peters – to us half-funny, half-witch – lived in the Court, at number four. Her gooseberry bushes were laden with golden, hairy goosegogs.

Lowered voices.

JACK. Look, Ken, it's best if Elsie keeps watch here and we crawl across the paths.

KEN. Yes. I vote for that.

ELSIE. I want to come with you.

KEN. You can't.

ELSIE. Why?

KEN. Because you're useless.

ELSIE. You're mean you are, you sod.

KEN. You always make a noise or get seen or something.

ELSIE. I can't help it if people notice me.

KEN. She makes me sick.

JACK. Well, Terry's the smallest. He can get under the prickles and pass out the goosegogs.

TERRY. Yeah, no one'll see me.

JACK. Then you and me, Ken, can get round the back there and get all them.

KEN. O.K.

JACK. And Elsie can stay by the corner and see all the windows and if anybody comes to the bogs.

ELSIE. I'm not staying there, it smells.

KEN. Stop moaning or we won't give you any.

ELSIE. Don't want any.

JACK. All right, come on. Terry first.

NARRATOR. We wriggled round the odorous privies on our stomachs with an excess of secrecy that would have excited attention from a mile away. We boys slid in among the bushes while Elsie kept watch and communed with her changing body.

Rustling twigs and leaves.

JACK (*low*). Come on, Terry. Pass 'em out.

TERRY. I am.

KEN. He's eating 'em.

GRANNY PETERS (*distant shout. Broad Cornish. Very old*). Hey, you. You boys. What you to?

Silence. The boys whisper.

JACK (*panic*). Oh, no. That's her.

GRANNY PETERS. What you doin' in there?

Agitated rustling of foliage.

JACK. Where's your sister?

KEN. She's gone.

GRANNY PETERS (*overlapping*). Why you lying down in there?

TERRY. Ow, I'm stuck.

KEN. Look out, you're squashing 'em all.

TERRY. I can't help it. It hurts.

GRANNY PETERS. Come on, you three. Out of there.

Cut to.

UNCLE JACK. So you two tried to steal Granny Peters' gooseberries, did you? (*Pause.*) Well, did you?

Mumbled assent from JACK *and* TERRY.

TERRY. We were only scrumping.

UNCLE JACK. Scrumping? What's that, then? Cockney for stealing?

JACK. Scrumping is when it's apples and things.

UNCLE JACK. I know what it is.

AUNTIE ROSE. I'll never hold up my head in the Court again. Ashamed, I am of you both. Poor old Granny Peters.

UNCLE JACK. What are we going to do with you?

AUNTIE ROSE. You're going to go in to her and say you're sorry to start with. And you take her in some of my rock cakes.

JACK. Yes, Auntie Rose.

AUNTIE ROSE. You know she makes jam from all her fruit and she earns her money from it and she do give us a jar every Christmas. And then you steal 'em.

UNCLE JACK. If you wanted some gooseberries why didn't you ask? Were you hungry?

JACK. No.

AUNTIE ROSE. You take my rock cakes and you go in there and you ask her if there's anything you can do to help her.

Timid knocking on door. Again, louder.

JACK. Granny Peters? Granny Peters?

Door opening.

GRANNY PETERS. Who's tha'

JACK. 's us, Granny Peters. Jack and Terry, the boys from Auntie Rose's.

GRANNY PETERS. Aaa-ah! (*The older, more other-worldly and strange she can sound, the better. She is very short of breath and wheezes badly.*)

JACK. We brought you some rock cakes from Auntie Rose.

GRANNY PETERS. Aun'ee Rose. Ooh. Her rock cakes. Aaah. Give 'em here. I'll soak they in my tea. You boys be from Lunnen, eh?

JACK. Yes.

GRANNY PETERS. I was to there once, with my Arthur. Too many 'osses. Everywhere. Hosses all round you. Worse'n Plymouth, twas. Come yere, my pretty. Come closer.

TERRY (*whispers*). Oh, no.

JACK (*whispers*). Go on.

TERRY. She smells funny.

GRANNY PETERS. Oh, you'm pretty 'n'no mistake. Don't wriggle, I won't hurt 'ee. You mind me o'my Billy. Ginger, they called 'ee. All down Dobwalls street. Ginger you'm barmy. You oughtta join the army! 'n he did. (*Weeps.*)

JACK. Auntie Rose said . . .

GRANNY PETERS. Oh Billy, my firstborn, my pretty, where you to now? South Africa, he went and the Boers shot 'ee. There's his medals. He warn't simple. The army took him. So he couldn't a' bin, could 'ee? They maids lead'n on. Twas they fault, not 'ee. He didn't hurt they. You wouldn't hurt a fly, would you, my pretty?

TERRY (*whispered*). She won't let me go.

JACK (*whispered*). Don't worry. I think she's all right.

GRANNY PETERS. His father, he was the simple one. I 'ad eight from 'ee. All gone to God. He took 'n all: three in the war; two when they was little like you, my beauty. Henry, he went on the railway. Working on the line. Down the valley. They threw a bottle from a train and it hit his lovely face. Oh. The 4.12 to St Austell, twas. (*She pronounces it Snozzle.*) Oh, I outlived all my own children. Tis not natural. Tis wonderful lonely.

JACK. Isn't Jimmy Peters' dad your son?

GRANNY PETERS. Oh, yes. Yes. I forgot 'ee. Huh. I don't count 'ee. He's still here.

TERRY. If you'll let me go I'll take your jug and get some water from the pump.

GRANNY PETERS. Wha' for? Tis half full.

JACK. Auntie Rose said we got to.

GRANNY PETERS. Oh, Aun'ie Rose. Yes. Rock cakes: they'm well named.

JACK. And we're sorry we tried to steal your gooseberries.

GRANNY PETERS. You want some gooseberries? Go on, then. They be yansome now. Take that bowl and bring me some, I'll make you some jam. Yere, come yere, little one. Let me touch your hair.

TERRY. I got to go. Auntie Rose is calling.

GRANNY PETERS. Give me a kiss, Billy. Henry, give your mam a kiss 'fore you go to work.

JACK (*calling as he goes*). We'll bring you some gooseberries in this bowl, Granny Peters. (*Whispered*.) Come on, quick.

Scuffle of feet and door opening.

GRANNY PETERS. The 4.12 Snozzle, twas. They shot 'ee.

Front door shutting. Cut to.

TERRY (*singing unaccompanied, second half of first verse of* 'The Ash Grove').
The friends of my childhood again are before me
Fond memories waken as

JACK *and* TERRY (JACK *joins in the alto line, harmonising with* TERRY. *They hold* 'roam' *for a moment*).

freely I roam;
With soft whispers laden its leaves rustle
O'er me.
The Ash Grove, the Ash Grove that shelter'd my
Home.

Range fire burning. Household sounds.

AUNTIE ROSE. That's lovely, boys.

UNCLE JACK. That's right, you both. You sound as though you're thinking what you're singing as well as making a beautiful sound.

JACK. You going to tell us now, then, Uncle Jack?

UNCLE JACK. Oh, well, I'm not sure.

TERRY. You promised when we got 'The Ash Grove' right.

AUNTIE ROSE. Promised what?

UNCLE JACK. I didn't say it was right. I said it's not bad.

JACK. Aah. That's cheating.

AUNTIE ROSE. Promised what?

TERRY. He said he'd tell us the story of the army badges, on the two shells on the mantelpiece.

JACK. And 'Ich Dien'.

AUNTIE ROSE. Oh, Jack, what do they want to yere all that old history for?

JACK (*quickly*). He promised.

TERRY (*overlapping*). Yes, he did.

AUNTIE ROSE. Horrible war stories. Isn't this one enough? Our Gwyn's out there, you know.

UNCLE JACK. They're boys, Rose, not wurzels.

JACK. Gwyn's a Desert Rat.

TERRY *makes machine gun and other battle noises.*

AUNTIE ROSE. To the chickens, me. Get the eggs. They hens do talk more sense than you.

Sound: door.

UNCLE JACK. I was in the Welsh Bantams, see. If you was under five foot you weren't accepted at first. Good enough to dig coal, too small to fight, they said. Then after our high Command had let the Germans slaughter most of the good men they needed more cannon fodder so they took us titches. We made a whole regiment: the Welsh Bantams. We was in the line up against the Prussian Guards, big fine fellers, all of 'em over six foot tall. How 'bout that?

JACK.   ⎫   Coh. That's not fair.
TERRY.   ⎬   That's terrible.

UNCLE JACK (*laughs*). Oh, no. Not so silly. Those big men was easier to hit, see. More of 'em. Every man's the same height when a bullet hits him. He's horizontal.

TERRY. That's brilliant.

JACK. Our High Command weren't so stupid.

UNCLE JACK. Don't let me catch you saying any good of our leaders boy. Especially that particular lot. They were just men like you will be sooner than you think. What were we doing fighting the Germans at all? Ernie Bevin tried to stop it with a general strike of all the German unions and ours. But they called him a traitor. Bloody patriotism beat him. Now he's in the government. Where's the sense?

TERRY. But the shells and the badges. What happened in the Great War?

UNCLE JACK. Great War, eh? Who taught you that?

TERRY. I heard it.

UNCLE JACK. Huh. Great. First we was up against the Saxons. They was all right. They didn't like the war no more'n we did.

JACK. But what does 'Ich Dien' mean?

UNCLE JACK. 's Welsh for 'I serve'. The prince of Wales's feathers and his motto. 's funny ich's like German. 's more German than English. But we're Celts, dark and small, different from you, Anglo-Saxons, fair-haired like them buggers.

TERRY. Are Jack and me Saxons?

JACK. Were the Prussian Guards fair, too?

UNCLE JACK. Some of 'em, yes. They were in one part of the wood. We in another. Mametz Wood near Ypres (*He pronounces it Wipers.*) Over a thousand of us, the same of them. Our artillery started shelling them. Their artillery started shelling us. Everyone got blown to bits. Who killed who? I don't know. Bloody fools. The wood was blasted away, too. Trees like used matchsticks stuck in the mud. Then it got cold, icy. Germans and Welsh dead frozen together, bayonets in each other. Frost made 'em all white next morning. It didn't look real, almost. Seventeen of us came out alive. We got one of those insignia each.

JACK. But you've got two.

UNCLE JACK. One is my mate's, Ifor Davies, faceman from Ystrad, even smaller 'n me.

TERRY. But if Ifor Davies was one of the 17 why didn't he keep his badge?

UNCLE JACK. There were plenty more battles, boy.

JACK. Coh, you were lucky weren't you, Uncle Jack?

TERRY. I'll bet he was clever and kept his head down.

UNCLE JACK. No one was clever. The clever ones weren't there at all. No matter what happens to you in your life, just remember this: there's no justice; there never was and there never will be. But you got to pretend there is. We call that being civilized. Live your life like that and that's all you can do. Just remember two things: it's not fair and don't be late.

NARRATOR. I turned the massacre in Mametz woods over and over in my mind. I acted out the scene in our woods, below Doublebois, creeping through the undergrowth down by the river. I hid behind trunks as shells ripped through the foliage, tearing the boughs off, splintering the green wood, uprooting forest giants, converting trees and men to blackened stumps. Why did the thousand of our men go in here? And why did the Germans? Who wanted to capture a wood anyway? All those tough little Welshmen hugging the ground, getting blown to pieces in spite of their lack of inches. The event had horror, fascination and mystery which I could leave only briefly behind as I emerged from our woods into the rabbit field, one of 17 survivors going home to tea and the polished mementoes on the mantlepiece.

Interior noises.

UNCLE JACK. It was raining. Raining. Raining. The soaking summer of 1916. Everything was sodden. Your boots rotted on your feet. Mud, there was mud everywhere, chest deep sometimes. But there was no clean water to drink, of course. I had to draw ours from a shell hole nearby. Then it stopped raining. The water went down and we saw there'd been a dead Frog in there all the time. Just as well I boiled it.

AUNTIE ROSE. Oh, Jack.

TERRY. What's so terrible about a dead frog?

JACK. Stupid. He doesn't mean a frog. A Frog is a Frenchman. A French soldier.

TERRY. Uragh. Ergh.

JACK (*eagerly*). Was he all bloated like that cow in the river?

UNCLE JACK (*laughing*). I'll say.

TERRY. Oogh. I feel sick.

JACK. I'll bet he was rotting like your boots.

TERRY. Ergh.

AUNTIE ROSE. Now stop that, Jack. That war's over 20 years ago.

UNCLE JACK. This one's on now, innit? If it goes on long enough Jack could be in the army easy. Home by Christmas we was told. Over two years our Gwyn's been out there.

NARRATOR. Our war took on a new, dreadful fascination for me. It was no longer an imaginary 'bang bang, you're dead,' with sanitary corpses – mostly German – and bandaged, tidy wounds. It became headless and bloated, mutilated and disembowelled; like the rabbits we snared then messily gutted with our pen-knives.

CHILDREN'S VOICES. Elsie Plummer was a very good girl.
She went to church on Sunday.
To pray to God to give her strength
To kiss the boys on Monday.

Cut to interior hut sounds. close, intimate. The children's accents, while still London, have Cornish overtones and phrases. ELSIE now has seduction in her voice, learned from the cinema, where none was in the earlier scene.

ELSIE. Terry, let's play families.

TERRY. No.

ELSIE. Oh, go on. You be Dad and I'll be Mam. I love you Dad. You can tell. Listen to my heart. Feel it. No, inside. Undo them can't you.

TERRY. Don't want to.

ELSIE. You do.

TERRY. You're older'n me.

ELSIE. I'm only fourteen.

TERRY. Boys should be older'n girls.

ELSIE. Who said?

TERRY. They always are.

ELSIE. Not. Mrs Kitto's older'n Mr Kitto. By miles.

TERRY. How d'you know?

ELSIE. Everybody knows. So's all right. I like you best. You're the youngest. Have you seen my new knickers.

TERRY. Everybody has.

ELSIE. They haven't.

TERRY. When you do high kicks.

ELSIE. Want to see 'em now? (*Quiet and near.*) Want to touch?

TERRY. Don't know.

ELSIE. You knew the other day.

TERRY. Shut *up*.

ELSIE. You want to really.

TERRY. I'm going.

ELSIE. You're scared.

TERRY. Just stop *talking* about it. 's embarrassing.

ELSIE (*quickly*). Sorry. Yere. Lie down. By me. I won't speak again. Promise. (*Pause.*)

NARRATOR. Suddenly soldiers descended on Doublebois.

A military band playing Lili Bolero in the arrangement used frequently in forces broadcasts during the war.

The Big House was requisitioned and overflowed. Nissen huts appeared along the drives. Girls took to walking the lanes nearby with increasing frequency; Elsie, now fulsomely fifteen, lost interest in me. If the vaccies had shocked the village, the soldiers stunned it.

Chorus of soldiers' voices singing impromptu to the tune of 'Colonel Bogey'. Also lorry engine as though troops are riding and singing.

Hitler, has only got one ball.
Göering, has two but very small.
Himmler has something similar
And poor old Goebbels has no balls at all.

Lorry fade out.

MISS POLMANOR (*agitatedly*). Mr Buckroyd, Mr Buckroyd, have you heard –

MR BUCKROYD (*wearily*). Yes, yes. There's a war on, Miss Polmanor.

NARRATOR. Then a huge event: a camp concert. Professional entertainers and the Looe Fishermen's Choir performed in the long Nissen hut that was the camp canteen.

COMPERE. And now, led by the choir, a sing-song.

A small band strikes up and, instantly, and shatteringly, the audience bellows 'You Are My Sunshine' after two lines, fade down behind NARRATOR.

NARRATOR. Rows of soldiers and girls sang with a sudden, rolling, bellowing roar that gave the song an emotional power the composer could never have dreamed of. And on a long table at the back, legs dangling, I was tucked in between Elsie and another girl, each with a happy, grinning soldier on the other side. Oh, my wartime childhood: the stinging smoke and sickly beer smell; and in the comforting dark, rows of soldiers and not enough girls. It was my other childhood but it was their youth: hands tight round willing waists; male fingers pressing into thin summer frocks; female cheeks against harsh army tunics; all of them bawling out their fervour for the moment with a passion I could sense but not comprehend. Their passion was not to get at the Germans, of course – but to stay – forever if possible – in the warm half-dark, against the pressure of another body that might be snatched away. They had the threat of extinction to sharpen their senses.

Fade song out.

We kids hung round the soldiers constantly, cadging rides, holding their rifles, wearing their forage caps and swinging on the big iron gates at the entrances to the drives of Doublebois House to watch lorries and even tanks rumble in and out. Teddy Worthing, a six-year-old, evacuated with his mother, was one of a row of us sitting on the gate when a lorry came round the corner, caught the end of the gate, pulled it off its hinges and threw us into the bushes. But Teddy went under the gate. And the gate went under the lorry.

TERRY (*shouting*). Auntie Rose, Auntie Rose. Come quickly, Teddy Worthing's dead. He's dead. Teddy Worthing's dead.

AUNTIE ROSE. You're covered in blood. What's happened?

TERRY. They're bringing him.

AUNTIE ROSE. Bringing him. You mean –?

NARRATOR. A sentry, accompanied by the bemused driver and three children, was walking up the main road carrying Teddy's tiny, crumpled body to number 3 Railway Cottages, where he had lived.

Soldiers' measured tread.

AUNTIE ROSE. What are you doing? What are you doing, man?

SENTRY. Are you the mother?

AUNTIE ROSE. No, where are you taking him?

SENTRY. The children said he lives in the cottages, here.

AUNTIE ROSE. What are you trying to do? Give his mother a present, you bloody fool? Give him to me.

SENTRY. Here you are. I didn't know where to –

AUNTIE ROSE. Where's Mrs Worthing? Does anyone know?

CORNISH CHILD VOICE. She's coming Auntie Rose. She's seen –

AUNTIE ROSE. Oh, Teddy my little mite. What will she do?

NARRATOR. Auntie Rose took Teddy's mother into our house where she lay crumpled and sobbing on the sofa, watched by our detached, curious eyes until we were driven out. So much emotion seemed more than one person could contain. Her body jerked and heaved as her grief tore its way out of her. A day later a soldier appeared in the Court: Teddy's father. He stood mutely, arms pinned to his side by his wife as she clung to him and sobbed anew. Jack and I, Jimmy Peters, the Bunney boys and Ken Plummer were to carry Teddy's coffin to the station to put it on the 9.00 am express: a farewell gesture from us all. A military band was to lead us. The whole of Doublebois followed. A funeral march was considered inappropriate for so small a child, so some genius of military bandsmanship used his discretion.

Scratch band playing 'Early One Morning', shuffling feet. Very distant train arriving and stopping.

Because I was the smallest boy, I was in the middle and had to hold my hands up to reach the coffin. It was not long enough to accommodate three boys a side and nobody had taught us to walk in step, so, as we tripped and shuffled along, my heels and shins were skinned by the hobnail boots of the boys behind and in front of me while I inflicted similar injuries on them. The station-master, stout and self-important, held the train as we filed down the slope of station approach between two rows of soldiers.

Command voice 'Squad, Squad, present arms'. *Sound of order being carried out.* 'Squad, reverse arms.'

Passengers stared from the train as we clumsily put Teddy in the strong-smelling guard's van on straw that was laid for some tethered creature, a calf or goat, that stirred uneasily at the activity round it.

Train door slams. Guards whistle. Train drawing out. Then fade all these effects.

The train departed and we coffin-bearers turned and ran hard to school in Dobwalls over a mile away. But I was the only one from the Junior Vaccie class in the isolated tin hut.

MRS LANGDON. Terry Foster, you're late again.

All TERRY *can produce is heavy breathing.*

What's your excuse this time?

More breathing.

Look at the time. And your legs. All scratched and bloody. What have you been doing? Football? Fighting? Climbing?

TERRY. No, miss.

MRS LANGDON. No fibs. Forty minutes you're late. This is a record, I think.

JUNE. Please, miss. Miss.

MRS LANGDON. Be quiet, June Burford. Terry, come here.

NARRATOR. The dreaded ruler was produced. God knows how such a failure of communication had occurred in our gossip-ridden little community but Mrs Langdon knew nothing of the Doublebois ceremony.

Six whacks of the ruler on knuckles. Indrawn breaths from TERRY. *He is still breathless.*

MRS LANGDON. Now go to your place.

TERRY (*muttered*). 'es, Miss.

MRS LANGDON. And don't be late again.

JUNE. Please, Miss.

MRS LANGDON. Be *quiet*, June.

TERRY *starts to cry*.

And stop snivelling, Terry. You've had that much before and earned it.

JUNE. Please, Miss.

MRS LANGDON. Yes, what *is* it, June?

JUNE. Please, Miss. He's been carrying Teddy Worthing's coffin. They put it on the train this morning at Doublebois. My lady said. I heard.

Pause.

MRS LANGDON (*very faint*). Oh, my –

Fade.

NARRATOR. Jack and I used to go shopping with Auntie Rose once a week in Liskeard, four miles away. But the great events that filled us with excitement were the 22-mile train rides to Plymouth over Saltash Bridge

Background. Train slowing down then crossing the bridge with a hollow noise.

guarded by a sentry at either end. Local legend said that the bridge moved a foot every time a train crossed. I got the railway timetable and multiplied the trains by the number of weeks since the bridge was built then wondered why it hadn't either edged itself up the Tamar or sidled miles out to sea.

Fade out.

We stared at the warships, low, grey, and menacing, lying in the Tamar estuary; then Plymouth and the Hoe; the statue of Drake with his bowls, a stylish reminder of how to reduce the enemy to size; and pasties that tasted of potato and pepper but had never seen meat. Over these expeditions presided Auntie Rose with two loaded shopping bags. She wore old-fashioned clothes and walked as if always laden. A cameo brooch was pinned to her best blouse and a shapeless hat that required hatpins to hold it was crammed onto her long, thick brown hair done up in a bun. One evening, we were waiting in Plymouth North Road station buffet for a train that was very late. 'Bombing up the line', was the dark rumour.

Background. Buffet foreground. JACK *and* TERRY *very quiet.* 'Coh', ''s terrific' 'Let's see' 'Pull it out' 'No, leave it' 'Don't touch: it's mine'.

Jack had bought a miniature sheath knife in its leather sheath, something he had been coveting and saving for for ages. He kept taking it from the shopping bag and half-withdrawing the glistening blade. Our heads bent over it as we experimented how to hang it from his belt. At the side or secretly at the back like a hunter's knife? It was a formidable purchase. The date was March 21st, 1941, the first day of spring and the first of the three nights on which the Luftwaffe wiped the centre of Plymouth from the face of the earth.

AUNTIE ROSE. Come on, boys. Put that knife away till the proper time. When you get home you play with that, not in here. You'll lose it.

Distant air raid sirens. Background hubbub of buffet falls silent.

(*Softly.*) Oh, Dieu, what's that?

JACK. Air raid sirens.

AUNTIE ROSE. They're a long way –

There is the heartstopping, low pitched whirr and whine that develops into the shattering wail of a siren starting up very close to them. Voices raised in a new nervous hubbub. Door opening.

PORTER (*Devon accent. Capping the noise*). All passengers in the subway please. At once. Move along, please. All passengers in the subways at once. Come on my dears, down under the station. Move along, my yansome.

Cut to crowds moving along platform quickly.

AUNTIE ROSE. Come on, boys. Bring that bag, Jack. I got this one.

Noise of guns firing, not very near. General hubbub responds.

Come yere, Terry. By me. Come on, down these steps. We'll be all right down yere.

TERRY. Are they bombs?

JACK. No, they're our guns, shooting the Jerries down. Bombs whistle.

Guns nearer. Voices, hubbub in background.

(*Panic.*) Where's my knife?

AUNTIE ROSE. What?

JACK. My new sheath knife. It's gone.

AUNTIE ROSE. Perhaps it's in this bag. Yere, let's see.

JACK (*running off*). I left it in the buffet. Oh, I left it in the buffet.

AUNTIE ROSE. Come back, come back, boy you can't – Oh, (*Faint.*)

he's gone.

TERRY (*very fast, crying*). Here's the knife. Auntie Rose. It's in this bag. I got it here. Jack, I got it! (*Running off.*)

NARRATOR. I flew between the huddled groups of people, turned a corner and started up the slope towards platform level.

Sound: overlap. Whistling followed by big explosion. Glass crashing. Bits dropping. Followed by the very near repetitious thump of naval guns firing, rapidly, and rockets.

I stopped and stood bawling, afraid to move, when hands grabbed me.

PORTER. Yere, boy, come yere. I got you. You can't stand out there.

TERRY (*sobbing*). Let me go. My brother. My brother's up there.

PORTER. What? Your brother.

TERRY. He lost his knife.

PORTER. What you talking about?

AUNTIE ROSE (*approach*). Here Terry, here he is. With me – he came back.

NARRATOR. And there stood Jack. His courage, too, had failed him at the sight and sound of the real war.

AUNTIE ROSE. You give me heart failure you did. Both of you.

NARRATOR. We spent the night sitting on a bench while the inferno raged above us. My principal memory, after the initial knife-panic, was that no matter how I shook with fright the bench, which sat about ten people, always quaked at a different rythmn and I couldn't get my bottom synchronised to the common tempo of terror.

Fade our air raid noises through above. All clear sounds. Then slow train.

The next morning we stood among debris on the platform till a train took us across the miraculously unscathed Saltash Bridge. Plymouth was ablaze, smoke hung everywhere. At each station crowds of people met the train to ask for news or just to stare at us.

Background. Hushed Cornish voices. 'Is anything left?' 'How many killed?' 'Have they sunk the fleet?' 'How d'you get over?'

As we pulled into Doublebois station, there right at the end of the platform, stood Uncle Jack looking ridiculously small and vulnerable till he saw the three of us waving wildly from a window. Then his shut face burst open into a grin that threatened to tear it in two.

Train stopping. Engine releasing steam.

UNCLE JACK. Oh, Dieu, girl. There you are. There you are. There you are. There you are. There you are.

AUNTIE ROSE (*pleased*). Of course I am. What d'you think? Let me go, you fool. People are watching.

UNCLE JACK. Give me those bags, I'll carry 'em. You looked after her, boys, did you, for me?

JACK.   }   It was triffic, Uncle Jack.
TERRY. }   I was ever so scared.

UNCLE JACK. I thought I'd got rid of you all at last. But there's no peace for the wicked, is there?

Fade.

NARRATOR. The bombing continued for three nights but Plymouth burned for longer than that, under a pall of smoke all day, and by night, making a red glow to the east like a false dawn.

Faint, but growing German bomber, propellor driven, slow, very slow.

One morning, during this, I stood in the Court unable to believe my eyes.

TERRY (*excitedly*). Auntie Rose, Auntie Rose. There's a German plane coming. Look. It's ever so low.

AUNTIE ROSE (*running*). Where, boy? Oh, don't be daft. It's Red Cross. Look.

TERRY. It's not. They're German crosses. See?

AUNTIE ROSE. I tell you, it's Red – look, they're waving. You can see him, plain.

TERRY. He's the gunner. Look, one engine's not working.

AUNTIE ROSE. Wave back, boy. Woo-oo.

TERRY. I think he's going to crash.

AUNTIE ROSE. If they're Germans they'd shoot us.

TERRY. Look, it's coming down in the valley.

Distant crash.

AUNTIE ROSE. Oh, my God. D'you think they were Germans?

TERRY. 'Course they were.

AUNTIE ROSE. Why didn't they parachute?

TERRY. I think they were too low.

AUNTIE ROSE. Those poor boys. I saw him. Young, like my Gwyn. Why didn't he shoot us if he was German?

TERRY. I think he must've been a Saxon, one of Uncle Jack's friends.

Lorries driving past in background.

NARRATOR. But Dobwalls and Doublebois were due for more shocks: the soldiers piled into their Bedford lorries and rode away.

Fade out.

The district just had time to heave a corporate sigh of relief when the roar of different motors was heard,

Background. Approaching heavy lorries.

vast, high-bonneted, high-sided lorries which the occupants called trucks, with names like Dodge and Chrysler. Yes, it was the Americans.

Music. 'Over there' military bands. Lorries and music.

1ST MALE CORNISH VOICE (*slowly and amicably*). Hallo there, my lovelies. Where you been to, then? 'Tis nearly all over.

NARRATOR. In that part of Cornwall, people from the next village were strangers; Englishmen from across the Tamar were foreigners; these men might have been from Mars.

1ST MALE VOICE (*quietly, awed*). Oh, my good God.

MISS POLMANOR (*quietly, then getting hysterical*). Oh, my, oh my, oh my – Mr Buckroyd, Mr Buckroyd, Mr Buckroyd – Mr Buck – buck – buck – buck (*She should finish clucking like a hen.*)

MR BUCKROYD. Yes, Miss Polmanor, I know. But, you see, there's a war –

MISS POLMANOR. But have you seen?

MR BUCKROYD. Yes, Miss –

MISS POLMANOR. They're BLACK. All of 'em; black as night; black as the ace of spades.

Hubbub of voices. Overlapping.

1ST MALE VOICE. All over? All the way up'n'down.

2ND MALE VOICE. So they do say.

1ST FEMALE VOICE. They can see in the dark.

2ND FEMALE VOICE. They'd need to, wouldn't they?

1ST MALE VOICE. What? Their backsides, too?

2ND MALE VOICE. Ar. Everything.

Men chortle.

1ST FEMALE VOICE. And their hair. They cut it with crimping shears, they do.

1ST MALE VOICE. Scissors aren't strong enough.

MISS POLMANOR. Creatures of the Devil.

1ST MALE VOICE. They'm Fuzzy-Wuzzies.

2ND MALE VOICE. They got white palms to their hands, I saw when I shook hands wi' one o'they.

1ST FEMALE VOICE. 'twas worn off, that's why.

2ND FEMALE VOICE. Does it wash off?

MISS POLMANOR. And their lips!

1ST MALE VOICE (*whispered*). They got John Thomases like Crago's bull.

2ND MALE VOICE (*whispered*). Twenty-two inches of uncontrolled flesh.

MISS POLMANOR (*shrieks*). Ah! They oughtn't to be out loose. We're not safe.

2ND MALE VOICE. They was very civil wi' I in the shop the other day.

1ST MALE VOICE (*laughing*). They're mad for white women, Miss Polmanor.

MISS POLMANOR. We'll all be raped in our beds.

1ST MALE VOICE. Don't worry, Miss Polmanor, they'll make an exception in your case.

One beat of silence.

ELSIE. I think they're lovely boys. Nicer'n our lot.

NARRATOR. It's no good thinking in terms of colour prejudice. The village wasn't prejudiced – it was astounded. And we kids, we loved them. We wore their hats, chewed their gum, held their strange hands and ate their candy. Rides on army vehicles doubled. Jeeps were the big treat: tooth-loosening, rebounding, joy-rides across the fields. And these smiling, gentle men who came from God-knows-what-Hells in southern segregated U.S.A. let us pat and pull their hair, rub them to see if it came off, examine their pink palms, marvel at their very existence – and then they were gone just as suddenly as they appeared and were replaced by other Yanks, white ones, no less friendly, no less generous, but with not a tenth of the exotic appeal of their delightful black comrades.

JACK *and* TERRY *singing* 'Sheep may safely graze' *in two parts:* JACK *alto*, TERRY *treble*.

Door opening.

AUNTIE ROSE. Jack, Jack, I want you. I want a word –

UNCLE JACK. Shush, girl. Can't you yere?

AUNTIE ROSE. This is important.

UNCLE JACK. And this isn't? Listen, they're a pair aren't they.

AUNTIE ROSE. Important *now*.

UNCLE JACK. All right, you two. That's all for today.

TERRY. Can we go out now, Uncle Jack?

UNCLE JACK. Yes, go on.

JACK. Uncle Jack, my voice keeps going funny.

UNCLE JACK. Don't you dare let it break till after the Silver Voice competition at chapel. You both wipe the floor with all them Christians. We'll show 'em heathens can sing better. Especially Cockney ones, eh? Go on.

Sound: feet door.

AUNTIE ROSE. Elsie's pregnant.

UNCLE JACK. There's a surprise. Who knows?

AUNTIE ROSE. She's told Mrs Steer who she lives with.

UNCLE JACK. Everybody, then.

Exterior woodland.

Rustle as he enters their hut.
Interior, hut. ELSIE *crying.*

TERRY. Elsie, don't cry. I love you.

ELSIE. Oh, shut up.

TERRY. I'll stay here with you.

ELSIE. Bugger off – Go on, bugger off. Leave me alone. (*She sobs.*)

Door crashing open TERRY *running into kitchen.*

TERRY (*out of breath*). Auntie Rose, Auntie Rose.

AUNTIE ROSE. Calm down, boy. What's up?

TERRY. Elsie's crying.

AUNTIE ROSE. She'll do a lot more of that.

TERRY. Have I got to marry her?

AUNTIE ROSE. What?

TERRY. I'm the father.

AUNTIE ROSE (*laughs*). Don't be silly, boy.

TERRY. But I am. I love her.

AUNTIE ROSE. Go on out and play.

TERRY (*starting to cry*). She told me she loved me.

AUNTIE ROSE. 'tisn't what she said to you that matters. It's what she did with someone else.

Cut to hut.

TERRY (*close, quiet and intimate*). Your stomach's getting 'normous.

ELSIE (*quiet and close. Giggles*). That's the baby. D'you remember when you didn't believe me about babies.

TERRY. I was young then.

ELSIE. Feel. It moves.

TERRY. Errggh. 's like a frog, squirming.

ELSIE. I hope 'er's a Yank. They was best.

Interior of full chapel.

MR BUCKROYD. This is a happy occasion that brings us here together, this evening: the East Cornwall Silver Voice Competition, in which we will try to decide which of our children has been blessed with the voice that will win this splendid trophy plus five shillings-worth of National Savings stamps. And now, let us pray.

Shuffle of everybody in church kneeling. BUCKROYD's voice goes to background.

Oh, Lord, bless the efforts of these, your children, who will try to bring beauty in the midst of destruction. Give our judges fair and clear minds, guide our organist's fingers and bless all our troops wherever they may be. Amen.

Through the prayer we hear in close-up. Voices lowered.

UNCLE JACK. Feeling nervous, boys?

TERRY. Yes.

JACK. A bit.

UNCLE JACK. That's good. You take good breaths, you'll see 'em all off.

AUNTIE ROSE. Here, boy, put your tie straight and pull that sock up. That's right. Now you both look a proper pair.

ELSIE (*arriving*). Here move up, can you? There's no room.

UNCLE JACK. Come in yere, Elsie. By me.

ELSIE. Cor, 'n arf crowded, innit.

At the end of the prayer everyone sits.

MR BUCKROYD. Our first contestant this evening is John Lavender from East Taphouse. John is going to sing 'Jerusalem'.

MISS POLMANOR. Mr Buckroyd. Mr Buckroyd.

Background buzz at this interruption.

MR BUCKROYD. Yes, Miss Polmanor?

MISS POLMANOR. In view of the fact that most of the children of the district are here this evening, I wonder if you fully approve of the congregation.

MR BUCKROYD. I don't think I understand, Miss Polmanor.

MISS POLMANOR. This is a children's occasion. We should be protecting them. From corruption.

Background reactions.

ELSIE (*whispered*). Oh, no. She's looking at me. Oh, no.

MISS POLMANOR. While our menfolk are away fighting God's Holy War we womenfolk should be setting an example not pointing the way down the primrose path to damnation. I think you all know to whom I refer.

ELSIE (*panics*). I'm sorry, Mr Buckroyd. I am, honest. I just came to hear the boys sing, I'll go, I –

UNCLE JACK. You bloody sit down and don't move.

ELSIE (*crying*). No, I –

MISS POLMANOR. *I saw her.* She slipped in while we were all at prayer.

MR BUCKROYD (*overlapping*). Please, Miss Polmanor, I am sure there is no need –

General background hubbub. ELSIE *crying.*

UNCLE JACK (*topping the noise*). What's she supposed to have done then, eh, Missus?

AUNTIE ROSE. Oh, Jack, don't make a scene.

MISS POLMANOR. Sinned. As well you know, Mr Phillips. Sinned again and again.

MR BUCKROYD. Please, please, this is a House of God.

MISS POLMANOR. Daren' we not mention sin in the House of God now, Vicar?

MR BUCKROYD. Miss Polmanor, I'm surprised and disappointed. Elsie may have transgressed . . .

UNCLE JACK. Let him that is without sin cast the first stone.

MR BUCKROYD. I was about to use those very words.

UNCLE JACK. Then what's all this transgressing? She did what come natural.

MR BUCKROYD. I intended no censure.

MISS POLMANOR. Then why *not*, vicar?

UNCLE JACK. And if anyone should leave this house, you should order *her* out –

MR BUCKROYD. No, Mr Phillips, I'm not ordering anyone out. That's not my –

UNCLE JACK. – for the sin of envy. We all know she'd like to have been in this state years ago only no one'd touch her, bloody, dried up, old haybag.

Hubbub.

MR BUCKROYD. Oh, now, Mr Phillips, that is not Christian.

UNCLE JACK. Well, I'm not a Christian, thank God. Come on, Rose. Come on, boys, let's breathe some clean air outside. Elsie, my lovely, you want to walk home with us, is it?

Fade.

NARRATOR. East Cornwall never did get its Silver Voice for that year, 1943, but the voice of propriety, the voice of conformity, had a strength then that went far beyond the ourbursts of frustrated old maids as we all discovered when the vaccies' billeting officer came and went one day. He missed Uncle Jack which was just as well.

UNCLE JACK. What the hell did he mean? Moral surroundings?

AUNTIE ROSE. He wanted to know if Terry was still allowed to play with Elsie. He's ten and she's fifteen and she's a bad example and –

UNCLE JACK (*in a contained, but growing, rage*). Oh, God. God save us all from the clutches of the bloody Holy ones.

AUNTIE ROSE (*simultaneously*). Jack, Jack, bach, ssh . . . don't . . .

UNCLE JACK. The sooner they all go to Heaven and leave us down yere in peace –

Village street. Walking feet, TERRY's.

MR BUCKROYD (*distant call*). Terry, Terry!

TERRY (*near, mutter*). Oh, no.

MR BUCKROYD. Hey, boy. Stop. I want you.

Boy's feet stop running. Man's feet approach.

What's up, cat got your tongue? (*Pause.*) I haven't seen you at choir practice lately. Not coming now? (*Pause.*) I see. Well, give Mr and Mrs Phillips my regards, won't you?

TERRY. I hate you.

MR BUCKROYD. What?

TERRY. They're taking Jack 'n' me away.

MR BUCKROYD. Who is? Your parents.

TERRY. No. You. The Holy ones. And Elsie, too.

MR BUCKROYD. What the Devil are you talking about?

TERRY (*accusingly*). See? You swear, too.

NARRATOR. The Reverend Buckroyd took a swift hand in our affairs. A phone call from him to Welling police station sent a constable to call on Mum and Dad – frightening the life out of them into the bargain. A return phone call from Dad soon settled where we should stay. But Buckroyd couldn't wave his hand over Elsie. Her foster parents couldn't face a new-born illegitimate baby and that was that. Elsie's father was a prisoner of the Japanese. Her mother was nowhere to be found – whether through enemy action or allied attraction, I don't know – and so Elsie was bound for a home. Homes for unmarried mothers appeared all over the country during the war. Meanwhile, great events were taking place in the world: North Africa was taken from Rommel; the Russians were turning defeat into triumph.

NEWSREADER. British forces under the command of General Montgomery and American forces of the 6th Army under the command of General Dwight D. Eisenhower have landed on the island of Sicily. The invasion of Europe has begun.

Mix to extract from Churchill's 'Soft underbelly of Europe' speech. include those words.

NARRATOR. Our three-year, other-childhood came to a swift climax. With air raids more-or-less over, Jack returned home to go to Woolwich Polytechnic and I was awaiting the results of my exam for Dartford Grammar School.

TERRY (*entering excitedly*). Auntie Rose, Auntie Rose, the letter's come. Look. It's come. It says Kent Education Committee.

AUNTIE ROSE. Well, open it, boy, let's see.

TERRY. There's a telegram, too.

AUNTIE ROSE (*voice changes*). Telegram? What's it say on it?

TERRY. Just 'Telegram. War Office.'

AUNTIE ROSE. Open it, Terry. The telegram. Open it.

Tearing paper.

Read it. No, no, bring it yere. No, read it. I can't.

TERRY (*reading*). The War Office, Whitehall, London. 2.35 pm, 14th July, 1943. We regret to inform you that your son Gwyn has been – (*Indrawn breath.*)

AUNTIE ROSE (*almost a whisper*). Does it say it, boy? Does it say it? Does it? Say it doesn't.

Silence.

Ooh. Come yere, boy. Put your arms round me. Hold me for a minute. Oh, Gwyn, Oh, Gwyn, my little – I was always afraid for you. Oh, Gwyn, Gwyn, Gwyn.

TERRY. Shall I go and tell Uncle Jack?

AUNTIE ROSE. No. No. He'll be home in an hour. Time enough for his world to end then.

Cut to pen being put down, rustle of paper.

TERRY (*reads*). Dear Mum and Dad, Just a line to let you know that Auntie Rose and Uncle Jack's son Gwyn has been killed in Sicily. They are very unhappy. Auntie Rose keeps crying and Uncle Jack keeps going to the bottom of the garden and sitting there instead of going to work. And as Jack is home with you now I thought it would be a good idea if I stayed here and became Auntie Rose's and Uncle Jack's son and you had Jack. Then you've both got one each. That's fair. I could go to the County school in Liskeard and get the 4.12 home. I like it here so it would be all right. Love Terry.

Summer exterior. Rural. Distant shunting engine.

Can I come and sit with you, Uncle Jack?

UNCLE JACK. Yes, come yere, boy. Time you had a 'aircut, is it?

UNCLE JACK *grabs him by the hair.*

TERRY, Ow. 's not that long.

UNCLE JACK. Little blondie, Anglo-Saxon. Gwyn was dark, you know, like me: a Celt. Hm. The soft underbelly of Europe. Hm. The mud was soft in Flanders, too. Didn't save anybody. What was he doing in Sicily, eh? What did he have to do with them? Twice we've had to fight the Germans. I bet they wonder why, too. (*Slowly.*) Remember, boy: never, never, never, never, never, trust your leaders. Never. Montgomery's a hero. Churchill's a hero. Gwyn is dead. Rose thinks the Germans killed him. Huh! And it's not just this war or the last. It's all history. 'Into the Valley of Death Rode the Six Hundred'. Huh! Who sent 'em there? Don't ever trust 'em, boy, not any of 'em.

AUNTIE ROSE (*distant, calling*). Jack, Jack. Mr Buckroyd's here. He'd like to see you.

UNCLE JACK. Oo-oh, no, not the bloody vicar. They don't just kill you. They send someone to tell your next of kin it's all for the best.

MR BUCKROYD (*getting nearer*). Good afternoon, Mr Phillips. Hallo, Terry.

TERRY. 'lo, sir.

MR BUCKROYD. I can't tell you, Mr Phillips, how sorry I –

UNCLE JACK. Then don't try, vicar.

MR BUCKROYD. Hm. Yes. I suggested to your wife a memorial service . . . ?

UNCLE JACK. What she say?

MR BUCKROYD. She would like it if you don't mind.

UNCLE JACK. No, let her have it. I'll be there.

MR BUCKROYD. Good. I'm sure you've made the right decision.

UNCLE JACK. Only, vicar, nothing about souls, eh? Or heaven, eh? Or eternal life, or any of that, eh? A memorial service; let's just remember him.

MR BUCKROYD. I'll vet everything myself. I'm sure he died a hero, Mr Phillips.

UNCLE JACK. Are you, now? I seen a few o'them die. Ashes to ashes and mud to mud.

MR BUCKROYD. Yes, well, good afternoon, Mr Phillips. I think Mrs Phillips would like me to have a word with her.

UNCLE JACK. Yes. Thank you. You're a good man, vicar. In spite of being a Christian.

Feet receding.

I like it yere, boy. Look at the wind on that hayfield. And the valley. And the compost heap, there, to remind us what we're coming to.

TERRY. And the railway. That's good.

UNCLE JACK. Yes. Let's have a service here for Gwyn. You and me, eh? An Anglo-Celtic service. You know that song you learned last week? That song you sang for us?

TERRY. Yes.

UNCLE JACK. Sing it, boy. Now that's – suitable. Go straight to the third verse. You know? 'And death is printed on his face'

TERRY (*sings to the tune of* 'Barbara Allen').
And death is printed on his face
And o'er his heart is stealing.
Then haste away to comfort him . . .

Interior parlour at breakfast time.

AUNTIE ROSE. I've got a letter yere from your Mother.

TERRY. So've I.

AUNTIE ROSE. You don't want to go home, is it?

TERRY. 's not that.

AUNTIE ROSE. Well, you see, you can't stay with us. As it is you'll have to sleep down in the front hall, there, for a bit, till you go home to your Mam and Dad, cos we must have your room at once. (*Smile in her voice.*) Don't look so pained. Guess who's going in there.

TERRY. Soldiers?

AUNTIE ROSE. Elsie.

TERRY (*pleased*). Honest?

AUNTIE ROSE. We're going to have Elsie and her little one. And she'd better move in quick or they'll be shunting her off to that home, that workhouse place. That's fit for nobody, certainly not Elsie and her baby, eh?

TERRY. No.

AUNTIE ROSE. So you go up and get your things out.

TERRY (*excited*). Can I go and tell Elsie?

AUNTIE ROSE. She knows, silly.

TERRY. Well, can I go and tell her I know, too?

Crash of chair. Running feet.

TERRY. Elsie, Elsie! You're coming here, Elsie.

AUNTIE ROSE. Watch out, boy, you'll break something.

NARRATOR. A week later I lay in terror on my mattress on the hall floor listening while Elsie up in my room, gave me another lesson on the facts of life.

Background ELSIE *in labour screams and gasps.*

No excuse for me to disbelieve any longer what went where or to puzzle how a whole baby came out of there.

Baby's cries, weak at first, growing in strength.

I crept fearfully into the kitchen and there was Uncle Jack with a glass in his hand.

UNCLE JACK. Hallo, boy, too noisy to sleep, is it? She always was a noisy girl. Now's her chance.

TERRY. Is Elsie all right?

UNCLE JACK. Right as rain. Here, have a sip of this. Drink the baby's health. say 'Good health and long life to you, Sambo.'

TERRY. Is it a boy, then?

UNCLE JACK (*laughs gently*). Black as pitch. Pretty little thing. I'm going to learn some Negro spirituals to teach him for the Silver Voice Competition, eh? They're good singers those darkies.

TERRY. Is it black all over?

UNCLE JACK. Just about. Well, 's a good thing. He'll do a lot for Rose, being yere. (*His good humour turns bitter.*) The Lord giveth and the Lord taketh away – as the bloody vicar would say.

Steam train stopping. Station sounds.

NARRATOR. A few mornings later, on Doublebois station, I boarded the 9 am express for Paddington. I was ten-and-a-half when my other-childhood ended. I had fewer peope to see me off than Teddy Worthing, but there were enough: Elsie with her baby and Auntie Rose and Uncle Jack. Oh, Auntie Rose and Uncle Jack, Uncle Jack and Auntie Rose. Ten shillings a week per vaccie was the official allowance, and in return they had given themselves without stint. Was there ever such a bargain? Yes, they were about to give Elsie the same, for nothing. They were without guile and without self-interest; 'the salt of the earth' was the saying . . . and whenever the earth needed salting Auntie Rose and Uncle Jack were there to do it.

Guard's whistle, porters' shouts.

AUNTIE ROSE. Goodbye, Terry, give my respects to your Mam and

Dad. Write soon. Oh, we'll miss you, boy.

ELSIE (*overlapping*). Bye, Terry. See you in London one day. Say good-bye, Louis. Bye-bye. Say bye-bye.

TERRY. Bye, Elsie. Bye, Louis.

Baby makes a noise. Train starting.

Goodbye, Uncle Jack.

UNCLE JACK. Goodbye, boy. Look after your – you be –

AUNTIE ROSE. Oh, now don't cry, Jack, for God's sake. You'll start me off.

She starts to cry.

UNCLE JACK. Just remember what I said, boy. Two things. Don't ever forget: it's not fair and don't be late.

Their goodbyes fade as the train gathers speed. Fade down to background, then out as: fade in from far away.

TERRY and JACK (*sing*).
Time like an ever-rolling stream,
Bears all its sons away.
They fly forgotten

Pause.

as a dream dies at the opening day.

CIGARETTES AND CHOCOLATE

by Anthony Minghella

Anthony Minghella was born in 1954 on the Isle of Wight of Italian parents. Until 1981 he taught at the University of Hull and since then he has written for the stage, screen and radio. His plays include *Whale Music*, *A Little Like Drowning*, *Two Planks and a Passion*, *Love Bites* and the television trilogy, *What If It's Raining?* *Made in Bangkok* was first seen at the Aldwych Theatre, London in a Michael Codron production and was winner of the Plays and Players Award for Best Play of 1986. More recently he has written the Emmy and New York Film Festival's Gold Medal award winning series *The Storyteller*. His short radio play *Hang Up* won the Prix Italia for Radio Drama 1988 and his work has been highly acclaimed in Europe and America.

Cigarettes and Chocolate was first broadcast on BBC Radio 4 on 6 November 1988. The cast was as follows:

GEMMA	Jenny Howe
ROB	Bill Nighy
LORNA	Juliet Stevenson
ALISTAIR	Alex Norton
MOTHER	Joan Campion
GAIL	Jane Gurnett
SAMPLE	Christopher Ravenscroft
CONCEPCION	Sally Eldridge

Directed by Robert Cooper and Anthony Minghella
Running time, as broadcast: 57 minutes, 23 seconds

Telephone ringing.

GEMMA (*a taped answerphone message*). Hello, you've rung 341 6293.
If you'd like to leave a message for Gemma, please do so after you
hear the tone.

Tone. Then Gemma's messages are heard.

ROB. It's me. Listen, did I leave my new toothbrush with you? The one
with the, it's got a, you know, the big head . . . I think it was in your
bag for some reason. Don't brush your hair with it. And don't open
the olive oil, I need something to give my sister. Can I come round
later for sex?

Tone.

LORNA. Hi, it's me, are we on for tonight? Will you ring me before
we meet and remind me to bring my glasses, because I can't read the
subtitles without them. Two reviews are in favour, one against. Ring
at seven, six forty-five, and say glasses. Ta ra.

Tone.

ROB. It's Rob. I'm leaving home for the office, and I don't know what
time I'll be home, late possibly, probably, probably ridiculously late.
Best thing would be to stay with you otherwise I'll have to drive the
extra seven hundred yards to my flat. Take pity on me.

Tone.

ALISTAIR. Gemma, look it's Alistair, you know, if you had anything
from me this morning, you know, like a letter, don't read it, you
know, if you haven't already opened, and if you have, if you have, if
you have, don't think of it as a problem, you know, think of it as a
not very good poem . . .

Tone.

MOTHER (*sceptical*). Gemma? It's your mother. Are you there? If
you're there and not answering can you pick up the telephone?

Gemma? I suppose you're out. Could you please telephone when you get in.

Tone.

ROB. Rob. Two-thirty. I'm at work. Call me.

Tone.

GAIL. Gemma, it's Gail. I hoped you'd be in because I wanted you to come and look at a flat with me. I'll read you the details, I can never remember whether your machine cuts you off after thirty seconds, I hope not because that drives me crazy, anyway, listen it's in, well the postcode is N19 but it's really Highgate Borders, I mean the Agents say Highgate which it isn't, but it's not inconvenient and anyway Highgate's ridiculous, as bad as you, it's impossible and this place has got a garden, it says pretty west-facing garden, although it doesn't say a length which is a bad sign, yesterday I saw a place in Camden with a Nice Town Garden, this is true, the details said Nice Town Garden and there was nothing, there wasn't one. There was a back yard where this guy had his bicycle and even that wouldn't stand straight, it was sort of bent up to squeeze it in.

Cut off. Tone.

Me again. I hate it when that happens. It makes you feel terrible, terribly rejecting, where was I? It's in Hornsey, did I say that, but I measured in the A-Z and it's really no further than, it's not as far north as Muswell Hill, say . . . it's about two inches above the Post Office Tower. I can't stand Muswell Hill. I hate the architecture as much as anything else: all those porches and it's smug, it's got smug porches. Gem, will you come and look at this place with me? Two bedrooms, plus a bedroom/study so there's room for the baby, there'll be room for the baby, plus the garden as I said . . . reception: fireplace, cornices, 16 by 11 which is okay, and dado rails, dado rails, (*Pronounces the A differently, first as in baby then as in far, then sing-song to the tune of 'Let's Call The Whole Thing Off'.*) You say Dado and I say Dado, whichever it is, who cares, so, I must hurry before I get cut off . . . I've got a scan at three tomorrow and I could go straight from that, so will you phone and let me know yes or no so I can make the appointment? It's much easier when you've got someone with, and Sample has a horror . . . actually if I could choose you'd come with me for the scan as well, would you hate

Cut off. Tone.

LORNA. It's Lorna, Gem, where are you? I'm in a callbox opposite the cinema. Are you on your way? Well, I'm assuming you're on your way. If for any reason you haven't left, I'll leave your ticket at the Box Office, or should I wait? There's a queue, Gem, and it's starting, what do I do? Just hurry up, will you!

Tone.

ROB. It's Rob.

Tone.

ROB *sighs, puts the phone down.*

Tone.

GEMMA's *flat. Morning.*

We hear the sounds of a spring morning in England. Larks, grasshoppers.
Music begins, the opening bars from Bach's 'St Matthew Passion'. But we
might feel we're hearing it through open French windows, because
GEMMA *is speaking from her small, walled garden in North London.*

GEMMA. The day I stopped talking was one of those perfect days we
have in England. They come in the spring and in the autumn,
differently, the one full of entrance, the other full of exit, but the
same in the way the air thins and you can see the edge of everything.
And somehow green is more green, blue more blue. I wish I'd had
another week, but there it was, a big red cross on my calendar, and
everything was ready . . . I'd had my holiday, in Italy, wonderful,
wonderful, as if I'd put my tongue on a small pile of salt . . . or a
glass of wine. Italy was a glass of dark wine swilled in the mouth.
And I'd spoken to them all, in turn, carefully, loving them all, like
suicide in a way: to stop talking. Like killing oneself.

Music and garden out.

Interior cafe, day time.

Cafe with sophisticated background music, jazz.

ROB. Hi, have you been waiting?

LORNA. No.

ROB. Am I always late?

LORNA. I think so, yes.

ROB. Yes, I think I am. Not very good is it?

LORNA. I adjust. Your coffee's cold. Actually, I don't think you were
late in the beginning.

ROB. You look nice. I'm supposed to be at a meeting.

LORNA. Really, and what? What? Do you mean – ?

ROB. I'm not going. I made some excuse. Sod it.

LORNA. What? You were meeting your lover?

ROB. Exactly. That's exactly what I said.

LORNA. I can believe that.

ROB. Lorna, she's stopped talking.

LORNA. What? Who? Gemma?

ROB. She's not talking. I went there this morning and she has just ceased to talk, she won't answer the telephone, she won't return calls, she won't say a single word to me.

LORNA. Why?

ROB. Well, obviously, because of this . . .

LORNA. Why? Did you tell her?

ROB. No.

LORNA. Well I certainly haven't told her.

ROB. She's very intuitive, she's very acute about these things.

LORNA. Really? I wouldn't have said so.

ROB. I'm telling you.

LORNA. I've just been on holiday with you both and we managed to –

ROB. There's no need to –

LORNA. I'm not being anything, I'm just pointing out –

ROB. I didn't say you were being anything – anyway, let's –

LORNA. Would you rather we stopped seeing each other?

ROB. No.

LORNA. What then?

GAIL. Rob!

ROB. Gail! Hi! Hi! Lorna and I are having an assignation! Ignore us!

GAIL. Oh hi, Lorna, I didn't realise it was you, wonderful coat, is that new? Where's Tom?

LORNA. It's ancient, it is nice though, isn't it? Sit down. Tom's with Gerti. (*The Nanny*.) Have you met Gerti?

GAIL. I thought it was Anna?

LORNA. No, Anna's gone. Gerti's wonderful.

GAIL. Can she speak English?

LORNA. She's Danish. She speaks better English than me.

ROB. Have some coffee.

GAIL. I thought you were off coffee for Lent?

ROB. This is mostly froth.

LORNA. Have some froth. You look wonderful.

GAIL. Thanks. I've put on fourteen-and-a-half pounds.

ROB (*to the* WAITRESS). Excuse me, could we have another coffee? Actually, I'll have another, make it three could you? Cappucino. Thanks a lot.

GAIL. Any more I'm going to have to make bras out of duffle bags.

LORNA. Is it going well?

GAIL. Apparently. The amniocentesis was, you know, clear.

LORNA. Terrific. So do you know what sex it is?

GAIL. I do, Lorna, but I've got to keep it a secret. Sample doesn't want to know.

LORNA. Right.

GAIL. How's Stephen? What are you two doing here? Is this really an assignation?

ROB. Seriously.

GAIL. How exciting. Is a threesome out of the question?

ROB. Jump in.

GAIL. How's Gemma?

ROB. She's great.

GAIL. She doesn't ring back when you leave a message on that bloody machine. What's the matter with her, the old bag? I wanted her to come and look at some places with me. I've only discovered this cafe since I've been flat-hunting. It's really nice, isn't it?

ROB. Yeah.

GAIL. I know what I wanted to ask you, Lorna . . . (*Deflected.*) Look at you both, I forgot you were all in Italy together, look at you, it's not the coat, well it is the coat, but it's the colour . . . it's February and you've both caught the sun! Was it wonderful?

ROB. It was. Tom was wonderful. The grown-ups were okay. Stephen cheated at Scrabble.

LORNA. So did you.

ROB. I cheated openly. Stephen pretended he wasn't. I always cheat. If you always cheat, it's hardly cheating at all, is the way I look at it.

GAIL. Did Gemma have a good time? Oh God, you pigs, I love Italy.

LORNA. Gemma was fine. Political.

ROB. She wasn't political.

LORNA. She wanted to adopt a Vietnamese baby we saw outside the Uffizi.

GAIL. Why?

LORNA. Why, Rob?

ROB. That's not fair. The context was . . . that's not fair, Lorna. It was because we were having such a good time.

GAIL. I'm having a nice time I think I'll adopt that Vietnamese boy? Was he up for sale?

ROB. No. No, of course not. No, he had Dutch parents. At least we assumed they were Dutch. They wore those funny shoes that you can get in Covent Garden: so ugly you can convince yourself they're good for you. Only Dutch people wear them.

GAIL. You mean clogs?

ROB. Not clogs. Those shoes which look like somebody ran over a pair of Nature Treks. And they had this Vietnamese boy, extraordinarily beautiful. (*Consulting* LORNA.) Wasn't he? (*To the* WAITRESS *who's arrived with the coffees.*) Thanks. Do you want anything else, Gail? We could get you up to fifteen pounds if you're interested.

LORNA. I'm going to have to get my skates on shortly.

ROB. Really? Should I cancel the hotel room?

LORNA (*saying 'Yes'*). Sorry.

GAIL. I'm completely confused about this Dutch Vietnamese boy.

ROB. Ask Gemma. It was her idea. She just said, actually she didn't just say – she went on about it all night. Did I tell you this, Lorna? You know we carried on the conversation the entire night? She kept saying 'How much do we give back? Expressed as a percentage of what we have: how much do we give back?'

GEMMA's *flat. Evening. Bach's 'Matthew Passion'*

ALISTAIR. Oh God, Gemma, I feel terrible now, I'm going to have to tell the others, I'm going to have to tell Rob, I'm going to get my wee nose bloodied, this love I have for youse, this love I mentioned in my letter, it's not a big obstacle type of love, it's not a trip over me on your front doorstep type of love, it's not a, it's small, it's a kind of very irrelevant passion, it was hardly worth writing down, it started off as a PS and got bigger in the letter, I'm speaking of proportion, I love you in brackets is what I was saying, oh-by-the-way type of thing; on a scale of one to ten, you know: one- and-a-half when I'm feeling really badly about it, it's a hot water bottle, 'I'm feeling terrible but at least Alistair loves me', when the fellow walks out on you, 'You're by yourself Gemma but at least that little chappie nurses a crushette. I can cry on his shoulder while I wait for Mr Right to come along'. It was not, repeat not, and block capitals IT WAS NOT INTENDED TO MAKE YOU STOP TALKING TO EVERYONE! Oh God, Gemma.

A restaurant. Day.

ROB. Italy. Italy was the trouble, was where it started, I realise that now, this wonderful restaurant we kept going to, we went with Stephen and Lorna and Tom who's their, who's two or something, well you know Tom anyway . . . Sample, have I told you this?

SAMPLE. I don't think so, was this when – ?

ROB (*ploughing on*). The food was, God, the first time we went they brought, there was no menu, they just brought food to the table . . . – *do you want these mushrooms? Fantastic wild mushrooms* – and there was fish, really fresh, these people were terrific, we kept going back, you could see the river from the table, oh God, it was a great holiday. Gemma was, she had the best time, we were talking about kids, she kept holding Tom and, who's really nice, in as much as a two year old, although they, Stephen's always making him wear these ridiculous, but he's remarkably, in the restaurant, perfect, of course that's the Italians they make you feel as if anything is perfectly, so no, and then she (*Distracted suddenly.*) Do you notice the central heating?

SAMPLE. I don't know. I'm not cold. Are you cold?

ROB. No. No. I'm hot. I'm too hot. Is it on?

SAMPLE. I expect so. It's February. I expect it's on. Feel the radiator. It's just behind you.

ROB. Well it isn't on. As it happens. I don't know, but there's vestigial central heating, do you know what I mean? The plants. The plants here are dying of it, and they're just plants, imagine what it's doing to us, I really noticed that when we came back here, of course the first thing you notice is the traffic which is now ridiculous, it is ridiculous, imagine a Martian . . . the traffic, the streets, I think that must be a strike, I'm sure it's not absence which has made them so dirty, not my absence, our absence, but the absence of street cleaners, my flat when I got back, outside, you know the place outside where we leave the rubbish so you arrive and wade through the armadas of black bags, well there's somebody who lives in the flats who clearly has psychopathic tendencies, really, during the election somebody delivered a Labour Party car sticker and it was in my letter box, you know where the letter rack is, with the dominoes, you know where the dominoes are . . .

SAMPLE (*he does*). I love that, was that your idea?

ROB. It might have been the psychopath who used the dominoes, must have been when I come to think of it, you have to have a psychopathic turn of mind to use dominoes to number the letter boxes, so anyway I get home in the evening and the sticker is still there in my letter box, except now it's in a thousand little pieces, literally, thousands of little pieces, which is psychopathic.

SAMPLE (*agreeing*). God. (*Pause.*) Gemma hates your flat, doesn't she, because of that, because she said the people who live there, the other people, she's always saying that, the Porsches . . .

ROB (*irritated*). There's only one Porsche, the secretary of the Labour Party lives there as well, as it happens, she's always doing that . . . there's only one Porsche in the entire building. It's a left hand drive, it's an old left hand drive Porsche, it's actually rather beautiful, and it's got the park. When you've been somewhere healthy you really appreciate that, somewhere sane, even fresh air, even that is no longer freely available, even that's political. My point is, about the flat, my flat, is that with this strike, I'm assuming it is a strike, instead of being careful, the psychopath has lost all self-control and has abandoned the black bag regime . . . you know they won't take the rubbish unless it's in black bags? Well that's all out of the window and there's this kind of deluge of little shopping bags, plastic carrier bags with stuff spilling out, bits of pizza and God knows what, the guy clearly is the Take Away king of North London, when they catch him there will be serious economic problems in the Indian Restaurant trade, and it's all there, the evidence, and each time I get home I want to kill him, I want to wade in to his little plastic bags and discover his name, I know somewhere between the polystyrene and foil containers, between the Chicken Tikka Masalla and the, I'm sure there's abandoned pornography as well, stuff which is delivered in plain brown envelopes, there are a lot of bits of plain brown envelopes and stuff from American Express, there will be his name, he will have left his name somewhere on an envelope, and once I've found it I intend to scoop up an armful of this crap and ring his bell and dump it over his mentally deranged psychopathic little head.

SAMPLE. That's awful. Because it's a beautiful flat.

ROB. I know, I'm really lucky, I'm really blessed to have it. I feel terrible. All my friends come round, this is my paranoia, my friends come round and they think sod him.

SAMPLE. I always think that. I think sod him for having such a terrific flat.

ROB. Except Gemma. Who hates it.

SAMPLE. Well, I expect she means the windows. Because there aren't really any windows.

ROB (*raging*). Of course there are windows! There are loads of windows!

SAMPLE (*conciliatory*). I suppose she, I love it, I keep telling you, I love it, I'll swap, but you know she loves light.

ROB. I love light! This makes me really angry. She doesn't have copyright on liking light. Light is very important to me, and my flat is often very light, but she does this, she makes a decision about something and that's it, finished, my flat has no light and is full of Porsches. If she'd agree to live with me, which after all this time is one of the more tired jokes among our friends, right? If she'd move in with me we could buy somewhere really special which was all windows if that is what she wants, we could buy a huge greenhouse and make babies. Vietnamese babies if that's what she wants, that's another thing I have to tell you about, the Vietnamese baby . . . Christ . . . her place is not that light as it happens and it's damp and then she has the central heating, this is my point, this is what I was saying just now . . . she has the central heating up full blast and then everyone feels ill all the time. Since we got back from Italy I have felt ill, physically ill, all the time, which is what's wrong with her, probably, something as simple as the central heating and instead of turning it down, turning it off, or agreeing to buy a flat with me, she has this whatever it is, this . . . what do you think it is? I don't know. She won't speak to me. Has she spoken to you? She hasn't spoken to anyone. Has she said anything to you? Has she said anything to Gail?

SAMPLE. Nothing. No. I don't think so.

ROB. Well, if she does: tell her to turn the central heating off. Sample, honestly, she has not said a word to anyone for a week. I mean, it's ridiculous. Now she's turned her machine off. The phone just rings and rings.

Phone ringing and ringing.

GEMMA's *flat. Evening.*

GAIL *with* GEMMA, *music. Bach's 'St Matthew Passion'.*

GAIL. Sample says I'm to mention the central heating to you although I can't think why, it's not on is it? Is it because there's something wrong with your central heating and because you're not speaking you can't do anything about it? Why don't you write down something on a piece of paper? That wouldn't compromise you would it? Is it a love affair? Who is it? Or is Rob fooling around? I have to tell you Lorna and I and Sample spent an entire evening on Friday speculating, your ears must have been burning! It's a great way to become the centre of attention, that's my problem I talk too much and then nobody's interested, although I think you could say a few words and still be mysterious, if it's a bit of mystery you're after. Anyway for the record: I thought you were having an affair, Lorna thought it was Rob, I mean something to do with Rob, – I'm trying to read your face, Gem, you're so inscrutable! It's not the baby, is it? It's not my baby, is it? (*She thinks it might be.*) I don't think it is. I can't think it could be that. I know you – I know that's something you'd eventually, but, (*Doesn't pursue it.*) I can't remember what Sample thought, if indeed he did think, impending fatherhood is making him all sort of fey and gloomy and concerned, I can't get him to come anywhere near me, he's gone all reverent which is a bit ridiculous, I think he's given me up for Lent, I'm only eighteen weeks, I mean I like holding hands as much as the next girl but, anyway I know you think I'm too smutty, to tell you the truth, Gem, it'll be quite nice not to feel obliged to every five minutes; I mean enough is enough, particularly if you're sort of saying we'll be doing this for donkey's years. It's like serving up spaghetti bolognese every night. Who needs it? I mean I like my spag. bol. as much as the next girl, that is not my point, this is what I was trying to say to Sample last night, I don't know how it started as he's even started coming to bed in track suit bottoms, but probably because I said something like 'this is nice holding hands', which'll teach me for not saying what I thought which was, you know, 'I won't break,' but he said something like 'I hope you don't like it more than our wild nights of passion,' Well! apart from I imagine your finding it as tricky as I do to imagine Sample in a wild night of anything, he can be very sweet to me, I mean for God's sake I love the bloke, I'm having his baby, so the point is last night he starts sulking right after I've lied about liking holding hands with him in his track suit bottoms and me in my sleep bra and so he starts this huge sulk about us never doing it ever again because he's got the calendar out by this time and is sort of saying well it's at least five months after this and ten weeks after that and stitches, which of course puts the fear of God up me and before you know it we're both really miserable but to tell you the truth I'm quite relieved because it means, I mean do you know anybody, any woman, who deep down, I mean really deep down under the first deep down where you admit to being insatiably lustful about everybody, what I'm saying is under that layer have you met anybody who actually would rather, I mean I'm not saying to begin with when you're courting and sorting out whether or not he fancies you, he's got to not be able to keep his hands off you at that stage, then that's fine: up the stairs, in the back of the Renault, every five minutes, I mean great, that's sort of required, but once you've said to yourself 'okay you'll do', well it's what I said about the old spag. bol., isn't it? See! if you don't shut me up look what happens! Tell you the truth, Gem, I'm getting a bit worked up about this baby, it's the hormones, obviously, look, these are all new, I never had a mark on my face, that's one thing I've always had is my skin, Gem, you know I may not be a beauty but I've always had fantastic skin, that's not vanity, and now suddenly look at all that and I just know I'm going to have stretch marks like a deflated balloon, which is fine, but that's always been my strong point, Gem, you know so it seems bloody unfair, but that's not it anyway, it's just I've been pregnant before, right, so now I've said, oh shit, not a big deal I have been pregnant before, I expect if the chips were down I'm not alone in this, which is neither here nor there, you know I'm not one of those women who, (*She's crying.*) you know I was speaking to this American woman the other day who has got everything, pool in the garden, holidays in Hawaii and she kept saying – you don't know her, it's got nothing to do with a swimming pool, she kept saying 'fill your house up with babies, Gail, fill your house with babies, like flowers . . .', great, I haven't even got a flat yet, and if I do I'll fill it with myself and – because Sample won't live there, will he? I mean he's never wanted to live with me before, so . . . I'm just saying the abortion thing which I'd do again if it were the same circumstances because I was like a kid at the time myself, I mean I wasn't a kid according to my passport, but in every other respect and the guy would have run a mile, of course, which all just goes to making this baby very important, because I can feel it and it feels like a big sob

in my stomach, all day I keep thinking it's there like this great
sobbing in my stomach . . . fill your house with babies, like flowers
. . . I think you should say something, Gemma, because it's not fair is
it, all these confessions, I bet you're getting all these wonderful
confessions, is there a tape recorder? Have you seen the size of my
tits? Pretty impressive, eh? Anyway, I've passed on the stuff about
the central heating. Do you think anybody could survive in
Holloway, I mean off the Holloway Road? I don't think so. (*Bleak.*)
Actually, it's bloody awful.

The music plays.

Soho office. Day.

ALISTAIR's office. ALISTAIR and ROB.

ROB. How could anyone so beautiful do that to himself? I swear, Al.
That is what she said. Those were her words. Such a beautiful face.
How could he set fire to himself? I have to say it made me pretty
angry.

ALISTAIR. What? That the monk was beautiful?

ROB. No, come on: Gemma. Come on. I got angry with her, because
there we were, the entire day poisoned, and I thought well okay, this
monk has done this to himself and he felt that was important.
Obviously, I mean, obviously he felt it was crucial or something, it
was obviously not just a gesture, and so fine it screws up all our
plans and we send everybody home, including my sister who already
thinks Gem is, and okay it's important, but then she says such a
beautiful face and I'm afraid that made me furious. And she's got
him up on her noticeboard, the beautiful self-immolator, and frankly,
Alistair, I almost burned his photograph with my lighter.

ALISTAIR. Why? I don't follow. Because she thought he was
beautiful? Sorry Rob, I don't follow you.

ROB. I'm just saying we're talking about a woman who went to
Greenham Common, okay, which is fine by me, great, but she has to
drive back here and find out where Greenham Common is on the
map. That's all.

ALISTAIR. And?

ROB. Well, you know, if you're going to have principles, Alistair, buy
yourself a map and a noticeboard.

ALISTAIR. If I'm getting your gist you're complaining because Gemma
didn't know where Greenham Common was before she went there, or
that she was upset when a beautiful monk committed suicide because
of what was happening in Tibet . . . am I right, pal? I mean she knew
Greenham Common was in England. That would do for me. Or do
you need a woman with Geography 'A' Level?

ROB. And what's all this about? The silence? I mean what is all that
about?

ALISTAIR (*thrown*). I don't know, Rob. I mean if you don't know. (*Shrugs.*) I don't know.

ROB. Italy. Italy must have something to do with it. And the Vietnamese baby. Who was probably Dutch. (*Despairing.*) You know. I can't go round there, Alistair. I can't bear all that music. The 'Matthew Passion'. I keep thinking it must be a clue. Have you been round? Does your ioniser have any effect do you think? I lie in my room with mine in my mouth. You can get tiny electric shocks on the tongue.

ALISTAIR. You should talk to Concepcion.

ROB. Should I? Who's Concepcion? I thought your cleaner was called Concepcion?

ALISTAIR. That's right. She's my cleaner. She's terrific. She's a psychiatrist.

ROB. Great. What? You talk to her? What are you talking about, Alistair?

ALISTAIR. I just said, she's a psychiatrist. She trained as a psychiatrist in Argentina. She's only a cleaner in London. In Argentina she's a psychiatrist.

ROB. Your cleaner is a psychiatrist.

ALISTAIR. That's right. I've told you before, actually. She's amazing. I get my shirts ironed by an amazingly beautiful Argentinian psychiatrist.

ROB. Listen, would you mind if I opened the window, I find it difficult to breathe in here, do you notice that? I think it's just very stuffy at the moment. How can you work in here with all these dead plants? (*Opens window to a deluge of traffic.*) I got clamped this morning. You can't drive off. Nothing happens. I thought I'd just drive off with that notice in front of my face, on the three wheels. But you can't. It is pointless driving in London. There is absolutely no point. There is a man directly below your office in a very big car and because the traffic has clearly unhinged him, he is stuck sideways across the road. His nose is touching a parked BMW and his tail is touching another parked BMW. In about two sec – the blue BMW has a dent . . . and now so does the black one . . . (*We hear the appropriate clunks and thuds and engine chorus.*)
blue 2 black 1
blue 3 black 1
blue 3 black 2
(*Car squeals off.*) and off to the gym, to the Tai Chi, to the aromatherapy, to the . . .

ALISTAIR. No, I've got this great deal going with Concepcion because I'm paying her three fifty an hour right? Which is not cheap but is the going rate for domestic help, so fine, but thrown in I get a little therapy, it's limited vocabulary therapy, but I get to talk over the vacuum cleaner or the washing machine, I feel everything's being tidied up at once. It's a wonderful deal. I've made all sorts of discoveries.

ROB. Such as?

ALISTAIR. Such as the vacuum cleaner whistles when the bag is full, such as you put a tennis ball in the washing machine for some obscure but deeply helpful reason, such as I harbour this desire to murder my cousin. Which was not a discovery but I've owned up to it. No, Concepcion is perfect, or would be if she would sleep with me.

ROB. Sounds great. Which cousin?

ALISTAIR. Such as I am in love with Gemma.

ROB. She told you this, or you told her?

ALISTAIR. I'm serious, Rob. I wrote to Gemma and told her. I had to. I know it's not how you treat your mates but this was serious. I wrote her a letter, not a big deal or anything you know, in the third paragraph of this wee note, and next thing she's not speaking to anyone.

ROB. Alistair, only you and your psychiatric cleaner didn't know you were in love with Gemma, it's got nothing to do with your letter. I don't mean to belittle the depth of feeling and, but it has nothing to do with this confession.

ALISTAIR. Right.

ROB. Because Gemma knew, is what I am saying. She knew. You wear it on your sleeve, you come to dinner and it's 'Could you pass the wine, Gemma, and I'm in love with you.' 'Oh Gemma, do you really think so and I'm in love with you.' 'Gemma, fantastic kidney beans and I'm in love with you.' So listen: don't feel badly because it's fine, Alistair, really, and I'm delighted you're in love with her, it made her feel nice, I'm sure it still does, she's probably a little bit in love with you.

ALISTAIR. Yeah, but you know Rob I really love her. Oh God. I cried when I told Concepcion. Oh God, it was just the relief of admitting it. I think I'm going to cry again now which would be embarrassing, I am not famous in this office for laughing on the wrong side of my face as my dad would say. Don't laugh on the wrong side of your face, son. Oh.

GEMMA's *flat. Morning. The 'St Matthew Passion'.*

ALISTAIR *and* GEMMA *are listening. The work finishes. We hear applause.*

ALISTAIR. No, I like it. I'm really getting to like it.

The recording starts again. Side 1 of a piece which is very, very long.

ALISTAIR (*taking a deep breath. The price of love*). Again? Great.
  Great.

He hums and half sings.

ALISTAIR. Terrific.

GEMMA's *flat. Evening. The 'St Matthew Passion'.*

ROB. I am actually very aggravated, you know, I find it very
  aggravating, I find it childish, I find it shocking and aggressive, very
  aggressive, actually
  because you know what it says to me
  Gem
  because by all means don't speak to the world,
  go right ahead.
  but with me, it says, I include you with the
  others, I exclude you from anything private,
  or intimate or
  plus, I'm pretty certain I know what, why,
  what's behind all of this, and I feel like
  I'm being put in the stocks for it
  so, if there is a problem, instead of talking
  about it
  you

The music plays.

I don't know if you're eating, or sleeping,
I don't know what you're thinking.

The music plays.
ROB *is suddenly agitated.*

what?
and please don't stare at that bloody
photograph!
because you know I have a particular
antipathy towards that picture, we've been
through this.
I don't think it's very clever, or brave, or
effective, or real, or real! to set fire to
yourself,
in fact, it's very similar.
what you're doing, what he's doing.
it's very similar,
it's like a kind of major sulk, isn't it?
in fact, I am going to burn that picture,
I should have done this the last time,

He tips the photograph off the noticeboard holds it up threateningly.

well talk to me then, talk to me, talk to me (*Pause.*)

okay.
okay.
okay.
okay.

He sets fire to the photograph with his lighter

this is just so . . . (*It burns.*)
sod it
look, I'll get you another picture, I shouldn't have
done that.
I shouldn't have done that,
you know, but I'm frustrated. I'll find the photograph
and get you another one,
I'm sorry, I shouldn't have done that.
Look, I'll go.

Pause. The music plays, ROB *sighs.*

Gemma? (*The music plays.*) Gemma? (*The music plays.*)

ALISTAIR's *flat. Day.*

ROB *to* CONCEPCION.

ROB. Is it . . . do you mind if . . . I . . . I should have brought my shirts
round . . . I'll give you an example. This is one, there are loads of
others. We had a visitor from the States, and we'd taken him out,
we'd taken him to the South Bank, no what it was, sorry, we had
collected this guy from Heathrow, and it was this time last year,
actually, it was Good Friday, and this guy had arrived from San
Francisco and was completely jet-lagged, but what had happened
was that Gemma had gotten us tickets for the *Matthew Passion* at
the Festival Hall and didn't want to miss it, if you knew her you'd
understand because it's like a very important thing, annual event to
go there and she sits with the score and is completely . . . music gives
her something which I certainly could never, I look at her sometimes
when she's listening to music and I'm frightened, I feel lonely, I'm
frightened because it's a lover's face, and I never really see it . . .
would you mind if I just opened the window a little? I think it's the
iron, the steam, am I speaking too fast for you? Sorry, I'm sure I'm
completely incoherent . . .

CONCEPCION (*heavy accent*). No, no . . . you were at a concert with
an American friend . . . it's okay, I'll do the window . . .

ROB. Well, of course, you'll know about jet lag and this guy he was
very game and sort of sat there propped up, but I don't know if you
know the *Matthew Passion*, it's not short, it is in fact the opposite of
short, it is fantastically long, I mean it goes on and on you get an
interval of about two hours, it's a marathon, okay? But of course
wonderful, even I see that, Gem's always saying it has more good

tunes in that one piece than in the rest of, it's great, and she's there following every bar in her book while this poor American guy is sitting bolt upright and then every now and then swaying and then catching himself and going back to upright, then lurching, then swaying, then bolt upright in this terrible torture of staying awake . . .

CONCEPCION. Uhuh.

ROB. . . . and then we get to the interval and go off to find some food, because I also realise this guy must be famished, Alistair won't mind if I make a cup of tea, will he?

CONCEPCION. Sure.

ROB. He's eaten me out of house and home many a time, so I'm sure he won't . . . I think I'll pinch a banana, it's ripe anyway, so, mmm, actually I'll just have juice, I'm not supposed to be drinking tea, is there any herb? No look: juice is fine, great, so anyway, where was I? This is really nice of you, you know.

CONCEPCION. It's no problem.

ROB (*flirting a little*). I'd really like to, I really appreciate it, I do (*tails off.*) Where were we? Oh yes, so we toddle off to find something to eat, and it's now the middle of the afternoon and our American friend is sleep-walking and we get to some patio or other, with all kinds of things going on, do you know the South Bank? by the NFT and the National Theatre, well there's always stuff going on, clowns and those funny dancers and stalls and stuff and buskers and this is all great for Felix, the American, who, – 'cause there he is first time in London and he can see the Thames and all the monuments – and we queue up for ages and get sandwiches and sit out in the sunshine having, eating, and getting some fresh air before plunging back into the Passion, which of course is now getting very heavy and moving and stuff, so like it's a very welcome break and Felix is reviving a little with the food and there's buskers playing, a really nice flautist. I can see it so vividly, this guy comes round with a cap to collect for this flautist, who's really wonderful, beautiful sound and you know what it's like sometimes when you're in the fresh air and there's music playing it's really lovely and with a glass of wine and so of course I dug into my pocket and gave a pound or something, some money for this flautist who's probably a student at the Royal College, I think it's standard practice for them to go out and busk and stuff, so . . . I give him some money and then we carry on eating and I'm not alone in this there are loads of people there from the concert, too, all eating and being entertained and they all give generously and . . . anyway the point is about ten minutes later, maybe five minutes, or even sooner, I can't quite remember, anyway I don't know if you know that area but it's a real haven for dossers, you know: down and outs, there are lots of people down by Waterloo Station, homeless, who can't get accommodation, it's really awful of course, you drive by at night and there are these huge fires, particularly in the winter, there are a lot of people there, there are a lot of homeless people . . . I'm sure you know all about this, and what happens of course is that one of these people, a woman, who has a drink problem, I mean she was carrying a bottle of cider and she had on a duffle coat and she smelt and, of course – it wasn't her fault, but you can't help those people by giving them a pound coin, you know, because they go and buy a bottle of cider and get pissed and it's not helping, so I didn't respond to this woman, and obviously, it was awkward for Felix, because she kept kind of pestering him, he looked, you know how all Americans look wealthy, they sort of exude dollars, and I was quite firm, I suppose, and anyway, this woman went off, in fact I did give her 50p, as it happens, but it was just to get rid of her, I really feel strongly that it wasn't helping her in the slightest, it was just another dousing of the liver, I gave her 50p and in fact she looked disgusted, she looked so disgusted I wished I'd just ignored her . . . so . . .

and Gem is watching all this and saying nothing and we finish our food and go back to the concert, of course as I'm telling you this the symbolism is all absolutely transparent but at the time, as we wander back to the concert I'm thinking about Felix, who is going a kind of pale grey at the prospect of another two hours of Bach; you know I find it quite a strain to sit through however wonderful but we go back in and all the singers stand up and of course it's riveting in a way – no, it's wonderful – and Felix does fall asleep and then it finishes and we're on our way back to the car – great banana thanks – I was just a little peckish, and Gemma starts wandering around this area looking as if she's lost something, which would not be unusual, and so I stand there holding Felix up, Felix has by this time given up pretending to be with us, he is in rapid eye movement dreaming of futons and California and sanity and Gemma is hunting around the back of benches and – sort of urgent and anxious and uncommunicative – and then she walked down a side road by the Cut, near the station and sure enough, by one of these huge open fires, the clusters of tramps, getting near the violent hour, the windscreen smashing hour, the abuse hour, Gemma wanders amongst these people poking around in their sacks and their sleeping bags and their cardboard boxes and yes there is our lady from the interval, settling down with her cider in a black dustbin liner filled with newspaper, essentially we'd walked into somebody's bedroom, I tried to make this point later, unsuccessfully, and Gem bends down and starts talking to her, 'What's your name? Where do you live?' I'm not joking, 'Where do you live?' and she said, of course, 'I live here.' Her name was Muriel. 'I'm Gemma,' says Gemma 'and this is Rob and this is our friend Felix. Are you hungry, Muriel?' Muriel was hungry. 'Let me give you some money. Muriel, I'm going to give you ten pounds, okay, and I want you to go and buy yourself a meal.' And out comes this ten pound note. Ten pounds to the Muriels of this world is not a note, it is a pale hot liquid in a big bottle. It is half an hour of a delicious burning sensation. It is not a meal. So I say this, I am, of course, embarrassed and uncomfortable and I am propping up Felix who would not turn a hair before slipping in beside Muriel in the black plastic bag. Actually what I am is furious, I am choking with anger. 'Okay,' says Gemma, who has gone that kind of, you know what it feels like to write with a pencil just after you've sharpened it, like that, like that is how she went, she yanked Muriel out of the sack and then we were wandering along the South Bank, because Gemma was going to find Muriel a place where she could have a meal, which we would supervise. Felix hasn't spoken for about seven hours, he's disappeared into his jacket, he's asleep in his pocket, Gemma walks purposefully staring ahead dragging Muriel, who is leaning on me, stinking to high heaven, like a hung rabbit, like a jugged hare, I can still smell that . . . ach! anyway, and Muriel is saying 'I'm thirsty, I'm a bit thirsty, where are we?' and she pulls out her little bottle of liquor from one of her many carrier bags which have devolved into my safe keeping and is about to swig from it when down comes Gemma's avenging hand, yanks this full bottle from Muriel and sends it flying into the Thames. We listen in silence as it hit the water. Splash. Restaurants won't serve the homeless, or drunks, it puts customers off, they see the bags, they smell the jugged hare and they're suddenly fully booked or closing or don't speak English. Eventually we are in the car, driving in to the West End. Gemma has begun speaking about taking Muriel home and giving her a bath, giving her some clothes, oh God, listen Concepcion: I admire her, I love her, she's extraordinary, she really does, she means what she's saying, and I admire her, you know but she's also a complete pain in the neck and the car is like a medieval kitchen and Felix is getting car sick and Gemma is getting into a rage, we stop at one restaurant which is empty and has WE ARE OPEN UNTIL TWO across its lights, the sign, the façade, and suddenly it's out of food, and Gemma starts yelling and kicks out at one of the tables and Muriel is crying and the manager of this place is ringing the police and it's all very ugly and Felix is sitting in the back seat of the car, perched with his head in his hands and his stomach emptying into the pavement and back go Muriel's bags and Muriel in beside him and I'm driving along with Gemma consoling Muriel who is crying and Felix groaning and I can feel this violence uncoiling inside me and then Muriel says I want to come and live with you and again we all listen in silence as this hits the water. Splash.

We drove to the nearest Macdonalds, bought her a Big Mac with everything on it and left her there eating it. She was about three miles from where she lived and it was after midnight. She had beautiful eyes. I suppose she was fifty, she could have been any age, I suppose she could have been forty or fifty or sixty, but she had these beautiful grey eyes and they rested on you as you spoke. And hoped. With such longing. Whenever I've witnessed atrocities on television, people starving, tortured, degraded, abandoned, they've always had Muriel's

eyes, and the same look: Disappointed. I can't think of a better way
of describing the look. Just disappointed. Disappointed.

GEMMA's *flat. Evening.*

The 'St Matthew Passion'.

LORNA. It's like uh . . . this is like therapy, isn't it? . . .
I hate analysis, I hate, I hate the idea of undressing myself, you
know, like making love with a stranger, worse, worse than that,
actually.
We went, Stephen and I, we both went, we went together, that was
to a counsellor and then we went to see different people, separately,
in fact,
I was very humiliated, I was, it was very humiliating for me, so I,
well I've told you, Gemma, about the sunbed, going for my sunbed,
in fact I've got my own sunbed, which I hide, I've got my own
sunbed, which I do in the evening, and the appointments at the
sunbed were, in fact, appointments with my woman, with this
woman, and I think it was the same for Stephen, although I think
men are able to gloss their day more easily, aren't they? . . . A screw,
the shrink, a drink, can all fit under meeting. I had a meeting, there
was a meeting, it was a meeting.

No, so there was no sunbed appointment, there was a therapist, and
then of course, as I frantically got brown in the middle of the night I
realised the half-hour under the lamp was better than anything that
was going on in that terrible room in Swiss Cottage with the blasted
alarm clock and the venetian blind and the joss stick or whatever it
was, and the voice she had, the voice, it was like, what was it like? It
was a sort of a whisper, like you'd talk to a person who was dying,
a sort of whisper for the very sick and I used to, honestly, I felt
violence towards her for this voice, and I felt violence for the silence.

I used to cry, sometimes I would go in and I would cry for forty-five
minutes, and, really, the whole forty-five minutes, and she would sit
and make sympathetic noises, sympathetic clucks, you know, while I
cried, and then the alarm clock would ring and it would be finished,
but you'd be very good, Gem, because you have the eyes,
you have the eyes.
do you just sit here all day? what are you doing with yourself? are
you reading? what? writing? I thought of writing to you. I thought it
would be quieter. I had this theory perhaps the silence was connected
with noise, I know you're sensitive to noise, and music, I love this
(*The music.*) . . . is it, what is it, is it Bach? So I thought it might just
be that you wanted some peace. When my mother died I went to
Greece and just lay in the sun for two weeks and let the sun
anesthetise me, let it just, I just lay on the sand for two weeks and let
the sun press on top of me
this is before I had the sunbed

can I smoke? I won't if, thanks, Oh God, I gave you this ashtray,
didn't I? This is the Greek experience ashtray, isn't that funny? This
is from the lying in the sand holiday, ha! It's beautiful, isn't it?
So I can thank my mother for something, can't
I? Paid for that holiday and the car
and the ashtray

I made a list, that was one of the therapy
things, my therapist didn't ask me to do it,
but I did it during that period, I made a
list of all the things I got as a result of
my mother dying, what I did with the money;
holiday
car
I had my hair streaked,
I opened an account, a sort of indulgence
account.
So I had my hair streaked, and a manicure,
and a facial and I bought some silk underwear
and what else? Well I used most of it for the
house, I paid for the bathroom, our bathroom,
which means that every time I take a shower,
I say thank you, Mum, whenever I brush my
teeth, whenever I take a pee, thank you, Mum,
and the sunbed of course,

in fact
this is our biggest bond, Stephen and I, what
has kept us at least legally as one,
the fact that we both come from suicide families.
isn't that interesting?
we were married before we found that out,

it wasn't until my mother killed herself that
I discovered his mother had too.
It was like he suddenly came out with it,
snap,
and both so cruel, really, very cruel, very
cruel
his mother, he found her, his father had been
dead for some,
and he went round, or went home, I think he
was still a student, I don't know all the
details, anyway he found her and she had a
note pinned to her dress, and it said,
'Stephen, put the rubbish out.'
that was all,
Stephen, put the rubbish out.'

which was very
harsh,

I think . . .

my woman called suicide an act of homicide on
the living

look at that cat!
the two of you
big cat, little cat.
purring, curled up,
it's quite unnerving, ha!
she'll never sit on my lap, will she?

I've got an incapacity to love, Gemma,
that's the
that's the
I think that's the

my ma was wearing one of my dresses
did you know that?
when she killed herself
at least she didn't leave a note
it was a summer dress and it didn't fit

it's very hard to think your way out of
something like that
to be honest

at least she finally managed to do it
she was the Sylvia Plath of South Hampstead,
my ma,
one year in ten
that's where the limp came from
known as the riding accident limp
known as the falling off the horse limp
was in fact the
throwing herself from the high building limp

she, this was when I was eleven,
she booked a room in a five-storey hotel
that was her joke when she told this nasty
little tale
I booked into a five-storey hotel in
Eastbourne,
and she
do you know I think that was the most heart
breaking thing to think that she would have
been the most beautiful woman, her face was
so, I can remember before this happened, or I
think I can, but she was so twisted and, her
spine was, well you know that sort of hunch
and she had to teach herself to walk again,
and what was so pathetic
which is a feature of our lives, of our

deaths, isn't it? of our gestures, our grand
gestures, is that they are so human, and so
trite,
she couldn't find a clear space to jump from,
she got this top room
with a balcony, but the angle or something,
there were balconies and ledges and she had
to do some sort of impossible clamber to get
into a position where she could hit the
ground and then she couldn't do it, she said
she hung by her hands for
I don't know, she said an hour

and then she let go

I think she was just tired,
and of course she hit everything on the way down
apparently she didn't lose consciousness and
this chap came to her, he was one of the
kitchen staff, she fell outside the kitchens,
that was her favourite part of the story
I don't know why
this chap came rushing up
when he asked her her name
and she told him a lie
she'd just jumped from this building, she'd
broken her back, her legs, her arms, her
skull, and she told him a lie
she said her name was Angela Carpenter
which was the name of the girl she'd sat next
to at school

anyway the next time she managed it
– another week and they would have converted
the cooker to North Sea Gas and that would
have been another fiasco –
I'm not sleeping with Rob any more, Gemma
We haven't for a long time, really,
I'm not sure how you found out, but I wish
you hadn't
It makes something which wasn't important
become important
with me
you know, it's a thing I do
it rates with not having bra straps on my tan

this is not what I wanted to say
I wanted to say sorry
and say don't worry

well, I wanted to say sorry

what are you thinking?
Gemma?
what are you thinking?
do you want me to go?

to tell you the absolute truth, for the past
ten minutes I've wanted to slap your face

GEMMA's *flat. The garden. Morning. No music.*

GEMMA. When you stop speaking, it's like stopping eating. The first
day there's something thrilling, and new, before the pain begins. The
pain where you want to give up, where you can think of nothing else.
Then the second day, you feel wretched, the third delirious, and then
suddenly there's no appetite, it shrinks, it shrinks, until the prospect
of speaking, the thought of words retching from the mouth, how ugly
and gross it seems.

Nothing changes.

How to stop people in their tracks, and make them think. Only if
you're starving, if it's your son lying in your arms, or you think he
might be in that discarded pile of mutilated bodies, or there's no milk
in your breast and the baby's crying, or the radiation is leaking into
your child's lungs, or the lead or the nitrates or the, or the, or the
and all the while skirts get longer, skirts get shorter, skirts get longer,
skirts get shorter, poetry is written, the news is read, I buy a different
butter at the store and have my hair permed, straightened, coloured,
cut, lengthened, all the while my hair keeps growing, I throw away
all my skirts, a black bag to Oxfam, lately I've been at Oxfam
buying back my skirts, I've stripped the pine and painted the pine,
pulled out the fireplaces and put them back in, I'm on the pill, I'm
off the pill, I'm on the pill, I'm off the pill. I'm listening to jazz,
swing, jazz, swing, I'm getting my posters framed. I'm telling my
women's group everything. I'm protesting. I'm protesting. I've
covered my wall with postcards, with posters, with postcards, with
posters. No this. Out them. In these. Yes those. No this. Out them.
In these. Yes those. The rows. The rows with my friends, my lovers.
What were they about? What did they change? The fact is, the facts
are, nothing is changed. Nothing has been done. There is neither
rhyme nor reason, just tears, tears, people's pain, people's rage, their
aggression. And silence.

Look, already it's happening here, the weight of words, the torrent,
all the words being said seep into each other, the rage, the protest all
clotting together, sit and listen to the wireless and run the wheel of
the tuner, spin the dial, hear them all at it, in all languages, pouring
out. This is, after all, our first punishment – Babel – saying so much
to say nothing. Doing so much to do nothing. Because the power to
arrest, to stop us short in our tracks, what does that?

Pause.

but the silence, listen, how rich it is, how pregnant, how full . . .

Pause.

What do you remember? When all is said and done? A kiss? The taste of someone's lips? A view? A breath? A tune? The weight of your grandmother's coffin? The veins on your mother's legs. The white lines on her stomach.

Don't speak for a day and then start looking.
The senses are sharp. Look at the world
about its business. The snarl. The roar.
Skin stretched over the teeth. The madness.

The law is frightened of silence. It has
words for the defendant who becomes mute.
The wrath of God. Mute by malice. But it's
not silence which is the punishment. Words.
WORDS are the punishment.

The silence.

A silence.

beautiful
last year it was cigarettes,
the year before chocolate
but this is the best

The aria. 'Mache dich, mein Herze, rein' from Bach's St Matthew Passion. Magnificent. Released.

THE DIRT UNDER THE CARPET

by Rona Munro

For my partner in quines – Fiona

Rona Munro was born in Aberdeen in 1959. She went to Edinburgh University where she studied History. When she left University she worked as a cleaner and later as a receptionist before she got her first professional commission for *Fugue* at the Traverse Theatre in 1982. Since then she has written for stage, radio, television and several community theatre projects. Her work includes *Watching Waiters* for BBC Radio, *Biting the Hands* for television and *The Way to go Home* which was commissioned and performed by Paines Plough Theatre Company. She travels as much as she can, including trips to Nicaragua, Turkey and South America. She also performs with Fiona Knowles in *The MsFits* a feminist double act who perform their shows in Aberdonian and have toured all over Britain.

The Dirt Under the Carpet was first broadcast on BBC Radio 4 on 11 February 1988. The cast was as follows:

LORRAINE	Fiona Knowles
MURIEL	Alison Peebles
SGT DONALD	John Buick
MR B	

Director: Stewart Conn
Running time, as broadcast: 58 minutes

A street in Aberdeen 4 am. The sound of the docks very distant. Occasional ship's horn, lorries unloading, this fades. Sound of soft-soled shoes on cobbles. LORRAINE *speaks in voice over.*

LORRAINE. It was cauld that morning. Tell you that morning you wouldnae hae been safe oot in contact lenses, you'd've come hame wi' frosted glass eyeballs. All the milk was frozen half way doon the bottles an' the blue tits were all gaen aboot wi cracks in their beaks. It was freezin' I'm telling you. Skiting doon the street after the cats, they were all flying hame tae the cat flap and the storage heater and the bowl o' Kit-e-Kat, trying tae get there while they could still bend their whiskers. Monday morning, my hands couldnae keep hud of a' I was carrying, nae gloves, it's better that way, I like tae get a feel of fit I'm daein, I've tough fingers, I mean fa needs oven gloves ken? But that morning the frost was chewing my finger nails faster than I was. It was cauld. Cauld, dark, dark as the bottom o' the harbour, a freezing bit o' haar, thick and wet as smoker's cough, and I was gaen tae my work. That's right, 4 am and I was up and working. A' the rest o' the law abiding world tucked up layers deep in duvets and downies and dreams o' Christmas and I was walking doon the back streets frae shadow tae shadow, my feet street wise in flat, soft shoes, quiet on the cobbles, slippery quick oer the frozen gutters. I was awa tae dae fit I dae every morning, nae a job you'd fancy, naebody would.

   I let mysel in the backdoor. I'd got the key, it's easier that way. I didnae pit the light on, I kent my road in the dark. So fan he grabbed my fit I didn'e ken fit it was, just that his fingers were caulder than my ankle and I didnae like the feel o' it at a' and . . .

Cut to Interior cafe, it's 6.30 am, but the place is hotching with cleaners, cups, clatter and conversation.

MURIEL. He couldnae hae grabbed your fit.

LORRAINE. Fit wey?

MURIEL. He was deid, a corpse canny grab onything.

LORRAINE. Fa's ankle wis't?

MURIEL. Yours.

LORRAINE. An' fa's telling this story?

MURIEL. You're nae telling it right.

LORRAINE. An you were there were you?

MURIEL. I was up the stair.

LORRAINE. That's right, up the stair, nae in the basement, nae at the scene o' the crime. Fa found the body?

MURIEL. Falling oer it in the dark is nae the same as finding.

LORRAINE. Fit is't then?

MURIEL. Aye well, you werenae looking for it were you?

LORRAINE. Na but . . .

MURIEL. So nae credit tae you, you fell oer him. Now I was expecting it. I'd deduced, I'd deduced he'd be there een o' they mornings. (*Calls off.*) Rita . . . *Rita*, when you've a minute pet, twa mixed grills an twa coffees . . . (*To* LORRAINE.) An a couple rowies eh? (*Calls off again.*) Aye an a couple rowies Rita, thanks pet.

Sound: cutlery.

LORRAINE. Well . . . you canny say I was surprised.

MURIEL. You've nae the imagination tae be surprised.

LORRAINE. I was remaining calm in the face of a crisis.

MURIEL. You were jist aboot passing oot.

LORRAINE. I got a wee bit dizzy, you'd've got a wee bit dizzy if you'd stepped in fit I'd stepped in.

MURIEL. Worst mess I ever saw on that flaer.

LORRAINE. I was in shock I was near up the doctor wi' it.

MURIEL. Oh here I was up the doctors again yesterday efternoon, twa hoors, twa hoors I was in that waiting room, an' folk ahead o' me in the queue wi' nae mair wrang wi' them than a cauld in the heid an I says . . .

LORRAINE. Am I telling this story or fit am I daein?

MURIEL. Get on wi' it then, an' pass the salt fan your aboot it.

Interior. Office 4 am. LORRAINE *speaks in voice over.*

LORRAINE. In my line o' work you get tae expect onything, onything so five cauld fingers fan I'd only thocht tae find twa inches o' cream shag pile an the draught under the door wis jist anither o' life's wee surprises. I backed off. I pit the light on. I looked. An he was deid, nae doot aboot that, flat on his back in front o' the door I opened the door, I yelled . . . MU . . RI . . EL!!!

Cut to Interior. Cafe.

MURIEL. Na, na, na.

LORRAINE. Fit!?

MURIEL. It doesnae mak sense if you tell it like that, gae back a bit.

LORRAINE. You want tae tell this?

MURIEL. Na you tell it, I'm haeing my breakfast. Just gae back a bit.

LORRAINE. Back tae far?

MURIEL. Back tae the beginning.

Sound: scrubbing louder and louder cut to.

LORRAINE (*voice over*). A'body you meet that does this job has some kind o' excuse for it. 'I wouldnae dae this but . . .' Well my excuse was obvious. (*Shouting off.*) An next time you're oer the north sea I hope you fall oot the helicopter.

Slamming door.

Twa years. Brian was O.K. He was good value ken, there was a lot of him, and maist o' it was muscle. (*Sigh.*) An' he'd a great flat. But . . . I moved oot the flat in Rubislaw wi' my non stick wok, the pot plants Brian bought me for my Christmas that were deid by February an half the records an I moved in wi my mate Wendy an her pals Morag an Brenda. It was a'right ken but eh . . .

Sound: pounding on bathroom door, running water other side of door.

VOICE. Morag, *Morag*, will you get oot o' there! I've tae be up the road in five minutes.

LORRAINE (*voice over*). Crowded. Three rooms up the back o' Schoolhill. The inside o' the windy's was always fogged up wi' steam frae the shower an the kettle an' the hot breathed types Wendy dragged hame wi' her . . .

Sound: hairdryer, sound of frying in background, LORRAINE speaks over hairdryer.

LORRAINE. Nae thanks Wendy I'm still a bit . . . ken . . . Brian an that . . . think I'm off men jist at the minute.

LORRAINE (*voice over*). And the same windys mid January they had frost on them an inch thick that naething could thaw oot, nae the blaw heater, nae the hairdryer, naething, every windy was like a bathroom windy, and naething tae dae aboot it. And my bed was damp.

Sound: hoover, LORRAINE *talks over it.*

LORRAINE. 'Sustain a relationship'. Of course I canny sustain a relationship, that's got naething tae dae wi' my stars, it's tae dae wi' the climate. I'd get an electric blanket but it'd be like sleeping in a steam bath.

LORRAINE (*voice over*). But we had a good laugh ken, it was a'right.

Interior. Bathroom moving rapidly and violently.

LORRAINE. Morag . . . na quit it, Morag . . . Wendy she's got my Harrison Ford toothbrush . . . na dinny, dinny . . . oh you wee shite, foo am I supposed tae use fan it's been doon there?

LORRAINE (*voice over*). An fan the money got really tight, which didnae tak long. Brenda got me work, jist turn up she said, bring a duster . . .

Alarm going off.

LORRAINE (*waking up*). Oh G . . . o . . . o . . . o . . . d.

LORRAINE (*voice over*). An I became an invisible woman. There's nae skill tae it. It gaes wi' the job. It gaes wi' the pinny. It gaes wi' the hoors you work.

Interior. Cafe.

MURIEL. Fit are you on aboot?

LORRAINE. Being invisible.

MURIEL. I see you.

LORRAINE. I see you.

MURIEL. Well?

LORRAINE. We're baith invisible women.

MURIEL. Aye we've baith got problems an mine's haein tae work wi you. Invisible naething. (*Calling off.*) Rita can I hae they rowies noo.

LORRAINE (*voice over*). I was green, I was clueless, I kent naething. I thocht dirt was something you got in the Sunday papers. I thocht dust wis fit you wiped off your records afore you put them on the stereo. I'd cleaned up the hoose a'right but I didnae ken onything aboot . . .

Interior. Cafe.

MURIEL. Industrial grime.

LORRAINE. Dinny you get technical wi' me Muriel.

Sound of scrubbing getting louder and louder.

LORRAINE (*voice over*). They gie you green slime tae get it up wi'. Green slime that gets the scuff o' shoes and slush oot o' stane flaers, that swallows a' the stains in stainless steel. An the women that use it they wipe up the world wi' lotions that remove all known germs and the skin off their hands.

Start to fade scrubbing and mix in hubbub of female voices.

They bleach acres o' enamel wi' chemicals that shrivel their lungs up till they breathe fire, they ride brooms an mops and polishing machines wi' engines in them like diesel trains. An I was tae join them.

Female voices at crescendo. Cut.

First day. 4.30 am start.

Paper rustling with echo.

Early morning streets, I learnt a secret. I learnt aboot paper. Some time fan a' the streets are empty the chip papers cam oot an' roll aroond an whisper tae each other till they meet the empty newspapers an the battered cardboard boxes hurling along the cobbles trying tae be drums. They a' joing together intae big snakes, rustling and thundering and wriggling along the gutters trying tae rise up and take over the world . . . but the dust cart always gets them first.

Footsteps on pavement faint hum in background.

The street lamps leak yella light, an they hum tae theirsels. A high kind o' hum like a whistle – like the silence in your ears.

Approach and receding a car moving slowly on a wet road.

Polis watch you frae ahint their windscreens wi' eyes as deid as their dipped head lamps sweeping the road . . . I'd tae gae doon the steps and rap on the basement door o' a building as blind and dark as a deid end. I never expected onybody tae answer the door . . .

Exterior. Office door. 4.30 am
Sound: door.

MURIEL. Fars your dusters?

LORRAINE. Fit?

MURIEL. Have tae get your ain dusters, they dinny gie you onything in this place, I'm telling you, *naething.*

LORRAINE (*voice over*). She talked oot the corner o'her mou like she's a cigarette clamped tae the ither side, but there was nae cigarette, jist her twa lips tighter shut than a mussel at high tide . . .

Interior. Cafe.

MURIEL. I'd gied up the fags, I've my health tae think of ken.

LORRAINE (*voice over*). But she still talked oot the side o' her mou like she could let the sense oot but was feart tae let the sound oot as well.

Interior. Cafe.

MURIEL, Canny be too careful, never ken fa might hae come in early tae work.

LORRAINE (*voice over*). She was wee, cam aboot up tae my nose.

Interior. Cafe.

MURIEL. That's nae wee.

LORRAINE. Wee-er than me.

LORRAINE (*voice over*). Walked wi' a swagger like she'd a Shetland pony 'tween her knees. Cams frae scrubbing too mony flaers wi' her bum in the air.

Interior. Cafe.

MURIEL. Here listen you . . .

LORRAINE. Am I getting tae tell this or fits happening?

LORRAINE (*voice over*). Dirt. She'd an eye for it. X-Ray eyes and a steel wrist. One dicht, WHAP! Oot wi' the clout, flashing it thrae the air sae fast you couldnae catch the colour o' the cloth. Left nothing ahint her but a shine.

Interior. Cafe.

MURIEL. That's mair like it.

LORRAINE (*voice over*). I didnae like her.

Interior. Cafe.

MURIEL. Fit?

LORRAINE. You heard.

MURIEL. You never telt me that.

LORRAINE. Fit wey would I? Muriel? . . . I like you now, you ken I dae . . . Muriel?

MURIEL. That's a terrible thing tae say.

LORRAINE. Fit wey?

MURIEL. It just is.

LORRAINE. Did you like me?

MURIEL. Fan?

LORRAINE. Fan I first cam tae work.

MURIEL. Na.

LORRAINE. Well then.

MURIEL. Get on wi' it then.

LORRAINE. I'm trying, can you nae hear me trying? . . . I liked you nearly straight away.

MURIEL. Fan?

LORRAINE. Fan I cut my finger.

Interior. Office 4.45 am.
Sound: breaking glass.

LORRAINE. Ooooyah!

MURIEL. Fit have you done you daft lassie?

LORRAINE. Ow!

MURIEL. They're crystal they water glasses. Do you ken the price o' crystal?

LORRAINE. My finger!

MURIEL. Oh god . . . dinny hud it there, hud it oer the sink. Have you got a plaster?

LORRAINE. Na.

MURIEL. A hankie?

LORRAINE. Na . . . God it's stinging!

MURIEL. Run the cauld tap oer it then tie it up wi' this . . . tight mind . . .

LORRAINE. It jist fell oot my hand.

Sound: running water.

MURIEL. Ach weel, I'll carry the bits oot wi' me. We'll get anither een oot the cupboard, they'll niver ken the difference, no till they hae six people in all efter a glass o' water and that canny happen every day can it?

LORRAINE. Look at the mess, it's all oer the carpet!

MURIEL. Aye well . . . I'll show you foo tae get it oot.

LORRAINE (*voice over*). It wis white. The carpet was white. Hale place was white. White as an arctic night. If it'd snawed inside naebody wouldn've kent till their feet cam up in chilblains, that's foo white it wis. A white carpet. Fa would pit a white carpet in an office? Some fiel that thocht dirt was something that cam in the mornings wi' the post and a'body's shoe leather and went oot the door again every night, polished awa hame by the pixies. Well . . . speaking as een o' the pixies its nae jist as simple as that.

Interior. Office.

MURIEL. Aye well, you canny use bleach, naethings as white as bleach. It'll be worse stain fan you've done wi' it.

LORRAINE. Oh god, fit'll I dae?

MURIEL. Hud on noo, dinny fash, dinny fash . . . mebbe a wee bit bleach in water if we could blend it in wi' the rest o' the carpet . . . na na . . .

LORRAINE (*voice over*). The walls were white, the skirting boards were white gloss, nae dust on the ledges, nae dust onywhere. The doors were white, you could see your face in the paint. The *desks were white* somebody's idea o' designer furniture, pale wood that gets a ring on it if onybody *talks* aboot coffee within ten feet o' it. And the lino, god help me, the lino in every ither room, toilet, kitchen, corridors . . . Torvill and Dean might hae kent fit tae dae wi' it but I didnae. White . . . lino. Only thing that wasnae white wis . . .

Interior. Office.

MURIEL. Christ lassie you're an awfy colour . . .

LORRAINE (*voice over*). An' I wis close.

Interior. Office.

MURIEL. Now jist you sit doon a minty till we sort wirsels oot. First day eye?

LORRAINE. Aye.

MURIEL. Ken fit wey I kent that?

LORRAINE. Na.

MURIEL. I hinna seen you afore . . . Fits your name?

LORRAINE. Lorraine.

MURIEL. Well Lorraine, pass us oer that litter bin.

LORRAINE. This een?

MURIEL. Na, that een you've got hinging aff your lug, just gie us it eh? Well empty it first will you, fit dae you think you're here for?

Nae wonder your name's Lorraine.

LORRAINE. How?

MURIEL. Fit?

LORRAINE. How is it nae wonder my name's Lorraine?

MURIEL. 'Cause that's fit your mammy calt you. Ken fit you are?

LORRAINE. Na.

MURIEL. Jist as well. Now look in that top drawer, see if you can find ony glue.

LORRAINE. Glue?

MURIEL. Fit are you? An echo? Jist get it oot. Aye that'll dae. Bonds in twa minutes eh? That'll dae us fine.

LORRAINE. Fit are you daein'

MURIEL. It'll jist stick doon fine there.

Movement of metal litter bin, scrubbing at carpet.

Lucky you decided tae cut your wrists near the desk there. If you'd done it in the middle o' the flaer we'd never hae got awa wi' this.

LORRAINE. They'll find oot.

MURIEL. Will they though? Fa ever picks up a litter bin in this place but us?

Fade.

LORRAINE (*voice over*). So I started work in the white basement o' the whiter than white offices o' Texas Oil Exploration Services, (U.K. Ltd.). Far Mr B. Rode the range o' his ambitions wi' his creamy buckskin jeacket firmly buttoned oer his wallet and his black wee heart . . . far Lonely Lillian languished oer her geology periodicals and dreamed aboot research grants and a real career, far Dreamy Derek sharpened his pencils a' the day, wi' nae thocht o' fa might be watching him, and dished oot jokes and dreams and distractions the best o' those being his ain beautiful wee bum . . . and Nervous Nora smoked and stopped and smoked and stopped and chewed a'thing she could get her hands on . . .

Interior. Cafe.

MURIEL. Hud on, hud on, that doesnae mak ony sense does it? You've got tae gie them the background tae it a' you canny jist . . .

LORRAINE (*interrupts*). Muriel.

MURIEL. Fit?

LORRAINE. That wis ma rowie.

MURIEL. Och no . . . it wasnae.

LORRAINE. We only ordered the twa.

MURIEL. Och *no*. Oh I'm sorry pet. I'll get you anither een.

LORRAINE. Na. 'S O.K. I hinna got room left efter a' that eggs an bacon an stuff.

MURIEL. You need tae watch yor strength.

LORRAINE. I need tae watch my figure.

MURIEL. Fit wey?

LORRAINE. I dinna ken, gies me something to dae.

MURIEL. I'll get the next coffee then.

LORRAINE. Well get me mine the now.

MURIEL (*calling*). Rita, *Rita*. Twa coffees. Plenty o' milk in mine Rita . . . Aye but fit I wis saying tae you, you canny jist jump intae the middle o' it like that, gie us the background.

LORRAINE. Och no. I'm wanting tae get tae the interesting bit.

Interior. Office.

LORRAINE (*shouting upstairs*). MU . . RI . . EL! He's deid!
    Cut.

Interior. Cafe.

MURIEL. Start a job at the beginning.

LORRAINE. I've done the beginning, now let's dae the end.

MURIEL. It's no the right way. You ken that.

LORRAINE. Well you dae it.

MURIEL. I'm no wanting to dae it.

LORRAINE. I dinny ken far tae start wi' the rest o' it.

MR B. (*echoey*). Remember to dust door ledges!

MURIEL. Na, leave that for now.

Interior. SGT DONALD's room.

SGT DONALD. So you found the body?

LORRAINE. Aye.

Interior. Cafe.

MURIEL. Na, that's later as well.

LORRAINE. Och, that's the good bits.

MURIEL. Wait now.

Interior. Office, echoey.

LORRAINE. Look at the state o' this desk.

Interior. Cafe.

MURIEL. That'll dae us, that's a good beginning.

LORRAINE *sighs.*

Go *on.*

LORRAINE. I ken fits goin tae happen, I'll get a' through it tae the
end, tae the good bit an' then you'll want tae tell it.

MURIEL. Go *on* Lorraine.

Fade.

LORRAINE (*voice over*). If evils got a smell tae it then it must be the
smell o' floor polish 'cause that's a' I ever snuffled in that place. Aye
but it wasnae evil, it was death, who's tae say they're the same
thing? I think aboot things like that. So should you. I cleaned doon
the stair Muriel cleaned up it. Three desks in one room, one big desk
all alane in anither. A kitchen, twa toilets . . . it was a' enough tae
gie you snaw blindness. I started every morning wi' the desks. First
desk on the left. Paper all oer it, letters, magazines, doodles,
drawings . . .

Interior. Office.
Sound: spray of polish.

MURIEL. Jist dust roond a' that. That's nae cleaning they're wanting
you tae dae, it's excavation.

Fade.

LORRAINE (*voice over*). Photos, postcards . . . *rubber balls?*

Interior. Office.

MURIEL. Those are juggling balls, no dinny ask, I'll tell you anither
time.

Sound: spray of polish.

LORRAINE (*voice over*). The seat a' covered wi' hairs, thoosands o'
wee goldy broon hairs . . .

Interior. Office.

MURIEL. Must be a labrador, mebbe a retriever eh? God knows fit his troosers look like must be mair hair on him than the dog. Tak the vacuum tae get them up.

LORRAINE (*voice over*). An pencil sharpenings a' roond the desk. Lovely lang pencil sharpenings, wee streamers o' jaggy wood, in a' diffrent colours.

Interior. Office.
Sound: hoover – they speak over it.

MURIEL. You iver tried getting a pencil sharpening that lang wi'oot brakin' it tae bits?

LORRAINE. Na, is it difficult?

MURIEL. Well, pit it this way, there's somebody in here spending an affa lot o' time sharpening pencils and nae much time daein onything else.

LORRAINE (*voice over*). That wis Derek, Derek's desk, we'll get back tae him. Then I'd dae the next desk alang. Naething but a blotter an a neat wee heap o' books. 'Petrology Today', oil derricks and gushers and guys in tin hats digging up deserts.

Interior. Office.

MURIEL. She's nae bother this een, a wee bit polish and you're done.

Sound: spray of polish.

LORRAINE (*voice over*). An a big lump o' stane, a fossil.

Interior. Office.

MURIEL. Look at that, a big, deid, stane snail. Nae my idea o' a paper weight.

LORRAINE (*voice over*). Spiral intae spiral intae spiral . . .

Interior. Office.

MURIEL. You'll need the feather duster tae get intae a' the cracks there.

LORRAINE (*voice over*). That was Lillian's desk. I couldnae mak her oot at a'.

Interior. Cafe.

MURIEL. I could.

LORRAINE. Is that a fact? Well tell us then.

MURIEL. Fan it's time, I'm jist waiting my moment. Could you gae a doughnut?

LORRAINE. You're jokin!

MURIEL. Oh I could, Rita . . . Rita . . .

LORRAINE. Far do you pit it?

MURIEL. In my belly, fars the sense in pitting it ony place else? Jist a doughnut Rita, thanks . . . On you go then.

LORRAINE (*voice over*). Nora's desk was next. It was a sight. If it wasnae the fag ash it was the sweetie papers.

Interior. Office.
Sound: dusting

MURIEL. There's nae answer tae it but tae tak a'thing off the desk and then dust it, you canny get it up'ony ither way . . .

LORRAINE (*voice over*). It looked like she cremated her hale family in the ashtray every Monday morning.

Interior. Office.

MURIEL. And dinny hoover till you've dusted.

LORRAINE (*voice over*). But every twa weeks or so a' the fag ends vanished and I had tae shift a mountain o' tinfoil and all the wee totty shreds o' chocolate that aye fall oot fan you unwrap your fruit and nut.

Interior. Office.
Sound: Hoover. MURIEL *speaks over it.*

MURIEL. She's aye trying tae gie it up, never does it though . . .

LORRAINE (*voice over*). Right enough three days later I wis shovelling up the stubs again. She had a' these books, gimy wee green and broon books. Kept them in the top drawer o' her desk. Well it was open ken, and onyway . . . Well we'll get tae that. She kept the books there wi' her emergency supply o' polo mints. Detective novels, ancient eens. I had a read at some o' them, they were rubbish.

Interior. Office.
Sound: Hoover.

MURIEL. Well all I can say is if the butler did it he must've had someone else tae polish the silver or he wouldnae hae found the time.

LORRAINE (*voice over*). An that was a' the desks except . . .

MR. B (*echoey*). Remember! Sweep into every corner.

Interior. Cafe.

LORRAINE. He wis a pain in the bum.

MURIEL. He wis, well . . . he kept fit he wanted.

LORRAINE. A pain in the bum. That's fit he should've got.

MURIEL. Fit he got wis a hole in the heid. An if onybody needed it he did.

LORRAINE. Oh aye, fas takin us on tae the juicy bits now?

MURIEL. That's jist a taster, tae keep up the suspense. You wanting ony o' this doughnut?

LORRAINE. Aye I'll maybe hae a wee bite. (*Bites.*) Bleuch! Raspberry jam, I canny stand raspberry jam.

MURIEL. My cousin used tae work in a jam factory . . .

LORRAINE. Oh aye?

MURIEL. Ken fit his job wis?

LORRAINE. Na.

MURIEL. He carved oot wee wooden pips tae pit in strawberry and raspberry jam tae gie it that natural look. You canny trust onything Lorraine, I'm telling you.

LORRAINE. I could hae telt you that jist by tasting it. Yeuch, far wis I?

MR. B (*echoey*). Sweep into every corner!

LORRAINE. Oh aye.

   Fade.

Interior office.
Sound: paper.

LORRAINE. Fits this?

MURIEL. Oh no, he's nae left anither een has he?

LORRAINE (*reads*). Remember, sweep into every corner . . . Mr B. Fa's Mr B?

MURIEL. The boss, fit dae they ca' it . . . eh . . . Regional Manager. Aye he likes tae keep an eye on us, if we get through a month wi'oot a complaint tae wir supervisor we're daein well. Wanted me oot my job one time cause I hadnae got a' the coffee cups clean . . . I'd left them soaking like, they were a' sugar and fag ends, ken fit that's like . . . Well I says tae the supervisor, Sheila I says . . .

LORRAINE (*interrupts*). Is that him on the wall there?

MURIEL. Aye.

LORRAINE. Funny how flash photys mak folks eyes gae pink eh.

MURIEL. His eyes are always like that.

LORRAINE. Fa's a' the rest o' them?

MURIEL. That's the chairman o' the company and some ither folk like that, they a' cm oer frae Houston last year. Come here I'll show you something else . . .

LORRAINE. Oh *God*.

MURIEL. Fit?

LORRAINE. Fa would pit a thing like that on the wall?

MURIEL. Mr B. would.

LORRAINE. God if I had a signed picture o' Sidney Devine I'd keep quiet aboot it.

MURIEL. Taks a' sorts, now . . . (*Sound: drawer.*) Look at that.

LORRAINE. Fit is it?

MURIEL. That's the Christmas card he sent tae a' they folk in Texas. See? 'Seasons Greetings from Aberdeen'.

LORRAINE. Is that him again?

MURIEL. Ay, wi' his femily.

LORRAINE. Fit are they a' done up like that for?

MURIEL. I think he likes country and western.

LORRAINE. That poor wee lassie, does he send her tae the school wi' rhinestanes roond her glasses like that?

MURIEL. Dinny ask.

LORRAINE. White, a' white. Fit does he think he is in a hat like that? The Lone Ranger?

Fade.

LORRAINE (*voice over*). A' in white wi' his wee pink eyes, like a rabbit. That's fit he wis, Mr B. was like the Magician's rabbit that thinks it's running the act, that thinks fan it's pulled oot the hat that a'body's clapping at him. He niver really kent fit was gaein on, he niver kent fit hit him till he was deid.

Interior. Office.

LORRAINE (*quiet, to herself*). So fits he keep in here then?

Sound: opening drawer, LORRAINE screams.

MURIEL (*distant*). God help us, fit hiv you done now?

LORRAINE (*voice over*). I wouldnae say I was the nervous type but staring a 45 in the face is enough tae mak onybody twitchy. I'm talking aboot a real 45, no the kind that maks Top o' the Pops but the kind you see on a film screen wi' Clint Eastwood attached tae one end o' it.

MURIEL (*approach*). You dinny want tae gae looking in too mony drawers, dinny ken fit might loup oot at you.

LORRAINE. Fit is it?

MURIEL. Fit does it look like?

LORRAINE. Fits he got it for?

MURIEL. Shootin folk, it gaes wi' the cowboy hat.

LORRAINE. Is it loaded?

MURIEL. I dinny fancy pickin it up tae find oot, dae you?

LORRAINE. Na.

MURIEL. It's for burglars.

LORRAINE. Is it?

MURIEL. Aye, hordes o' them, they're a' brakin in after his country an western tapes . . . They did hae a break in jist afore I started right enough. Ha's a ba' heid, that's a'. Come an dae the windys wi me.
    Fade.

Interior. Office a few minutes later.
Sound: cloth on glass, fade up on.

MURIEL. I wouldnae a had the three o' them, no if I'd kent I'd have tae dae it all mysel, my sister taks them some days right enough but you never get a break ken? Aye well, life never gies you fit you want eh? Let alane fit you expect. I jist expect the worst a' the time, that way I dinny get disappointed. They're a' in wi me every night 'cause the damps sae bad in the ither room, naebody's daein onything aboot it, they jist cam up an look, crowds o' them, cam an look an tak notes an gae awa an naething happens. I'm awa tae charge them a' entrance, £2.00 a peek, I'd mak mair than I dae at this job I can tell you . . .

LORRAINE. It's dangerous that ken.

MURIEL. Fit the damp? I ken it is, there's mair colds gaen roond the four o' us than a ton o' tissues could soak up, you canny hear the telly for us a' sneezing an . . .

LORRAINE. No, I meant haein' a gun like that, fits he reckon tae dae wi it?

Interior. Cafe.

MURIEL. Suicide.

LORRAINE. Is that fit you think?

MURIEL. You ken fit I think.

LORRAINE. Could hae been ony o' them.

MURIEL. Ony o' them.

LORRAINE. They a' hid a motive.

MURIEL. They a' hid a key tae that back door.

LORRAINE. Suicide, fa could ca' it suicide?

MURIEL. Sergeant Donald an the P. an J.

SGT DONALD (*echoey*). Death, it's a funny thing eh? In the midst o' life . . . Maks you think . . .

LORRAINE. Oh God dae I have tae?

MURIEL. Na. You can leave him till later.

LORRAINE. Och I'll get it oer wi'.

LORRAINE (*voice over*). Naebody talked tae us efter we found him, nae the polis, nae the papers. It was twa days later they hid me up the station an that's fan I met him, Torry's answer tae T.J. Hooker, Detective Sergeant Donald. I jist took one look at him an I kent he did for crime detection fit Dracula does for Blood Donors, looked like he enjoyed his work an a' . . .

Interior. SGT DONALD's *office, pm.*
Distant typewriters etc. Bring up sound of bluebottles briefly then fade.

SGT DONALD. So you found the body?

LORRAINE. Aye.

SGT DONALD. Horrible was it?

LORRAINE. Eh?

SGT DONALD. Blood all oer the place eh?

LORRAINE. There was a bit o' a mess aye.

SGT DONALD. An you recognised him?

LORRAINE. Aye.

SGT DONALD. Certain?

LORRAINE. Aye.

SGT DONALD. It was Mr Bruce?

LORRAINE. Aye.

SGT DONALD. You could tell?

LORRAINE. *Aye.*

SGT DONALD. He'd enough o' his face left had he?

LORRAINE *says nothing.*

So you could tell fa he wis, you recognised him?

LORRAINE. Well . . . nae exactly.

SGT DONALD. Oh?

LORRAINE. I never saw onybody that worked there. Nane o' them.
But I kent that's fa he wis.

SGT DONALD. How?

LORRAINE. I jist . . . kent that's a', it wis obvious.

SGT DONALD (*pause*). Gie you a scare did it?

LORRAINE. Fit?

SGT DONALD. Tripping oer his brains like that, bet you jumped eh?
. . . Scream did you?

LORRAINE. Na.

SGT DONALD. Did you no?

LORRAINE. Na, I never screamed.

SGT DONALD. Fit did you dae then?

LORRAINE. I called Muriel.

SGT DONALD. An fit did she dae?

LORRAINE. Rang the police an made a cup o' tea.

SGT DONALD. Wi him lying there? Lying there at her feet while she
was drinking it?

LORRAINE. Na . . . We hid it in the kitchen.

Sound: cup. SGT DONALD *takes a drink.*

SGT DONALD. Death, it's a funny thing eh? In the midst o' life . . .
Maks you think. Fits your name again lassie?

LORRAINE. Lorraine, Lorraine Tavendale.

SGT DONALD. This society is degenerating Lorraine. It's drugs, sex, I
ken I sound like the Sunday papers I'm nae ashamed o' it, that's the
kind o' horror I hae tae work wi' Lorraine. Think aboot that, I ken
fit I'm on aboot. This toon never used to hae these kind o cery ons, a
wee bit burglary mebbe, somebody daein his wife in, ken far you are
wi' crimes like that . . . Noo wi' a' these folk comin' in, God kens far
they've been half o' them . . . We've been infected Lorraine, nae
wonder respectable men hiv takin tae daein theirsels in . . .
Degenerating, hiv you seen the films their makin noo?

LORRAINE. Eh?

SGT DONALD. Like that eh . . . That 'Friday the Thirteenth' Part 3 wis the worst . . . definitely the worst.

LORRAINE. I think I saw een o' them on video.

SGT DONALD. And?

LORRAINE. Fit?

SGT DONALD. Fit did you think?

LORRAINE. Thocht it wis stupid.

Pause.

SGT DONALD. Stupid.

LORRAINE. Aye . . . Well I dinny ken, I wis makin the tea fan it wis on, I wasnae really watching . . .

Sound: bring up bluebottles, LORRAINE's *voice over, over this.*

LORRAINE (*voice over*). He hid wee black specks crawlin roon his window sill, I thocht it wis beetles, or ants. Fan I looked I saw it wis flies. Nane o' them hid wings.

Fade bluebottles.

SGT DONALD. Well Lorraine, we ken far tae get hud o' you.

LORRAINE. Is that it?

SGT DONALD. I think so, I dinny think we'll need tae bother you again.

LORRAINE. Do you nae want tae ask me onything else?

SGT DONALD. Aboot fit lassie?

LORRAINE. Aboot the . . . the gun . . . an stuff in the office . . . an . . .

SGT DONALD. Well we've plenty o' witnesses Lorraine, plenty o' ither folk tae see, an its nae like there was ony . . . foul play . . . is it?

LORRAINE. But . . . I ken things aboot them a' I . . .

SGT DONALD. Foo's that Lorraine?

LORRAINE. Well . . . O.K. I wis only the cleaner but . . .

SGT DONALD. Jist the cleaner, well, there's nae shame in that Lorraine, nae shame ava . . . Noo jist tak this cup alang wi' you an gie it tae the lassie oot the door there . . . (*Sound: cup.*) That's ma girl . . .

Fade.

Interior. Cafe.

MURIEL. Naebody asked me ony questions at a'.

LORRAINE. I hate daein him.

MURIEL. Hae a swig o' coffee, tak the taste oot your mou.

Sound: cup. LORRAINE *swallows.*

LORRAINE. Fit bit'll I dae now then?

MURIEL. It's time for wir suspects do you nae think?

LORRAINE. A'right.

Fade.

LORRAINE (*voice over*). There were never ony curtains in that place, jist white blinds left open like eyelids propped up half the night. Light and bright an white far we were, an dark glass an the dark street ootside. Onybody standing there, ootside in the dark would hae seen me and Muriel scrubbing awa like we were spotlit. But I never saw onybody roond there but policemen and ither cleaners. An we couldnae see ootside, we couldnae see onything but fit wis under oor noses . . . but then that telt us enough.

Interior. Office.
Sound: hoover, LORRAINE *speaks over it.*

LORRAINE. Well he's awa tae lose his job.

MURIEL. Fa?

LORRAINE. Derek.

Interior. Cafe.

MURIEL. Na, na, fit hae you missed oot noo?

LORRAINE. Och *Muriel*!

MURIEL. Tell them aboot the photy, then tell them aboot Derek.

LORRAINE. You said suspects. It was you that said get on tae the suspects!

MURIEL. Aye well, start wi' the photy.

LORRAINE *sighs.*
Fade.

LORRAINE (*voice over*). The office party. That's what the photo wis. A picture o' the office party, one Christmas auld an curling at the edges. There they a' were, my desks, wi' faces ahint them an names tae gae wi them an tinsel an misletoe making an awfy mess o' the paint work. All that was left o' that party was the photo an a Astis Spumante stain on the carpet. I kent it wis Astis Spumante by the bottles they were a' swigging oot ae. Great drink Astis but hell on pure wool. So there they a'were. Derek, Lillian and Nora. Sharing one kiss an twa glasses. 'DEREK, LILLIAN AND NORA FEELING FESTIVE, FESTIVE IS OUT OF SHOT'. Ha ha. Derek was tall and blonde and beautiful. He was the kind o' guy fa looked like he could loup frae one side o' the street tae the ither an no hae tae pit his fit doon halfway een tae keep his balance. An he had these jeans on that jist let you see foo he was pit taegether wi'oot screaming aboot it, and he was grinning like his face wis used tae being that shape. An his tie an his shirt an his jeckat were three different colours that should hae clashed but didnae an he had een o' they earrings, wee gold yin an kind eyes an I looked at him an I thocht well son you can water ma mistletoe ony time you like but I bet Mr B. doesnae like the way you clash wi' the paintwork ..

Interior. Office.
Sound: hoover. LORRAINE *speaks over it.*

LORRAINE. Well he's awa tae lose his job.

MURIEL. Fa?

LORRAINE. Derek. (*Sound: paper.*) Look.

MURIEL. Fit is it?

LORRAINE (*reading*), 'Dear Mr Caie', – that'll be Derek eh? – 'Further to our conversation about the correct demeanour and appearance of junior executive staff in this office I am forced to draw your attention once more to your apparel at yesterday's board meeting ...

Fade out LORRAINE *mix in* MR B.

MR. B. In particular I feel it has been made quite clear that the wearing of *ostentatious personal jewellery* is not appropriate and may even give rise to offence in certain quarters. I would further like to suggest that 'juggling' and similar activities are not appropriate to your working hours on these premises. One of the desks has already been marked by your 'antics' and this week's flow chart bears the distinct impression of a pink rubber ball in the top right hand corner. This kind of wanton damage will not be tolerated. I hope I will not have to speak to you about this again or we may have to review your future with the firm in view of your obvious lack of motivation ...

Fade MR. B.

LORRAINE. Derek's written all oer it in coloured pencil.

MURIEL. Fits he say? (*Sound: paper.*) Is that foo you spell that? I thocht there wis an 'R' in it?

LORRAINE. Me too, looks right enough eh?

MURIEL. Well ... he'll need tae watch his step eh?

LORRAINE. Fit dae I look like?

MURIEL. Eh?

LORRAINE. Look, it's his earring, he'd left it on the desk top there.

MURIEL. Hmmm. Looks better on him. Think he's turning oer a new leaf then?

LORRAINE. Fit wey does it look better on him? Sees your mirror . . .

Fade.

LORRAINE (*voice over*). I left the earring there, twa days later it wis awa. I thocht he'd taken it hame wi' his imitation fur bow tie and his origami models o' seagulls an his juggling balls . . . but he must hae pit it back in his ear. Fan Mr B. met the bullet that was efter an introduction tae his brains Derek was working oot a month's notice. We saw the letter . . .

Interior. Office.
Sound: clang of metal litter bin and paper.

MURIEL. Aye aye Lorraine, here it is . . .

LORRAINE (*voice over*). Well you canny empty a bin wi'oot noticing fits in it can you? . . . I says he wis a rebel. Muriel says . . .

Interior. Cafe.

MURIEL. He wis a nice looking laddie but daft, nae job, nae reference, nae future . . .

LORRAINE. Aye, I did it my way, that fit wey they chucked me oot on the street . . . He must have jist hated Mr B. Jist hated him.

MURIEL. He didnae smile like he hated onybody, he'd soft eyes, good eyes, but it didnae look like he'd ken fit tae dae if the world played him a bad turn, he could hae done onything . . . onything.

LORRAINE. That was Derek.

MURIEL. Tell them aboot Lillian now.

LORRAINE. I wis awa tae dae Nora.

MURIEL. No, save Nora.

LORRAINE. Aye right enough, it's a better story that way.

LORRAINE (*voice over*). Lillian. In the photy she's the one wi' the half smile 'stead of the grins that hae a'body else chewing their ain ears. She's wearing black. It makes her look sophisticated. It also maks her look like she's in mourning for something. Might as well hae been her career. You should hae seen her CV I did. She had it oot on her desk one morning.

Interior. Office.

MURIEL. Aye, aye, somebody's lookin tae change jobs.

LORRAINE. Foo do you ken that?

MURIEL. Well she's nae got all this on her desk jist 'cause she fancies haein' a wee gloat tae hersel has she?

LORRAINE. Twa degrees, she's got twa degrees!

MURIEL. Aye, I see them, pass us that bucket will you Lorraine if you're done wi it.

Sound: bucket.

Watch you dinny drip on her papers!

LORRAINE. It's jist a wee spot . . .

Sound: scrubbing.

MURIEL. You're lucky I've the time tae help you oot the morn. Chewing gum, folk that spit it oot on a carpet like this should hae tae chew it off again . . .

Sound: scrubbing.

LORRAINE. I canny get oer this, look at a' she's done . . .

MURIEL. Naething lifts it, nae detergent, nae that stain remover . . .

LORRAINE. . . . An she's only 28 . . .

MURIEL. It would hae tae be pink! It'll be bubble gum, that's fit it'll be, it'll be that Derek, he's the type eh? I'm forever blawin' bubbles . . .

LORRAINE. Fit wey has she nae got an office like Mr. B. Fit wey is she nae running this place?

MURIEL. Eh?

LORRAINE. Lillian. Fit wey is she nae oot there building oil rigs?

MURIEL. Building fit?

LORRAINE. Well something, if no oil rigs then something.

MURIEL. Gie us a look at that again . . . (*Sound: paper.*) No jist hud it oot my hands is wet . . . Aye, aye it reads well eh?

LORRAINE. Canny be mony women dae a job like that, engineering.

MURIEL. Civil engineering, you dinny get your hands sae dirty . . .

LORRAINE. . . . You'd think she'd want something better eh?

MURIEL. . . . Nae like this job. (*Sound: scrubbing.*)

LORRAINE. Is she no just like a secretary here? She's typing letters for Mr B. half the time . . .

Fade.

LORRAINE (*voice over*). Lillian looked like she smouldered. Wee tight lines hinging aboot her face like the half smile was half way tae showin a' her teeth and biting the heids off the lot o' them. A' black, like a bit o' smokeless fuel, you wouldnae ken she was on fire till you pit your hand on her . . .

Interior. Office.
Sound: polishing machine.

LORRAINE. O-o-o-oH! M-U-R-I-E-L!

MURIEL. Watch the skirting board! Dinny hit the skirting board!

LORRAINE. I canny hud it!

MURIEL. Switch it off!

LORRAINE. H-E-L-P!

MURIEL. The switch! LORRAINE HAVE YOU GAEN OFF YOUR HEID!

Sound: crash of polishing machine hitting skirting board. It is switched off.

LORRAINE. Oh shite. (*Pause.*) Oh . . . shite.

MURIEL. It'll tak mair than polyfilla tae fill that in.

LORRAINE. It's never done that before . . . I mean . . .

MURIEL. Foo mony times have I *telt* you aboot that polishing machine, you've got tae *balance* it.

LORRAINE. The balance is *off.*

MURIEL. Aye . . . mebbe it is.

LORRAINE. God it's heavy enough tae hud at the best o' times . . .

MURIEL. There was one time we put in for extra money for daein stuff like this, fair taks it oot o' your back using they machines . . . Here look, mebbe if we try and pull the carpet across a bit . . .

LORRAINE. Did you get it?

MURIEL. Fit?

LORRAINE. Extra money?

MURIEL. You're jokin'. They said if we couldnae handle the work there wis plenty that would. Naebody gets extra money wi' oor firm but the men that dae the station forecourt an stuff like that.

LORRAINE. Fit wey dae they get it?

MURIEL. Och . . . 'cause they say they use heavy machinery.

LORRAINE. Like fit?

MURIEL (*snorts*), Polishing machines . . . That's nae gaen tae hide it Lorraine, we'll jist need tae hope they dinny notice.

LORRAINE (*voice over*). He noticed, but that comes later.

MURIEL. Mr B'll probably leave us a wee note aboot it.

LORRAINE. Him?! Did you see o' his litter bin the day? Crammed full. I had tae drag the stuff oot ae it. Fit wey could he nae jist hae takin it a' tae the back door himsel if he'd that much tae chuck oot?

An Lillian . . .

MURIEL. Fit wis he chuckin oot?

LORRAINE. Books it wis, an magazines, a' brand new.

MURIEL. Fit aboot?

LORRAINE. Och it was jist books . . . aboot oil . . . an women.

MURIEL. Eh?

LORRAINE. Things like . . . 'Women in North Sea Industries' . . . an
. . . Oh I canny mind, they were frae Houston ken, the heid office . . .
something aboot improving the company's image . . . 'The female
face o' oil services' . . . that kind o' stuff. He hadnae opened ony o'
them . . . Och Muriel, fit'll I dae? I've the rest o' the floor tae polish.

MURIEL. Switch it on. I'll stand by the plug tae cut you off if it gaes
haywire again . . . We'll need tae get a new een.

LORRAINE. They'll say I brak it.

MURIEL. Well . . . they better nae say that . . . but they might. Jist
watch they dinny tak it oot your wages, they dae that wi'oot telling
you.

LORRAINE. As if I didny hae enough on my plate the day, aye I was
telling you, Lillian's got litter all oer her desk.

MURIEL (amazed). Lillian?

LORRAINE. Aye, look at it, she's left paper all oer the place, she's
smashed her coffee cup an left it lying there.

MURIEL. Lillian? (She moves to desk, then more distant.) What a state!
(Slight chink of broken china.) She must hae chucked that frae clear
across the room.

LORRAINE. She micht hae saved her tantrums till I'd time tae clear
them up . . . I'm nae switching this on again, Muriel, I'm feart . . .
Muriel?

MURIEL (absorbed). Hmmm?

LORRAINE. Fit is't?

Sound: paper.

MURIEL (reads). Dear Sir, with reference to your enquiry concerning
our employee Miss Lillian Ross . . .

Fade out MURIEL mix in MR B.

MR. B. . . . I can tell you that the standard of her work is usually
adequate if allowances are made for her abrasive personal manner.
Yours sincerely . . .

Fade.

LORRAINE. Fits that?

MURIEL. A refrence, a job refrence, fit you willny get.

LORRAINE. Fits it mean?

MURIEL. It means Lillian willny leave here 'less its tae sign on, you must ken the feeling. It means she's spent too much time chucking cups o' coffee about an nae enough time makin them for Mr B . . . It means we'll need tae get wir skates on if this desk's tae be fit tae look at afore 8.00 . . . God . . . I never thocht she was the type tae tak sugar . . . sticky mess it is . . .

Fade.

LORRAINE (*voice over*). I thocht aboot Lillian a lot. I mean twa degrees, she should hae had it made ken? An she was organised, I mean her desk used tae shine *afore* I'd been at it wi' the polish . . . An she looked good . . . smart ken. Well I thocht she did, I thocht she looked affa smart, like something oot a magazine . . . professional. She looked like a professional woman. So fit wey was the typing letters fae Mr B?

Interior. Cafe.

MURIEL. She canny hae liked him.

LORRAINE. Na.

MURIEL. Well would you?

LORRAINE. I didnae, an I didnae ken him.

MURIEL. Ruthless, she could hae been ruthless . . . an violent, you can tell by the eyes . . .

LORRAINE. An if onybody could hae planned it . . .

MURIEL. Aye let's no get ahead o' wirsels. Nora.

LORRAINE. O.K.

Fade.

LORRAINE (*voice over*). Nora . . . Look this isnae meant tae sound bad right? But eh . . . Nora didnae look much o' onything. It's no that she looked bad or she wasnae pretty or . . . well Nora looked like something that's been left at the back o' the cupboard so long you canny mind fit it is fan you get it oot . . . could be onything inside o' course but eh . . . the labels gone. E'en her smile said sorry. But then . . . some people canny keep their teeth oot ae folk like that . . .

Interior. Office.

MURIEL. Mr B. took her oot, I'm telling you Lorraine, I ken aboot these things.

LORRAINE (*sound: paper*). Muriel?

MURIEL. Aye?

LORRAINE. Have you looked at your pay slip?

MURIEL. Aye.

LORRAINE. I'm twa poonds less.

MURIEL. Aye, happens a' the time I'm doon six poond since I started here.

LORRAINE. Fit?

MURIEL. Well you see . . . this lot, Texas oil people, they pit this cleaning job oot tae tender an oor cleaning company has tae gie them the cheapest price tae keep the job, happens a' the time, only way they ken tae cut prices is tae cut oor wages . . . Aye but Lorraine listen tae fit I'm telling you.

LORRAINE. You reckon he took her oot? Mr B?

MURIEL. Someone pit on mair perfume afore they left here the ither night, tak a sniff in the ladies, an it wasnae Lillian she doesnae wear the stuff, tak a sniff roond her desk. An he must hae jist aboot drooned himsel in this stuff, look the bottles still here.

LORRAINE (*sniffing air*). Och that's terrible!

MURIEL. He took her oot tae that disco.

LORRAINE. Fit wey do you ken that?

MURIEL (*drawer opens*). Look, here's his credit cards still here, he's a tight bastard, think he keeps them here 'cause he doesnae want his wife getting hud o' them. Well if he didnae tak them he'll no hae been painting the toon pink will he? That place roond the corner does candlelight hamburgers an the lassies are in free an Thursday night is country an western night.

LORRAINE. Did he . . . I mean dae you think they . . . ?

MURIEL. She didnae. She wouldnae I reckon.

LORRAINE. Foo are you makin this oot?

MURIEL. Well look, look at her desk thrae there, a' cigarette ash again, she's smokin mair than ever, she's nervous. She's three books half read on her desk an she's cried on the lot o' them, you can see the marks on the page, an this een . . . hud on till I show you . . . (*Receding.*) . . . Aye here we go . . . (*Approach.*) Tak a look at this.

LORRAINE. That's Mr B's is it no?

MURIEL. Aye, his desk diary, he must hae pit it on her desk, an look here's her name in for last Thursday, it's nae in ony night afore that, an here it is for *next* Thursday . . .

LORRAINE. God he's just aboot the pen through the page crossing that oot.

MURIEL. I dinny think he's awfy pleased wi' her. He'll be lookin at her wi that look that says if you dinny come across next time I'll ken fit tae dae aboot it. That look that says you'll get fits coming tae you an I'll gie it you . . . He'll be hinging aroon her desk. He'll be standing in doorways so she has tae squeeze past him . . .

Sound: floor sweeper.

LORRAINE. Muriel, can you manage wi'oot that twa poond?

MURIEL. I'll jist hae tae manage . . . It was my Heather's birthday this week an a' . . . Och weel. I dinny fancy lookin for anither job the now, there's nae jist that mony aboot.

Sound: floor sweeper.

LORRAINE. Fit wey dae you ken that, aboot the looks he's giein her, an the standing in the doorway an stuff?

MURIEL. Some things you jist *ken.*

Interior. Cafe.

LORRAINE. God I've been there.

MURIEL. Fa hasnae?

LORRAINE. I hae been that woman . . . I tell you *now* . . . I'd've kicked him in the goolies, I'd hae dropped something on him, I'd hae . . .

MURIEL. Well somebody did . . . Somebody . . . did . . .

Pause.

LORRAINE. If it wis suicide fit wey was he wearing his Walkman?

LORRAINE *voice over mix in slowed down Sidney Devine.*

LORRAINE (*voice over*). It had an automatic rewind. That morning fan I found him spread oer his interior design the batteries were stone deid, an Sidney Devine wis jist aboot wore oot . . .

Sound: Sidney slows to a stop.

Interior. Cafe.

MURIEL. God if that's nae enough tae kill you fit is?

LORRAINE. He must hae lain there the hale weekend. Must've worked late on Friday.

MURIEL. Naebody left but him.

LORRAINE. And jist een o' the others . . .

MURIEL. Or mebbe somebody cam back, a'body his that basement key, that's fit wey we got een.

LORRAINE. Fit wey would he kill himsel? It's nae as if he wis bankrupt or onything.

MURIEL. Na, but the company wis.

LORRAINE. Fit? Texas Oil Exploration Services?

MURIEL. Aye.

LORRAINE. I niver kent that.

MURIEL. It wis in the *Evening Express* yesterday, well they've jist gone
under the now, nae all o' it, jist the Aberdeen bit ken.

LORRAINE. God they're a' closin' doon, we'll be a ghost toon 'fore
we ken fits happening . . . Did he ken that wis comin? Mr B?

MURIEL. He micht ae had a suspicion . . . but it still doesnae mak it
suicide jist explains fit wey they were sae sure he did awa wi himsel,
Sergeant Donald on the P. an J.

LORRAINE. Oh God.

MURIEL. Fit.

LORRAINE. I've tae talk aboot him again.

MURIEL. Aye.

LORRAINE. God I wish I hadnae had such a big breakfast . . .

Fade.

LORRAINE (*voice over*). I'm nae the suspicious type but if someone
sticks a tin o' sardines that's past its sell by date under my neb you'll
excuse me if I hat tae say I smell fit I smell. If I kent that gun wis in
the desk, onybody could hae found it an I thocht aboot them a'
workin' awa there under Mr B's eye an I *thocht* . . .

Sound: Very slow Sidney Devine music mix to interior SGT DONALD's
office. As before.

LORRAINE. Listen, there's something you need tae listen tae . . .

SGT DONALD. Now Lorraine jist stop a minty and think eh? Jist
think tae yoursel, why are you bothering aboot a' this, is it right, is it
healthy tae hae such a morbid fascination for the dead. It's difficult,
I ken, tae pit it ahint you, difficult for a lassie like yourself, your first
contact wi' that dreadful fact o' life . . . death. You've been brought
face tae face wi it, dabbling wi'it you might say, poking your
innocent wee fingers intae a' that gore an gristle . . . but its nae right
is it? Have you been dreaming aboot him, is that it?

LORRAINE. Eh?

SGT DONALD. Is his faceless body draggin thrae your dreams? Are
his bloody hands tapping at you a'times you pit your heid on the
pillow . . . ? Naebody's surprised you're upset lassie.

LORRAINE. I'm nae upset I . . .

SGT DONALD. Hiv you seen a doctor?

LORRAINE. I'm nae sick.

SGT DONALD (*sigh*). Well Lorraine now, I'd like tae . . . Look, give me a ring fan I'm nae workin eh? That's my hame number . . . I'm concerned for you Lorraine, dinny think o' me as jist a uniform, think o' me as . . . mebbe a faither. Is your faither living Lorraine?

LORRAINE. No.

SGT DONALD. I didnae think he wis, no, I could tell, I could tell. Well day or night Lorraine, you feel free, day or night . . .

LORRAINE. But can you nae see! You're missing it all!

SGT DONALD. I doot that Lorraine, I doot that, look lassie, we're professionals.

Sound: bluebottles. Fade.

Interior. Cafe.

MURIEL. Aye well, they missed the one thing that mattered. The one thing.

LORRAINE. Fits that?

MURIEL. The one thing that tells the hale story.

LORRAINE. Oh I kent this would happen, a' this time I've been wearing mysel oot and you're jist goen tae come in and tell the punchline. Aren't you?

MURIEL. So you tell it.

LORRAINE. I dinny ken it!

MURIEL. Jist one thing that hit me in the eye like that bullet hit him.

LORRAINE. Muriel are you goin tae tell us fit you're havering aboot?

MURIEL. Awa an get us anither coffee then, I think it's time right enough. Plenty o' milk mind . . .

Interior. Office.
Sound: sound of hoover. It stops abruptly.

LORRAINE. Muriel!

MURIEL (*distant*). Hud on I'm daein my flaers.

LORRAINE. Muriel get doon here! (*To herself.*) The bastard, he canny dae this, he canny . . .

MURIEL (*approach*). Fits up wi you?

LORRAINE. It wis on his desk.

MURIEL. 'To Isis Cleaning Contractors . . .' Oh God . . .

LORRAINE. Aye.

Mix in MR B. *echoey.*

MR. B. To Isis Cleaning Contractors, Dear Sirs, I wish to complain about the standard of service provided by your firm, not only has the cleaning of these premises been far from satisfactory but our furniture has sustained damages which will be difficult and costly to repair – I refer to a pure wool carpet which appears to have been deliberately vandalised with adhesive and a skirting board which has been irreparably dented by the careless use of a hoover or polishing machine. I do not know what sort of staff you employ but they are not the kind I wish to entrust with the responsibility for maintaining the appearance of these offices, Yours etc. Mr D. Bruce, Regional Manager . . .

LORRAINE. An there's a note for us.

MR. B. Remember the dirt under the carpet!

LORRAINE. I could just kill the bastard I could jist . . .

MURIEL. It's awa, this is a carbon, the ither eens awa . . .

LORRAINE. We'll be oot wir jobs won't we, *won't we*?

MURIEL. I dinna ken.

LORRAINE. Christ I've rent overdue, I've my share o' the electric, I've nae even paid Brenda for last week's food . . .

MURIEL (*dead*). I've three bairns an naething coming in.

LORRAINE. There's nae ither jobs, a'things gaen under, there's nae ither jobs . . . Oh I could jist *murder* the bastard!

MURIEL (*still dead*). Aye, me an a'.

Fade.

Interior. Cafe.
Sounds: cup on table.

LORRAINE. There you go. I dinny ken foo you can drink it that colour, there's mair milk than coffee in that.

MURIEL. Pass us the sugar eh?

Sound: spoon in cup.

LORRAINE. Well.

MURIEL. Well?

LORRAINE. Are you goin tae tell us or fit are you daein?

MURIEL. Ony o' them could hae done it . . . we ken that but fa's bothered? Onyway . . . they didnae . . . nane o' them. (*Pause.*) A scuff in the lino, a wee black scuff, you ever tried getting scuffs oot ae that lino?

LORRAINE. Have I? I near wore my airms oot trying.

MURIEL. I couldnae mak it oot. The day before I'd seen it, one wee scuff screaming at me oot ae that hale flaer like a deid fly in an operating theatre . . . one nasty wee bit o' dirt that'd lose us oor jobs for sure . . . you were trying tae get Blu-tak oot ae the shag pile mind? So I did it. Scrubbing awa, God I pit some elbow intae that, thinking aboot him, thinking it didnae matter foo hard I scrubbed now, 'cause we were finished there, time *I'd* finished I'd near worn a dent in the lino, hale thing shone, like the slides I'd mak on the opad road fan I was a bairn an my Ma'd aye skelp me, says 'You can kill folk wi' that kind o cerry on' . . . Day we found his nibs there it was . . . another skuff, near aboot the same place, a skid mark, a wee bit o' somebody's shoe . . . He'd hae been coming oot the toilet in his shiny, shiny cowboy boots, carrying his shiny, shiny gun that he'd been giein' a clean, slipping on the shiny, shiny flaer . . . whoops! His gun's in his hand, he trips oer his ain feet an shoots himsel in the heid. Falls doon neat as anything on his ain white carpet. (*Takes a couple of noisy swigs of coffee.*)

MURIEL. I kent it was trouble, a' that polish. It was only a matter o' time Lorraine, I kent . . . I'd *deduced* we were jist rubbing up trouble for someone.

Pause.

LORRAINE. But you didny ken he'd . . . Did you?

MURIEL (*another swallow*). I tell you this Lorraine, I ken mair than onybody'll ever tak the trouble tae ask.

Slow Sidney Devine mix to dock sounds.

LORRAINE (*voice over*). The firm shifted Muriel an me efter Mr B. was deid. Its longer hoors fir the same money bit we're daein it. We're up by the prison now. It's jist a wee bitty walk for me thrae the docks, that's always awake, hale place is awaken wi' the smell o' ice an fish an kippers, alive wi' folk in big, wet, red rubber aprons daein horrible things tae the fish . . . There's nae sae much fish now 'course, that all went for the oil, now the oil's gaein up an doon I dinny ken fit'll come after that. Ken fit Aberdeen is? It's a pipeline, full o' money, it's like the hale toon got a heat off o' a' that hot money jist by sitting on the pipe. Fit happens fan they switch the heating off? Fa gets the warmth o' a' that money then? I think aboot things like that. So should you. I think aboot it as I'm walkin past a' the fish an they're staring at me wi' wee deid eyes, I look back an say 'dinny you look at me like that, I'm practically a vegetarian, I canny afford tae be onything else . . .' An fan we leave oor work a'body else is gaein tae theirs . . . like gaein the wrang up a one way street, against the flow o 'a the people wi' nine tae five jobs an alarm clocks that niver wake them afore 7.30. Invisible people. We micht as well live under the ground . . . an naebody wants tae hear it the underside o' the world looks like.

Interior. Cafe.

LORRAINE. Did you ken oil was a' wee died creatures?

MURIEL. No.

LORRAINE. Aye, that's fit it is, wee deid creatures a' turned tae earth then rock an silt gets on top o' them and they jist lie there fir hunners o' years an turn tae oil.

MURIEL. Oh aye? Well maybe Mr B'll turn tae oil gie him lang enough.

LORRAINE. Fifty centuries frae now, somebody'll be filling up their Fiesta wi' a bit o' Mr B.

MURIEL. He might be some use in the world at last then. (*Sound: cup in saucer.*) Time I wis up the road.

LORRAINE. Aye, me an a'. I'll see you the morn Muriel, I'll try an make it for half four the morn.

MURIEL. Och dinny kill yourself, no for a poond an hour, it's nae worth it.

Fade.

Sound: hoover, mix in scrubbing, fade hoover, scrubbing gets louder and louder, echoey, cut.

APPLE BLOSSOM AFTERNOON

by Dave Sheasby

For Bill

Dave Sheasby was born in Sheffield where he worked as a teacher for four years. He joined BBC Radio Sheffield in 1967, making educational programmes and stayed there for 21 years. About ten years ago he started writing his first radio play and has written at least twelve more since then. He has also written plays for the stage and a TV film, *On the Palm* was shown in 1986. He currently works for BBC Network Radio, directing plays and making arts and general features for the BBC North East Region.

Apple Blossom Afternoon was first broadcast on BBC Radio 4 on 24 August 1988. The cast was as follows:

TED	Malcolm Hebden
JANE	Marlene Sidaway
DAVE	Ray Ashcroft
WESLEY	Louis Emerick
POVEY	Colin Meredith
BILLY	Philip Whitchurch
TANNOY	Christine Cox

Director: Tony Cliff
Running time, as broadcast: 44 minutes, 11 seconds

In betting shop.

TANNOY. At Cheltenham, it's overcast. The going is good to soft.
Non-runner in the 2.30, number 4, Lopside. Jockey change in the
three o'clock, number 16, Pyewipe, will be ridden by J. Blacker.

Fade.

TED. They were all looking at me. Their faces turned and fixed. Like
in a photograph. The tannoy was telling us the dogs were going into
the traps at Monmore. Marie was looking at me from behind the
counter, peering over the top of her specs. And the others, Indian
Jane, Back-pocket Dave, Big Tall Wesley, Mersey Billy and
Formbook Povey, all looking at me. I could feel the tears on my
cheeks and the pink slip of paper in my hands. I was 55 on that day.
It was a Saturday in November and the clock on the wall said twelve
minutes past four. And all this took place under the sign of
Ladbrokes.

Tannoy fades up under last.

TANNOY. And they're going down the far side of the course and
Pennysave takes them along. He's closely followed by My
Mackintosh; some two lengths behind these is Crème de la Crème.
Coming to the next. This is the one before the water . . .

TED. A Saturday between the Mackeson and the Hennesey when the
form is beginning to work out just that bit and you can feel the
winter really taking a hold. Anyway Saturday afternoons was
always a bit of time off. 'Enjoy yourself, Teddy, but be careful.' I
always was too, with the money side. Mum knew that. Not that I
ever have that much on. So I never win much either. I reckon there's
not many who do. Some people say that's why we do it but I think
that's rubbish. I mean, who wants to lose? Mr. Know-All Skeffington
at work, I've heard *him* say that. Never been in a betting shop in his
life but reckons to be an expert on human nature. Awful man. Still
only half past eleven. I leave the pussies some lunch, greedy lot, and

set off. I've bags of time so I call at Walcott's for some ciggies and take it easy down to the shop. Get there early. There's always the dogs to pass the time.

Fade.

Fade in.

TANNOY. At Hackney they bet 3–1 trap 4, 4–1 trap 5, 5–1 trap 1, 6–1 trap 2.

JANE. On the dot. The man himself. Morning Edward.

TED. Jane.

JANE. Nippy out there.

TED. On the cold side, certainly.

JANE. Perry Mason's out again. Second, second, second.

TED. I saw.

JANE. Today's his day. I've got him in my double. Better be his day.

TED. Last race at Haydock isn't it?

JANE. Right.

TED. Long time to wait then.

JANE. I'm all right today. Our Deirdre's got a neighbour in. I'm having one off. Well fair's fair. Saturday afternoon. Got to have a bit of time to yourself eh? Isn't that what you always used to say?

TED. Did I?

JANE. You're looking a bit washed out. Taking care of yourself these days . . . you know . . . on your own?

TED. I'm doing OK.

JANE. Er . . . you don't happen to have a spare . . . er.

TED. Fag? Sure.

JANE. Ta. My saviour. Perry Mason. It'll win today.

TED (*narration*). Indian Jane. I have these names for the regulars. Just a little thing with me. I used to tell mum. She loved hearing about it, especially when she got badly at the end and never went out at all. One of the regulars is Jane. The bit about Deirdre's very sad. She'll be eighteen now; the only child. Wheelchair job. Terrible business. She got knocked down in the school yard when she was ten. A delivery van reversing. It was in the local paper. Crisps and sweets, the van. She's never walked since. Then the mister walked out and that left Jane to cope on her own. She gave up her job, the lot, to look after Deirdre full-time. It hasn't been easy. I know that. Caring for someone. I call her Indian Jane because she's very free with her rouge. A few of the lads in here make fun and reckon she's 'mutton-dressed-as' but I admire her. She makes an effort when she goes out. She tries. Even to Ladbrokes on Saturday afternoons, she looks nice.

There is no neighbour. She leaves Deirdre to fend on her own a few hours. I don't blame her for that. I think she deserves a little break.

TANNOY. Later betting Hackney. They bet 2–1 trap 4. At Hackney they're going into the traps.

JANE. Never touch dogs. Can't fathom it.

TED. You only need to pick one from six.

JANE. This form guide here. 'Trap 2, Sally Rose, plenty of speed if she can get smart out of the box. Must watch her inside.' I mean, what kind of help is that?

TANNOY. Off Hackney. At 12.21.

JANE. My Uncle Stan owned a dog. It never won a race. A lovely name though. Starry Starry Tess.

TED. A bitch then.

JANE. What?

TED. It'd have been a bitch then. Tess.

Enter DAVE.

DAVE. Now then you sinners.

JANE. Morning David.

DAVE. Who's doing what and are you sure you should be?

JANE. Touch of frost I reckon.

DAVE. It's very quiet in here. Not mourning your losses already.

JANE. It's you that's early. Perry Mason's in the last race at Haydock.

DAVE. Cheltenham today. Always a nice little challenge is Cheltenham.

TED (*narration*). Back-pocket Dave. He's a plumber. Very busy man. Always in a rush. Pressed for time if not cash. Thing about Dave is, he wins. Not all the time, but enough. He seems to make it pay. You can't say that for many in here. Back-pocket of Dave's overalls, he's got this wad of cash. He gets tips does Dave and he's not selfish with his info. If you happen to be nearby you can click. A month ago he gave me Scorchlight. It won at 7–1. I had 50p on that. Very nice too.

DAVE. I've got this central heating job on. A real swine. Can I make that boiler fire on automatic time-switch? I've come here for a break from it. Little woman's going crackers about it. I've told her I'm trying my best. Very nice lady too. Lovely eyes.

JANE. He's off.

DAVE. Not yet; be right. Not yet.

JANE. Always fancying, you.

DAVE. Me? Why didn't you tell me darling?

JANE. All mouth and no trousers . . .

She moves off.

DAVE. And how's Edward these days? Got any winners? I'll tell you what *won't* win. Perry Mason.

TED. Any er . . . bits of news?

DAVE. I did get a little nod, as a matter of fact; yesterday. Stable job. No guarantees, mind.

TED. I know that.

DAVE. First race at Cheltenham. The one on the screens now.

TED. It's a novice hurdle with thirty runners, Dave.

DAVE. Right.

TED. Half of 'em have never run. I was going to give it a miss actually.

DAVE. Like I say, it's just a nod. The price might be very affectionate. Bally Ferriter. Number 30. Bottom of the shop.

TED. It's not even in the s.p. probables.

DAVE. I shouldn't let that put you off.

TED. Tricky race. All those unknowns.

DAVE. Listen. I've had ten nods from this lad and eight have gone in. OK, one was disqualified after a steward's enquiry but I'm counting it because it won by four lengths going away. So eight out of ten. That's no flat beer Edward. Think about it. Mind you, it could be the wrong day, do a wallop. No cast iron in this game.

TED. Tempting though.

DAVE. Please yourself. Know anything about boilers? Central heating kind?

TED. Not really, sorry.

DAVE. I just can't bear the idea of letting Mrs. Lovely Eyes down. Not when she's all on her ownio – with the kiddies, mind. Still, first things first.

TED (*narration*). And it's into the back-pocket and out with a wad thick as a book. Now I normally just do a 20p, 30p yankee, small bets, pay tax. Reckon on an outlay of £4 max. Just nice for a Saturday afternoon. Mum always knew I was careful with the cash side so she never had to worry. But today I'm 55 and I don't have a little outing in front of me tonight. For the first time. I've just realised – our little treat at the Maharajah. There's no point in going on my own. I don't want to sit in the corner like a lemon with all those folk jabbering and eating. So I won't go out. So, looked at that way I have spare cash . . . and it's my birthday and I've only myself to think about . . . I'll have a little roll up bet, a little accumulator. Why not. One down, all down. It's a dream bet really, if they all win. If it loses, well I can always have a double later. It's my birthday.

TANNOY. At Crayford they bet, 7–1 trap 6, 2–1 trap 2, 3–1 trap 5, 5–1 trap 4, 10–1 trap 1, 10–1 trap 3. All quoted Crayford.

Enter WESLEY.

WESLEY. Morning my friends and how's it all shapin' up this morning?

JANE. Morning Wesley.

WESLEY. Mornin' to you madam.

JANE. Joys of spring is it?

WESLEY. It's always joys of spring with Wesley.

JANE. How do you manage it?

WESLEY. Come back to the house one day and I'll show you.

JANE. Cheeky bugger. You men. In this shop. You're all the same.

WESLEY. It's you; making yourself look like a lovely lady every Saturday for Wesley. I miss you in the week you know.

JANE. You've seen Perry Mason's running again Wesley.

WESLEY. It'll win today. We've backed it and backed it, haven't we? It can't lose today. Sir Charles Dobson's the owner and he's got to have a winner one day.

TED (*narration*). Big tall Wesley. Reckons to be a joiner but his back went and it's not coming back he says so he spends his time in here most days. Saves on the electric he says. And he laughs but it's only half a joke. There's a few in here like that. They've got nothing and they do nothing and they need to keep warm and they like a chat. I don't think I could do that. Not all day, every day, all year round. At least I've still got my little job at Crossleys; like mum said, it keeps me out of mischief. Not that it's forever. What is these days? Skeffington's always muttering about cutbacks. He lets everyone hear just so we're all a bit afraid. I can see what Skeffo's game is, oh yes . . .

TANNOY. Opening show at Cheltenham. They go. 4–1 number 13 Crazyman Crazy, 5–1 number 2 Knittingley, 6–1 number 6 Cooper's Pet, same price, 6–1 number 13, Frenchman, 8–1 bar.

Fade.

DAVE. There you go . . . not mentioned.

TED. That's what worries me Dave.

DAVE. Take it or leave it old love. Eight out of ten remember. But don't blame me *if*.

TED. Right.

DAVE. I've done it anyway.

TED (*narration*). So I take Barry Ferriter as the first of my four. I need three others and I've only got five minutes. It's that kind of bet. You have to be on from the start. You choose the horses and that's it. One down, all down. It's a silly bet really. A pools-win dream bet. Still . . .

TANNOY. Approaching the traps Crayford. Later betting Cheltenham, they bet 7–2 number 13 Crazyman Crazy . . .

Enter POVEY.

POVEY. You've seen it then?

JANE. Here he is. Pens down everybody. Attention.

WESLEY. Seen what?

POVEY. The three o'clock at Chepstow.

JANE. Is this a tip then?

POVEY. I'm just saying – have you seen it?

WESLEY. You're going to tell us.

POVEY. Karenski. Number 16. Bottom weight.

JANE. Karenski. Bottom weight, he says.

POVEY. It's all the way from Dorset to Wales. Right? It's set to carry next to nothing. Right? And who's riding?

JANE. Boy George.

POVEY. Danny Smart. Right? Claiming four pounds. There'll be a gamble on it. You watch.

JANE. What *is* he on about now?

TED (*narration*). Barry Povey. 'Form-book' Povey I call him. Says he's a student. Economics he says. He's in here a lot I'll say that. Quite an expert. Certainly sounds like one. Very keen on form is Barry. All the details. Half the time I can't even understand him. He knows so much. And he's got all the jargon right. Students of horses, I don't know about economics.

POVEY. All right then, you tell me why Frank Henderson's gone to such trouble to run Karenski at Chepstow. I mean see the clues and solve the mystery. If you're doing a yankee I should make it your banker. Teddy, you do yankees.

TED (*narration*). Yes I do but I'm not doing Karenski. Instead I go for Pickles and Bardwell Boy – two I've followed before. They both owe me. Pickles has got to come good one day soon and Bardwell Boy was second at Ascot three weeks ago and was really unlucky. It was on telly, and you could see it was hampered at the second last. That was three. I needed one more for my accumulator. Then I saw it. In the last race at Cheltenham. Now I don't go on names. Mum used to. When she had a little flutter on the National or the Derby. She always went for a name. The ladies are like that, I've noticed. Indian Jane; a real case for names. They're influenced by all that sort of thing. Mind you it can pay off. When mum was on the National that time, she picked this horse ridden by Bob Champion because she knew a lad when she was a girl called Bobby Champion. He was in her class at junior school. And this horse went and won at 11 to 1. I put a pound on for her. She was thrilled. Aldaniti – that was it. She went and won on a name which was more than I did. So here I am this afternoon staring at this horse called Apple Blossom Time and saying to myself don't be daft Ted because you don't do names. Even so . . . There was this song mum always sang when she started cleaning on a Friday afternoon. I was supposed to keep out of the way. I don't think she even knew she was doing it but it was a sort of signal that she was going to have a go at 'corners, cupboards and carpets'. Always this song and there was this horse and it was my birthday and I was thinking of mum today a lot. I don't know. It just seemed to be right even though I know I never go on names. Horse number four for my roll-up bet. Apple Blossom Time. I put up a two quid stake. I wrote it out and I paid tax. Total outlay two pounds twenty pence. Daft bet really . . .

TANNOY. At the post Cheltenham. At Cheltenham they bet 3–1 number 13 Crazyman Crazy; 5–1 number 6 Cooper's Pet.

Enter BILLY.

BILLY. Now then. All set?

JANE. Trouble's here. Everybody say hello.

BILLY. Ta very much. You are saying hello to one of the all-time great losers.

JANE. Or not saying hello as the case may be.

POVEY. All right Billy? Not gone up in smoke yet?

BILLY. What have I done?

JANE. Didn't expect to see you.

BILLY. Not see me? I *live* here.

JANE. After last Saturday. You were in a right state.

BILLY. You would be. 47 losers on the trot I've had. Forty seven bets – 22 seconds, six thirds and the rest bloody nowhere. That can't be right. Not one winner in 47 bets.

WESLEY. Who gets winners? Only the queen and the rich folk get winners. The rest of us just have to scrape.

BILLY. I've kept a note. My black book. Here. Look at this Wesley.

JANE. Calm down. They've not even started racing yet Billy.

BILLY. Second, 3rd! Second, 3rd, nowhere: 2nd, last! Forty seven bets. No winners. That's not natural, that.

TANNOY. Orders Cheltenham.

BILLY. I'm doing Cooper's Pet in this. It'll be second. Bet you it'll be second.

TED (*narration*). Mersey Billy. Six foot four and half barmy. He's always like this. Always losing, always angry. Marie had to tell him off once a few weeks back. Not just the bad language. He went and jabbed his biro through the list of runners on the wall. Mind, he did say sorry afterwards. Funny but mum always liked hearing about Billy the best. She could never understand why he bothered to carry on with it. 'Why does he bother if he always loses?' she used to ask me. I couldn't explain that to her . . . too difficult.

TANNOY. Off Cheltenham. Off at 1.03. On the off they were betting 4–1 the field.

JANE. I've done nothing in this.

BILLY. Cooper's Pet'll be second. I know it.

POVEY. Novice hurdle. Thirty runners. You need brain surgery if you bet on this. Total bloody lottery. Thirty novices. Anything could win. Anyone for surgery?

JANE. He does go on, doesn't he?

WESLEY. I've done the favourite. One of Sheikh Tamrood's. He can be relied on, can Sheikh Tamrood.

POVEY. Crazyman Crazy? You've actually put money on that. You must be.

WESLEY. I must be what?

TANNOY. Going out into the country for the final time at Cheltenham and it's Cooper's Pet who takes them along. He's followed by Davos, two lengths back in second.

Fade under.

TED (*narration*). The shop's filling up now. Marie who settles all the bets sits at the back behind the counter, looking like a schoolteacher with those specs and her hair done up in a bun. It's all women of course, the staff.

TANNOY. Approaching the last at Cheltenham and Crazyman Crazy is racing with Bally Ferriter. These two have gone six lengths up on the rest. Cooper's Pet is a long way back in third.

TED (*narration*). Doris lives over Roebuck's butchers. She's a widow lady, and there's Miriam whose hubby brings her every morning in the little Metro on the dot at 10.15. It's a sort of club really. People know each other.

TANNOY. On the run in now at Cheltenham. Two furlongs to go and Crazyman Crazy and Bally Ferriter are stride for stride. It's eight lengths back to Cooper's Pet in third. Into the last 200 yards now and Bally Ferriter has taken a slight advantage. This one's holding on. As they go for the line it's Bally Ferriter by a length now. At the line it's number 30 Bally Ferriter the winner, second number 13 Crazyman Crazy . . . The third horse was No 10, Cricket Bat.

Fade.

DAVE. There you go Edward. Nine out of eleven. I told you he was a good lad. See you later old love. Must get back to my boiler lady. Those eyes . . .

TANNOY. Starting price of the winner at Cheltenham 25–1. The favourite Crazyman Crazy at 3 to 1 was second.

JANE. Twenty five to 1. That's a start to the proceedings.

POVEY. Told you. These races are a lottery. Leave them alone.

BILLY. Number 48. What happened to Cooper's Pet? Lost in fog. Still running. Forty eight losers. Is this a record?

POVEY. What did you do Ted?

TED. Well – that one actually.

JANE. You never . . .

TED. I had a tip.

JANE. Who tipped that?

TED. Dave.

POVEY. Plumber Dave? You kid?

TED. He said it had a chance.

POVEY. He might have let us all in on it.

JANE. Hark at him. You wouldn't have backed it if he'd written in ten foot high letters on the bloody ceiling.

POVEY. I wish he'd have said, that's all.

BILLY. Where is he anyway?

TED. On some job he said.

BILLY. Always on some job, Dave.

JANE. No mucky talk thank you very much.

TED. He said about a faulty boiler.

JANE. Bally Ferriter. 25–1. Nice one. Irish wasn't it? Irish name anyway.

WESLEY. They have some good horses over there.

BILLY. Pity they didn't tell us about 'em in advance.

TED. I've only done it in an accumulator.

JANE. Accumulator? What's got into you?

POVEY. That was not wise old son.

TED. No, well, I don't come in here to be wise, do I?

BILLY. I like it. I like it.

POVEY. He had a bit on himself I suppose? Dave?

TED. I suppose he did.

BILLY. How many to go then?

TED. What?

BILLY. In your roll-up?

TED. Er . . . three more.

BILLY. Nice start. Twenty five to one winner.

POVEY. See this one.

JANE. Here we go.

POVEY. Columbo Jumbo. In the 2 o'clock at Chepstow. I mean why have they sent it to run in a race of three miles when said horse has never, in its life, run more than two and a quarter miles and when it last ran two and a quarter it finished pulled up. I repeat, *pulled up*! Can anyone tell me why this horse is in Wales today running three miles against good class chasers like Vagabond?

WESLEY. You ask a lot of questions Mr. Povey.

POVEY. It's 5 to 1 possible s.p. in my paper. Do you reckon there's something they're not telling us?

JANE. It's that University – your trouble.

POVEY. Polytechnic.

WESLEY. You think Columbo Jumbo's going to win? Let me get this straight.

POVEY. I'm just asking, that's all.

WESLEY. Asking? Tell me what's gonna win please.

BILLY. Ring him up.

POVEY. Who?

BILLY. This trainer. Illingworth. Ring him up and ask him.

POVEY. Don't talk so daft.

WESLEY. Lots of questions. But never any bleedin' answers.

TED (*narration*). Twenty five to one. Fifty quid! Silly man. Should've backed it to win. Still fifty pounds rolling on; well 52 with the stake back. Might as well enjoy the moment.

POVEY. I was begged off coming here this morning.

BILLY. You what?

POVEY. A bloke came up to me in the street and asked me for 'the price of a cup of coffee guv'.

BILLY. What did you do?

JANE. Told him about Columbo Jumbo!

POVEY. He had Nijinsky tattooed on his fist. Big thick blue letters.

Back of his hand.

BILLY. A racing man then.

JANE. How do you mean?

BILLY. Where've you been since rock 'n'roll old love? Nijinsky. Bloody brilliant racehorse. On the flat. Years ago. Come on, come on ... you must *know*.

JANE. I thought he was a dancer, Nijinsky.

BILLY. Don't be daft. Dancer? With a name like that.

JANE. You know *so* much.

WESLEY. All of it, total bloody rubbish.

TANNOY. At Haydock, they bet, 2 to 1 number 6 Crispin's Day, 3 to 1 number 13 Curly; 5 to 1 number 1 Barley wine; 7 to 1 number 20 Glassily ...

Fade.

Enter DAVE.

DAVE. Now then. All on Bally Ferriter were you?

BILLY. You might have told us.

DAVE. You never asked.

JANE. Twenty five to one. Where do you find them, Dave?

DAVE. It was a valve. Tiny as that.

JANE. What was?

DAVE. Causing all the trouble. *The boiler.*

JANE. Have you got any more like that this afternoon.

DAVE. I wish I had. And *ever* so grateful.

POVEY. Look at this. Now this is a nice little problem.

JANE. Leave me out, professor.

POVEY. Beatledrive. In the 3.45. Top weight right? 11 stone 12 lbs. Over two miles right?

JANE. I should've done Bally Ferriter. Lovely name.

POVEY. Won only once last year and this year has only managed a crappy fifth to Gringo at Worcester six weeks ago. Right? That said why is it quoted as 3 to 1 favourite in the s.p. probables in the *Sporting Life*?

WESLEY. Misprint.

POVEY. Don't be daft.

TANNOY. At Haydock they bet 7 to 4 number 6 Crispin's Day. They're going down at Haydock.

Cut to.

TED (*narration*). I pass this shop sometimes in the dark at night or on a Sunday when it's all shut up and it reminds me of a church. A church without the people and the prayers and the singing. Lonely and silent and dark and shut up. Out of place somehow and unreal. Ladbrokes is like that. It doesn't have any point when there's no-one there.

JANE. Now then Teddy, I can't cadge – er, another fag off you can I?

TED. Sure.

WESLEY. Another nail in your little coffin.

JANE. You don't mind do you?

TED. Go on.

JANE. You're a star only I'm not smoking anymore you see, so I can't buy any, can I?

BILLY. Not smoking.

JANE. Ta.

BILLY. Bloody marvellous.

WESLEY. Lady Waplington's got one in this next at Haydock.

POVEY. You what?

WESLEY. She's on holiday at the moment. In California. It's lovely over there this time of year.

POVEY. How do you know all this?

WESLEY. Everybody knows about California.

POVEY. No, I meant . . . never mind.

WESLEY. She gets some winners, does Lady Waplington. She knows horses, you see. Worth following.

POVEY. What do you reckon for this next then, Billy? At Cheltenham.

BILLY. Bulbrook should piss it.

POVEY. Bulbrook? Doubt if it'll get up that hill at the end of three and a half miles.

BILLY. It's done the distance.

POVEY. But not that weight. Cheltenham can tire the fittest.

BILLY. You ever been like?

POVEY. Where?

BILLY. To Cheltenham. Know it personally do you?

POVEY. I had a girlfriend came from Cheltenham. I never got invited back home. She got a 2.1. Business Studies. Always in the rotten library.

BILLY. I went once. Twenty years ago. Festival meeting. Gold Cup day. I had twenty quid on the Laird.

POVEY. I wasn't born.

BILLY. Course it was second. I love being on the course. There's nothing like it. The flat's best. Nicer weather. Newmarket. June meeting. Ideal that is. Get there nice and early in some nice new clean clobber. Always take a lass. Some really smart piece with shoulder length hair and neat little figure. I'd get this room for us at a country hotel, somewhere really smart, in the environs of the course and we'd have a clean, light breakfast and look through the papers and then set off to get to the course nice and early to watch the private jets and big limos arrive, the sheikhs and the lords and ladies and the fat cats from the city and the jocks like Cauthen and Eddery and Carson. Stroll on the heath, the warm sun on our backs and then stroll out into the paddock to have a look at the runners for the first race – two year olds of course, and as they clip clop round the ring my lass'd just nod and smile at number 7 – something called Perfect Dream and I'd flip out five tens just for a starter and take a ticket on it from one of the bookmakers and I'd get 8 to 1 which is a nice price any day of the year. Then we watch the race from the stand, my lass holding her hat on as a little bit of breeze comes up off the rolling heathland. And we watch the knot of horses bang against the rail flashing up the five furlong course and then number 7 would come out of the pack, black and gold sleeves with gold cap and it's across the line some two lengths clear and we collect a cool 400 quid. But we've still the rest of the afternoon ahead, me and this lass and the way it feels it's never going to end . . . never going to end.

WESLEY. Shut that door, man, there's a big draught in here.

JANE. Anybody bung me a spare cig?

POVEY. Now this is what I call an interesting race.

TANNOY. At the post Cheltenham. At Cheltenham they bet 2 to 1 number 14 Chromosomes, 3 to 1 number 6 Stag Night, 4 to 1 number 17 Coomber Boy; 6 to 1 number 7 Raringtogo, 8 to 1 bar.

JANE. Mine's not even in the betting.

POVEY. What's that?

JANE. Pickles.

POVEY. No chance.

JANE. Says who.

POVEY. Suspect over fences. Look at this form. 'Fell.' 'Unseated rider.' 'Fell.' It's nearly a cripple.

JANE. That was last year. And watch your mouth young fella . . .

POVEY. What have I said!

JANE. Never mind. I've said. That's all.

She goes off.

POVEY. What's up with her?

WESLEY. I'll tell you one day, man.

POVEY. Why can't you tell me now?

TED. Some other time eh?

BILLY. Raringtogo's got a chance in this.

POVEY. It's one-paced. Look at the form.

BILLY. Form says it's been second three times out of five. That's going close on my system.

POVEY. System?

JANE. It's a nice name, anyway.

BILLY. It'll do me.

JANE. Raringtogo.

POVEY. They're all nice names. Think about it.

JANE. I'm taking Pickles, even so.

TANNOY. Orders Cheltenham. They bet at Cheltenham 7 to 4 number 14 Chromosomes.

WESLEY. You got this race in your roll-up Ted?

TED. Er . . . yes. I've done Pickles.

JANE. It'll be 10 to 1 at least.

DAVE. You're always on about the price. Price is nothing to do with finding winners.

JANE. I'm not backing favourites, Dave.

DAVE. You want winners, don't you?

JANE. Can't afford favourites.

DAVE. That's daft. Winners are winners.

JANE. I can't back things at 7 to 4 and 15 to 8 and all that. Where's the return on that to 20p?

TANNOY. Orders and off Cheltenham at 2.03.

JANE. Did you see those penguins last night on the box? Scream.

WESLEY. I don't think you should treat animals like that. Tin hats. Bloody cruel.

POVEY. Which channel was that on?

JANE. How do you mean which channel?

TANNOY. And at Cheltenham there's been a faller at the first fence. Fallen, number 6 Raringtogo.

BILLY. Fallen at the first! My card is marked! Someone is trying to get me! Friggin' torture!! I paid good money for that.

POVEY. How do you mean, paid?

BILLY. I bought a system.

POVEY. Dicey.

BILLY. Advertised in the back of the *Life*. 'Win with Walt Thompson.'

POVEY. Con merchants.

BILLY. Who asked you?

JANE. How much? I've seen that ad.

BILLY. A tenner. Postage was on top.

POVEY. What did you get. A crystal ball?

BILLY. Shut it Povey. It's a book. Gives you horses to follow.

POVEY. Who's Walt Thompson then? I mean, what does he know?

TANNOY. A circuit to race at Cheltenham and it's Pickles who's clear by some ten lengths. In second place comes Chromosomes. Coomber Boy races in third.

Fade.

BILLY. Reckons on 60 per cent success rate if you pick the right race with the right horse. It's all in this book. I mean he's printed his bank account in the back. You can see what he won last year – six thou.

POVEY. Faked.

BILLY. You're getting to me son.

POVEY. I'm just saying.

BILLY. It's a proper book. Printed out.

POVEY. Doesn't make it genuine, does it? I mean, Raringtogo. Fell at the first.

BILLY. Bleedin' clever dick students! I was backin' horses before you were on the planet.

TANNOY. One left to jump at Cheltenham and it's Pickles with a ten length advantage. This one's led from the start. In second place is Chromosomes who's racing half a length up on Beverley Sister. Coming to the last and Pickles is up and over safely, still some eight to ten lengths clear. Running on strongly into third is Stag Night. But on the run in it's Pickles holding his lead; at the line, it's number 8 Pickles the winner. Second number 14 Chromosomes.

JANE. There you go. Another little winner. We're laughing, Ted.

TED. Nice, yes.

JANE. At least 10 to 1.

TED. Do you think so?

JANE. Two up, two to go, eh?

POVEY. Pickles should never have won that.

BILLY. Here he is. The wise man of the turf.

POVEY. How can a horse that finished twenty lengths behind Chromosomes last time out come here today and beat it by ten! Can anybody tell me the answer?

JANE. Some of us were on it.

POVEY. I know you *were* on it. We *all* know you were on it. *Why*, I'm asking, did it win?

JANE. Form, lovey. It changes. Horses change. Like people.

POVEY. Disgraceful.

BILLY. You'll have a nice lot going on, Teddy.

TED. Not bad. I won't win though. Not all four.

BILLY. Two winners. It's a start. I've not had one for weeks!

TED. It won't come off – accumulators never do.

BILLY. You haven't done Caressing in the three o'clock at Chepstow have you?

TED. Why?

BILLY. Cos I've done it, that's all.

JANE. You'll get a winner Billy, don't worry.

WESLEY. Try Lady Waplington's. In the three o'clock.

TED (*narration*). This is getting serious. £572 going on to Bardwell Boy! Most I've ever won's seventy pounds. On a treble about eight years ago. I can't believe this. 572 quid. On one horse. Bardwell Boy. I never gave it a thought. It's just one I'd done before. I'm loyal like that. Mum used to say too loyal. A weakness, Edward. Too loyal to Mr. Skeffington at work who's just a pig; too loyal to those cats who run rings round you and too loyal to me, your old mum. Yes, well, we made a good team, you and me, mum. We were all right. We looked after each other. If that's loyalty, then three cheers says I. Five hundred and seventy quid on Bardwell Boy . . . this is a real birthday afternoon Edward my son . . . Too late to go back. It's only a two pound bet after all.

TANNOY. At Chepstow they bet 13 to 8 number 14 Caressing, 3 to 1 number 6 Skinflinter, 4 to 1 number 4 Booklist, same price, 4 to 1 number 8 Bardwell Boy, 7 to 1 bar.

POVEY. They're tipping some cash on the favourite.

BILLY. Caressing? It's got to have a chance.

POVEY. One from your system, Billy? One from Walt?

WESLEY. Money doesn't win races, man.

POVEY. What does win races, Wesley?

BILLY. My grandad used to follow money. Poor old sod. Died

following money. He never caught up. And he was always out of breath.

JANE. What's he on about?

BILLY. I'm being friggin' poetic.

JANE. It runs in the family then.

BILLY. Poetry?

JANE. Betting. Your grandad.

BILLY. Every day he had the papers, pencil, form books.

WESLEY. He won a lot, did he?

BILLY. Course he didn't.

POVEY. Hasn't put you off the horses though.

BILLY. If I'd been an airline pilot it might have or a consultant in a hospital. I mean I wouldn't have had the time to get to the shop, would I? But with me being a hod carrier and general labourer it hasn't made no difference. I've carried on the tradition.

JANE. Losing.

TANNOY. Later betting Chepstow, they bet 11 to 8 number 14 Caressing . . .

TED (*narration*). Think of something else. Don't think of winning. Have a ciggy. It's worse than work this. When I get the summons from friend Skeffington – some bollocking or other. It's worse than waiting to see Skeffington.

TANNOY. Orders Chepstow. Off Chepstow 3.02.

JANE. You on Wes?

WESLEY. No. I'm skint.

JANE. What about Mr. Povey?

POVEY. I've done one.

JANE. Go on, tell us the secret.

POVEY. Skinflinter. Shall I tell you why?

JANE. If you must.

BILLY. Keep it short, eh?

JANE. I've done Caressing.

POVEY. Nice name.

JANE. Anyone got a spare ciggy?

TANNOY. At Chepstow they're going out onto the farside for the last time and Skinflinter takes them along. This one's some two lengths up on Raviolini. In third place comes Rena Rich.

Fade.

TED (*narration*). Two pounds. Accumulator. A bit more than I usually do but it is my birthday. And there's nothing much to celebrate this year. No little outing to the Maharajah with mum. I mean it wasn't much, just a regular little do on my birthday, a little ritual. But I'm not going on my own. No way. All those couples enjoying themselves and there'll be me sat in the corner on my own. I couldn't face all that. So think of it like that. I've had a little bit of a bet today . . . a little bit of a birthday treat. Bardwell Boy can't win this anyway. Loyalty never pays, does it?

TANNOY. Turning into the straight at Chepstow and Caressing still leads with Booklist now going into second. Bardwell Boy is making a forward move. At the second last and Caressing and Booklist jump it together with Bardwell Boy who's getting nearer in third. Behind these come Skinflinter. Cherry Riper is not out of it. They're coming to the last. There's three in a line. Caressing, Booklist, and Bardwell Boy. They jump the last together. All over it safely and on the run in now and it's Bardwell Boy who has a slight lead from Caressing. Booklist is dropping back. They're into the last furlong and Bardwell Boy still leads by half a length from Caressing. It's Bardwell Boy holding on, in the last hundred yards from Caressing. No 8 Bardwell Boy is the winner; second number 14 Caressing; the third horse was number 4 Booklist.

BILLY. I'll give it another race then I'm off.

POVEY. Skinflinter. Bloody terrible. It beat Caressing ten lengths at Ascot!

JANE. I must get some veg.

DAVE. I think you might be in the wrong shop.

POVEY. Bardwell had some form. I'll give you that.

WESLEY. Teddy's laughing.

TED. Yes, well, that's three up.

POVEY. You never did that winner?

TED. I've backed it before you see. I thought I'd give it another go.

DAVE. You'll have a fair old roll-up I reckon, Ted.

TED. Quite a bit.

DAVE. Yeah. More than quite a bit.

WESLEY. What's your last one then?

TED. Apple Blossom Time. Four o'clock at Cheltenham.

POVEY. It's done the distance.

TED. Has it?

POVEY. And it's got that Stewartson on it.

TED. Right, yes.

POVEY. He's riding some winners this year. Cocky sod. Saw him interviewed on TV. Welsh. Plenty to say, the Welsh.

TED (*narration*). Marie is looking over her specs. At me. And she's smiling. She knows the score. I've got two thousand, eight hundred quid going on to Apple Blossom Time. She'll have to ring her boss in Leeds. That's how it works. I've seen that before. I saw her on the phone a minute since.

JANE. Why did you choose that one? Apple Blossom whatsit?

TED. Nice name . . . Here . . . have a cig.

JANE. Ta very much. I should be getting back soon. And there's the shopping.

TED. You'll stay for Perry Mason.

JANE. Should get back really. You know . . . suspense though, Ted. Your roll-up. I can't leave.

BILLY. Forty nine losers on the trot.

DAVE. A bad run, Billy. We all have bad runs.

BILLY. This is not a bad run, it's hangman time. Skint. Total.

JANE. I need to get some veg before they close.

POVEY. This Apple Blossom Time.

JANE. The great man speaks.

POVEY. It had some nice outings last year. Second at Sandown. Second at Ascot. In good company too.

JANE. What price will it be?

POVEY. Fives or thereabouts. Dave?

DAVE. Fives. Yeah.

POVEY. Could be the big one Ted.

TED. It won't win.

BILLY. Don't get like that. Wait until you'd had fifty 'won't wins'.

POVEY. Karakoram'll be favourite. Three wins on the trot that one.

TED (*narration*). I didn't want to do my sums but I had to think about it. Two thousand eight hundred going on at 5 to 1 or thereabouts. With the stake back I'd be taking away . . . I didn't want to think about it. And I'm stood there in the shop and these people around me chattering away hadn't any idea. They knew I was winning. Three up, one to go. They knew that; but they didn't know just how much. I think Dave had an idea. He'd seen Marie on the phone and he'd probably guessed they'd got a charlady's situation. It's what they call a really lucky bet like this one. Four horses all at big prices. A total one-off. Like the pools. I was shaking. Shaking. I had two cigarettes on the trot waiting for the last race. I'd been coming to this shop some fifteen years. I'm the senior citizen of Ladbrokes. Burncross Road branch. I go back before Big Wes and Indian Jane and they're old-stagers. I go back before Marie. I stood in the corner of the shop I'd been coming to for fifteen years and tried to work out how many bets I'd had and how much cash I'd lost. It is all losses in the end. And now I stood there. And I wanted to savour it, taste it. So much on one horse. It would never happen again. I know that. It had to lose and when it lost I'd have the memory. But there was no-one to share it with: win or lose. It hit me suddenly, for the first time since, you . . . since . . . since I was on my own . . . there was no-one else. I felt, suddenly, so bloody alone.

TANNOY. At Cheltenham they bet 2 to 1 number 6 Holy Fellowship, 3 to 1 number 10 Karakoram; same price 3 to 1 number 11 Havers, 5 to 1 number 17 Ragtime Cowboy, 6 to 1 number 19 Apple Blossom Time.

POVEY. What do you reckon Dave?

DAVE. Karakoram'll do me.

POVEY. Not so clever at the big fences though, is it? Been on the ground twice this season.

DAVE. If you feel like that stick with Teddy here. Three up, one to go.

POVEY. Apple Blossom Time? It's too young. No experience at this class.

DAVE. Always something wrong, isn't there?

POVEY. What?

DAVE. You always find a fault. How do you ever make up your mind, Povey? Tell me that?

WESLEY. Dave's doing Karakoram. He knows how to pick winners that man.

JANE. He doesn't know everything, Wes.

WESLEY. Knows more than me, lovey. Lady Waplington's horse fell at the fourth.

JANE. Just 'cos they're rich doesn't mean they always win.

WESLEY. But it does you see.

BILLY. I think I might pack it all in forever, after this, win or lose. I mean, what's the point. I've lost thirty quid in the last ten days. I can't afford it.

JANE. Go with Teddy.

BILLY. What on?

TED. Apple Blossom Time.

BILLY. I fancy Holy Fellowship.

JANE. Not turning religious, Billy?

BILLY. I will. If it helps find a winner, I'm a Hindu tomorrow!

TANNOY. Orders and off Cheltenham. Running Cheltenham at 4.02.

JANE. You've done all right, Teddy.

TED. Yeah.

JANE. Are you OK?

TED. Bloody shaking. Look at me.

JANE. You've got a lot then? Going onto this?

TED. I can't believe it.

JANE. A real lot eh?

TED. Nearly three thousand quid.

JANE. . . . You . . . never have. Really?

TED. At 6 to 1. I'm faint.

JANE. So am I. Now. Never that much, is it?

TED. Keep it a bit to yourself though, eh? Please.

JANE. Course; er – can I pinch one . . . ta.

TED (*narration*). Keep it quiet? I should've known better. I could see the word going round. But it was like a dream now. I could see the people and hear the tannoy but it was all happening to someone else, out there.

TANNOY. Over at Cheltenham, Karakoram is taking them along. He's some two lengths up on Havers. Holy Fellowship is in third.

This fades as inner voices take over.

POVEY. He stands to win . . . stands to win . . . bloody hell fire.

DAVE. Four in a row. There's no law against it. Doesn't happen very often but still.

WESLEY. That is big money man, big big money.

JANE. Come on Apple Blossom. Come on, for Ted's sake.

BILLY. A friggin' fortune. Retirement to Spain. Goodbye hod carrying.

JANE. He looks like death. White as a sheet.

POVEY. The horse simply has not got the necessary ackers. Pity.

DAVE. Come on Apple Blossom. Give the lad a break.

TANNOY. Three left to jump at Cheltenham. And Karakoram continues to lead. Holy Fellowship has moved into second, Havers is dropping back.

WESLEY. Not even mentioned. Shit . . . not even mentioned.

JANE. It's not going to win; not now. Three *grand* down.

BILLY. Not Holy Fellowship; not now – after fifty losers.

POVEY. Duff form this year. I feel sorry for him; bloody near the big one I'll say that.

TED. What a story, mum, rolling in at five o'clock. You'd never believe it. Win or lose, mum, it would be a lovely tale. You would have laughed and cried . . .

TANNOY. Approaching the second last at Cheltenham and Holy Fellowship has taken it up. He's gone two lengths up on Ragtime Cowboy who's moved into second. Apple Blossom Time is starting a late run. Over the second last and Holy Fellowship takes it safely; number 19 Apple Blossom Time moves quickly through into second.

Fade quickly to inner voices.

WESLEY. It's there man; come on horse, come on, come on.

JANE. Apple Blossom Time. Lovely name.

POVEY. No extra at the finish, this one. It faded at Lingfield last year. Pity really.

DAVE. Long run in at Cheltenham . . . anything can happen now.

BILLY. Take this winner from me. Take this winner from me.

TANNOY. Coming to the last at Cheltenham and it's still Holy Fellowship by a length now from Apple Blossom Time with Casual Baby going into third. Over the last and Holy Fellowship is still a length clear of Apple Blossom Time. On the run in and Holy Fellowship continues to lead but he's being challenged now by Apple Blossom Time on his outside. They're in the last furlong and these two are stride for stride. There's nothing in it. Holy Fellowship and Apple Blossom Time. Apple Blossom Time and Holy Fellowship. They're coming to the line, and still nothing in it. They've gone past the post together. It's a photo-finish Cheltenham. Involved in the photograph number 19 Apple Blossom Time and number 6 Holy Fellowship.

POVEY. Holy's got it.

DAVE. Close. Very close. Very very close.

JANE. Are you OK, Ted?

WESLEY. Photograph . . . No problem Ted, no problem.

BILLY. I never thought I'd want a horse of mine to lose.

POVEY. Sounded like Holy Fellowship's got it. From the commentary. Pity really. Very close.

JANE. You would have to say that.

WESLEY. You still get half the winnings if it's a dead heat. No problem, Ted.

JANE. You might be all right, Ted. Luck anyway mate. I don't think I can bear to stay.

TANNOY. Going into the traps at Monmore. At Monmore they bet. 2 to 1 trap 4.

JANE. Dogs! Now!

TED (*narration*). All stood there. All looking at me. Indian Jane, Big Tall Wesley, Back-pocket Dave, Mersey Billy, Formbook Povey. I could feel the pink slip in my hand. I could see their faces. I could hear my heart bang-banging in my chest. Apple Blossom Time. That bloody tune. It was like a dream . . . *Mum* . . .

TANNOY. Result coming from Cheltenham. The winner, number 19 Apple Blossom Time; second number 6 Holy Fellowship. At Cheltenham Apple Blossom Time beat Holy Fellowship in the photograph.

TED. Twenty thousand pounds. This Saturday in November. My birthday. And I was suddenly crying and they could all see that and looked away. Nice people. My friends at Ladbrokes. Burncross Road branch. But none of them really knew why I was crying. Not really.

TANNOY. Starting price of the winner at Cheltenham was 6 to 1. Distances a neck and three lengths.